Prejudice in *Harry Potter's* World

A Social Critique of the Series, Using Allport's *The Nature of Prejudice*

Karen A. Brown

For the Reader who is passionate about Harry Potter politics

This book is a work of fiction. Any resemblance to actual events or persons, living or dead, is entirely coincidental.

"Prejudice in Harry Potter's World," by Karen A. Brown. ISBN 978-1-60264-153-2.

Published 2008 by Virtualbookworm.com Publishing Inc., P.O. Box 9949, College Station, TX 77842, US.

Manufactured in the United States of America.

PREJUDICE IN *HARRY POTTER*'S WORLD

PREJUDICE IN *HARRY POTTER'S* WORLD

A Social Critique of the Series, Using Allport's *The Nature of Prejudice*

Karen A. Brown

To my father, ***Dalvin George Brown***

For the countless arguments about politics
(even when I was not interested),
For companionship and all the little things
(like schoolbooks, lunch money and the daily Cheez Trix),
And for being such an enthralled Harry Potter audience,
Thanks.

Contents

Acknowledgements

I thank my parents, ***Mr. Dalvin Brown*** and ***Ms. Urcena Waugh***, for all you have done for me. And to my sister ***Yvonne Elizabeth Brown***, I say thanks for the many ways in which you contributed to my upbringing.

Special thanks to my uncle and aunt, ***Mr. Albert Evelyn*** and the late ***Mrs. Everyl Evelyn***, for having given me that all-important early start in education. Heartfelt thanks to ***Murlene Evelyn*** (or ***Doris Stewart***), for all you have done for me and my father. And to my uncle, ***Mr. Calvin Small***, I give much love and gratitude. Thanks for encouraging and supporting me throughout my studies in the UK. And finally, ***Aunt Freida Small***: You were once my savior; I will not forget it. Thank you!

I am grateful to ***Sarah Flemig***, ***Tricia Mohan*** and ***Aruna Nair***, who first prompted me to read the *Harry Potter* books, and discussed the social themes in the series with me. And many warm thanks to all the *Harry Potter* ***Readers*** who participated in the survey for Chapter 3.

Many thanks to my supervisors ***Dr. Toby Garfitt*** (Magdalen College, Oxford) and ***Dr. Jane Hiddleston*** (Exeter College, Oxford). Thanks for understanding my reasons for taking time off from my academic work to write this book. I am also very grateful to ***Madam Chantal P. Thompson***, who was my mentor at Brigham Young University.

Sincerest thanks to the various members of the academic and administrative staff at Brasenose College (Oxford) who have encouraged and assisted me over the years. Special thanks to ***Professor Richard Cooper***, ***Dr. Susan Lea***, ***Principal Roger Cashmore***, ***Dr. John Knowland***, ***Mrs. Wendy Williams***, ***Mel Parrot***, ***Mr. David Buxton***, ***Miss JanaLee Cherneski***, ***Dr. Giles Wiggs***, ***Julia Palejowska***, ***Mr. Peter Bushnell***, and our kind and ever-courteous ***Porters*** and the ***Accommodation Staff***. I take this opportunity to express how very proud I am to belong to Brasenose, and also to convey my gratitude for the *Clarendon* and *Hector Pilling* scholarships.

There are no words that can sufficiently express my gratitude to ***Mrs. Arlene Masters***. You never take any credit for my success, although you are the reason for it. But most importantly, you have always treated me like a daughter (You were certainly no Petunia!) I also thank ***Mr. Franz Masters*** and ***"Grandfather" Masters*** for all your kindnesses. ***Francine***, ***Kanisha***, ***Jodi*** and ***Danielle*** (the Masters girls) and ***Kerri-Dojhn Barret-Hall***: You are my sisters in all the ways that matter. Thanks for all your love and support over the years, especially when I was far away from home.

Many, many, many thanks and warmest wishes go to ***Chantal Ononaiwu-Robertson***, ***Akeem Sule***, ***Béatrice Clio***, ***David Magezi***, ***Alexandra Alexandridou*** and ***Tania Oh*** for having been so supportive during those troublesome DPhil years.

And many heartfelt thanks to my "Shire" (Wolvercote) friends: ***Marina Rose***, ***Judith Secker*** and ***Uwe Shönberger***. Thanks for having looked after me when I was ill, and also for the encouragement you offered when I first conceptualized and started the research for this project years ago.

And finally, thanks to ***J.K. Rowling*** for having created Harry Potter, and also to the ***Christopher Little Literary Agency***, whom I wrote to three years ago, to request permission to publish the essay "Harry Potter and the Minorities Issue." Although no official authorization was given for either that essay or for this work, Ms. Rowling's representatives declared their good will to hold no objections to the publication, as long as copyright rules were followed and references properly cited and accredited to the author.

Sincerest thanks to you all.

K.A.B.

He jests at scars that never felt a wound.
—William Shakespeare
(*Romeo and Juliet*, Act 2: Scene II)

It is by those who have suffered that the world has been advanced.
—Leo Tolstoy

Do not pity the dead ... Pity the living, and, above all, those who live without love.
—J.K. Rowling
(DH, p. 578)

Foreword

This book was written for *Harry Potter*[1] readers who are as passionate about social issues as the author of the series clearly is. The true magic of J.K. Rowling's creation lies not in its overwhelming appeal to the mainstream audience, but rather in the fact that so many people, from all walks of life, 'relate' to the books. What truly makes Rowling's success unprecedented is the fact that, it is the first time in history that a work of popular fiction has appealed to the international community and minority groups as much as it appeals to the Western mainstream audience. And I believe this is largely due to the important (and very current) social themes played out in the novels.

Curiously, however, when I first read the books and made this observation to some of my fellow *Potter* enthusiasts, many of them would say something along the lines of: "We know the books are a little political and the writer is trying to comment on discrimination in the real world; but that's not why people love *Harry Potter*." Although these readers acknowledged that Rowling's work referenced many of the social issues plaguing our world, they did not believe that her target audience was attracted to this particular aspect of her work.

In contrast, the response from minority-group readers (such as the Disabled, religious and racial minorities or people from severely stigmatized groups) was completely different. In fact, most of them insisted that *Harry Potter* was really about them. And so, I decided to write an essay on "Minority Issues" in the series against the backdrop of Gordon Allport's *The Nature of Prejudice*. But due to the enormous scope of Rowling's work and the detailed nature of her so-called "wizarding world," had so much material to work with that, what was intended to be an essay ended up being a short book.

---

[1] For international publishing reasons, the spelling in this volume will conform to the American Standard English format. However, I will be using the British (Bloomsbury) versions of the *Harry Potter* books for references. Page numberings are slightly different from the American (Scholastic) or other versions of the books.

Bearing in mind that Allport's thesis is an acclaimed sociology text, I set out to use it as a guide; but I wished to write something that was less technical and more accessible to a wider audience. This was not only because the *Harry Potter* novels are considered to be popular literature, but also because the prejudice and discrimination issues which are raised in them are relevant to people from all educational backgrounds. Therefore, this volume aims to appeal to both non-academic and academic readers alike. Anyone who is interested in prejudice as a social issue, or who enjoys reading *Harry Potter* because of its social themes, should find this volume useful.

Also, since I set out to write a critique of J.K. Rowling's novels, there was no scope for examining Gordon Allport's work in great detail. *The Nature of Prejudice* is used here merely as a reference point for different prejudice-related concepts. For a more in-depth analysis of Allport's acclaimed text, I suggest a recent work edited by Dovidio, Glick and Rudman entitled *On the Nature of Prejudice: Fifty Years after Allport* (Blackwell Publishing, 2005). Students and researchers in the social sciences should find this compilation of essays rather useful in terms of updating the research on prejudice that Allport conducted more than half a century ago.

Also, since this is a social critique, I do not deliberately seek to address previous (literary) scholarship on Rowling's work. Nor do I seek to comment or pass judgment on the literary merits of the author or her novels. The purpose of this volume is to simply highlight the prejudice-related themes in the series, and to comment on their relevance to our own world. Nevertheless, this book is not meant to be a perfect 'text-to-world' analysis: While it is true that certain events in the fictional wizarding world seem to directly refer to true historical events in our own world, there are no absolute parallels. For example, pertinent comparisons can indeed be made between the Holocaust and Rowling's "Mudblood" subplot, but it is not enough to say that Muggle-born oppression "*represents*" Jewish persecution during Hitler's Nazi regime. It is "*comparable*," or it might be a social parallel in some ways; but the one does not "*represent*" the other.

Finally, it would be impossible for me to use this book to analyze Rowling's novels and at the same time provide a detailed chronicle of each type of prejudice in the modern world (sexism, racism, homophobia, disability prejudice, ageism, religious biases, and so forth). And so, I wish to make it clear from the outset that this volume does not aim to treat any one particular type of prejudice as a 'pet subject.' Although I seem to have singled out the disability issue in Chapter 4 of this volume, this is only because I found Jane Sancho's article on the portrayal of disability in the British media to be extremely useful in terms of categorizing people's attitudes towards minority groups in general. Sancho's aptly-coined terms (*Issue-driven, Transformers, Traditionalists,* and so forth) and her observations on how each category reacts to the Disabled and/or copes with disability prejudice, can also apply to other types of prejudice affecting other non-dominant groups such as racial or religious minorities.

And so, I discuss prejudice here as a characteristic of human nature which is manifested in various ways depending on social settings, upbringing, and so forth. After all, a 2001 MORI survey found that "64% of people in England could name at least one minority group against whom they were prejudiced."[2] The report also stressed that many people who held prejudiced views towards minority groups (such as the Disabled) failed to acknowledge that their feelings were prejudicial....

And so, what is it about human nature that creates situations where glaring injustices can go unnoticed by society for decades, and sometimes centuries? And, according to the ideas put forth in J. K. Rowling's *Harry Potter* series, what can we do about it?

[2] Ouseley, 2001, p. 17, in his Foreword to the *Profiles of Prejudice* survey.

Definition of Key Terms

The terms "discrimination" and "prejudice" will be used repeatedly throughout this book, sometimes together. Therefore, I must first clarify the contexts in which they will be used, as well as highlight the subtle differences between the two.

Where the term *prejudice* is concerned, Allport considered both the positive and negative aspects of the word in the following definition:

> *A feeling, favorable or unfavorable, toward a person or thing, prior to, or not based on, actual experience.*[1] (Allport, 1954/1979, pp. 6-7)

Here, we can see that there is a difference between what Allport called "love-prejudice" (prejudice *in favor of* someone or something) and "hate-prejudice" (prejudice *against* a person or thing) [pp. 6-7]. But for the purposes of this book, we will focus on "*anti*-feelings," or prejudice *against* the out-groups or marginalized individuals in *Harry Potter*'s world.

Other definitions of prejudice include more descriptive elements such as "irrationality," "conformity" and "intent." For example, Ackerman defined prejudice as "a pattern of hostility in interpersonal relations which is directed against an entire group, or against its individual members" whilst fulfilling "a specific irrational function for its bearer."[2] Ackerman was clearly suggesting that prejudice always had what Allport described as a "self-gratifying purpose."[3] But this definition was somewhat misconceived...

It is indeed true that the expression of prejudice towards others often serves unconstructive personal objectives for persons who are prejudiced. Yet there are many occasions where people unconsciously sustain irrational, negative beliefs and attitudes towards outsider individuals and groups. In many such cases, there is no intent to harm or to place

---

[1] Allport uses the New English Dictionary definition here; but, bearing in mind that his work was first published in 1954, many later editions of that dictionary have been subsequently released.

[2] Ackerman, 1950, p. 4.

[3] Allport, 1954/1979, p. 12.

oneself above the social Other: The prejudiced individual simply "conforms" with the rest of society in his views, his words and his actions, without considering the consequences for himself or for the scorned outsider. And in such cases, it becomes more a question of conformity and indifference rather than the need for personal gratification.

In Allport's day, Black and Atkins provided the most relativistic definition of prejudice, distinguishing between social conformity and intentionally oppressive prejudice:

> A prejudice is a generalized anti-attitude, and/or an anti-action toward any distinct category or group of people, when either the attitude or the action of both are judged by the community in which they are found to be less favorable to the given people than the normally accepted standard of that community.[4]

Here, the writers seemed to be suggesting that prejudice was merely a "deviance from common practice," as Allport summarized.[5] But such a distinction is dangerous, as it might appear to have condoned anti-Semitism during the Nazi regime, or supported Black-White segregation in the pre-Civil War United States. After all, the oppression of Jews and Blacks, respectively, was "common practice" at the time.

In fact, the very purpose of this volume is to demonstrate how certain "common practices and beliefs" can be socially devastating—whether in the real world or in J.K. Rowling's fictional wizarding world. As we will observe through the various examples provided in the *Harry Potter* novels, harmful attitudes and beliefs sustained for long periods of time—often as a result of conformity to social norms—play a significant role in the development of institutional discrimination. And so, for the purpose of this volume, no distinction will be made between "conformity" prejudice and the more aware or "self-gratifying" expressions of prejudice.

---

[4] From their essay entitled "Conformity versus prejudice as exemplified in white-Negro relations in the South: some methodological considerations." *Journal of Psychology, Vol. 30*, pp. 109-121.

[5] Allport, 1954/1979, p. 11.

Finally, as far as opposites go, the aforementioned MORI survey (*Profiles of Prejudice*) declared the opposite of prejudice to be "respect." But there are also other terms that I will use throughout this volume. These include Allport's notion of "tolerance," as well as my own personal preference: "acceptance."

***

Discrimination usually results from prejudice, as Allport listed the term as one of the five main ways of "acting out" prejudice towards out-groups:

1. *Antilocution*: The free expression of antagonism towards the outsider or disliked group—through conversations with friends or even strangers.
2. *Avoidance*: The separation of oneself from the outsider or disliked group.
3. *Discrimination*: Decision-making that disadvantages members of the outsider or disliked group, including exclusion from job opportunities, political rights, and so forth.
4. *Physical Attack*: The use of violence or the threat of violence against the outsider or disliked group.
5. *Extermination*: The use of extreme violence such as lynching and genocidal activities against the outsider or disliked group.

([Paraphrased from] Allport, 1954/1979, pp. 14-15)

However, for the purposes of this book, the term "discrimination" will be sometimes used to denote all the ways of acting out prejudice. Other terms—including but not limited to the ones defined above—will also be used wherever there is need for further clarification. For example, terms such as "ridiculing" and "exploitation" are other ways of "acting out" prejudice.

Introduction

J.K. Rowling's views on all forms of social discrimination are clearly and emphatically expressed throughout the *Harry Potter* series. However, the author does not set out to simply tell her readership that prejudice and discrimination are social ills. More importantly, she shows the conditions in which prejudice spawns, thrives and prospers, sometimes unnoticed. And in doing so, she does not always use the characters that her readers expect to be inhumane or "evil." Instead, she often chooses the beloved and idolized ones—the characters with whom her readership identifies most—in order to demonstrate exactly how prejudice works, as well as how pervasive it is in human cultures.

For example, in *Prisoner of Azkaban*, we see Harry's faithful and good-hearted friend, Ron, becoming extremely anxious when he discovers that one of his teachers is a werewolf (p. 253). And later, in *Goblet of Fire*, Ron is similarly alarmed when he learns that Hagrid—a close friend—is part-giant (p. 374). Even though Hagrid contradicts everything that Ron has been raised to believe about people with giant blood, the boy is still frightened by the discovery of his friend's so-called 'racial' background (in wizarding world terms). We may even speculate that, if it were not for his friendship with Harry and Hermione, Ron might never have come to an understanding that Hagrid's blood or race simply does not matter.

It is worth noting that both of Ron's best friends (Harry and Hermione) have non-magical (or "Muggle") relatives, and were raised outside the wizarding world. In contrast, Ron is a so-called "Pure-blood" wizard who knows very little about other social groups—even those within the magical community. And because of this crucial difference, both Harry and Hermione remain uninfected by certain dominant wizarding prejudices. These include a predictable superiority feeling towards the non-magical community, as well as intense *anti*-feelings towards stigmatized magical beings such as werewolves and giants. And so, when Harry and Hermione ask Ron to explain why having giant blood is such a terrible thing, he struggles to clarify the reasoning behind his opinions. Instead, he simply explains that the general belief amongst wizards is that giants are "just vicious."[1] We later discover that, as a result of wizarding prejudice, the giant race has been isolated and excluded from co-existence with other magical beings.[2]

Ron's example is important for three reasons: First, the character helps to demonstrate how environment and upbringing affect people's beliefs about others who are perceived as different from themselves. Second, Ron's unexplained *anti*-feelings point to the fact most prejudicial behavior is irrational and further proof that prejudice is often the product of ignorance. Finally, and most importantly, because we know the character to be a good, kind-hearted person, Ron's example strengthens the argument that prejudice and tolerance are not a '*bad people versus good people*' issue at all. Most people have experienced some form of discrimination against themselves. And likewise, many people have actively participated in discriminatory behavior towards others—sometimes unknowingly, but usually by blindly embracing the sort of uninformed, erroneous beliefs which sustain *anti*-feelings.

As will be discussed in later chapters, other characters in the *Harry Potter* novels repeatedly demonstrate that *anti*-feelings resulting from misinformation and ignorance can have considerable social impact. Not only can this prejudice steer the direction and the tone of day-to-day interactions between people, but it can also influence the creation of laws, as well as a person's ability to access the most basic rights and social privileges. Furthermore, the belief systems, behavior patterns and modes of thinking that foster prejudice and discrimination in J.K. Rowling's wizarding world are similar to the factors which cause prejudice in our own world.

But before discussing wizarding world prejudice in depth, let us first (re)acquaint ourselves with the story of *Harry Potter....*

---

[1] *Goblet of Fire*, p. 374.

[2] Books Four and Five reveal that, on a global scale, wizards have almost persecuted the giants to the point of extinction. See *Goblet of Fire*, p. 374 and *Order of the Phoenix*, pp. 376-378.

Introductory Book Summaries and Their Prejudice-Related Subplots

If you have not yet read the *Harry Potter* books and do not wish to be spoiled, then perhaps you should read them first before going any further with this book. But those who have not had a chance to read the series and who wish to be quickly informed about the plot should find this section useful. Some readers might simply need a quick recap of the story, which spans over 3,400 pages. The following section provides concise (yet detailed) synopses of each book. And, in addition to the book summaries, there are seven separate synopses of the subplots that are most relevant to our discussion of the prejudice-related themes in the series.

Book 1: *Harry Potter and the Philosopher's Stone*

When we first meet Harry Potter, we find him living in a cupboard under the stairs in the Dursleys' home. The Dursley family is comprised of Harry's aunt Petunia (his mother's sister), her husband Vernon and their son Dudley. Dudley is extremely pampered, ill-mannered and overweight; and we are told that his favorite hobby is hitting Harry (p. 24).

A thin, underfed eleven-year-old orphan, Harry does not yet know that he is a wizard. Before they took him in, while he was a still baby, his aunt and uncle had decided to keep his wizard identity a secret in order to prevent him from becoming an abnormal "freak" like his parents (p. 44). And although James and Lily Potter had died protecting their son from the most dangerous Dark wizard of all time (Lord Voldemort), the Dursleys informed the boy that his parents had died in a car crash.

Fortunately though, the Dursleys can do nothing to stop Harry from discovering the truth and becoming enrolled at Hogwarts—a school for magical children, which his parents had also attended. As soon as the boy turns eleven, the Hogwarts Headmaster, Albus Dumbledore, sends his trusted gamekeeper Hagrid to fetch Harry. And so, on his eleventh birthday, with Hagrid at his side, Harry walks into an incredible world of wands and wonder. Hagrid takes him to a wizard bank called Gringotts, which is run by goblins. Here, he discovers a small fortune—the wizard gold that his parents had bequeathed to him.

Harry also learns that he is famous in the wizarding world for being the only known survivor of the Killing Curse—which presumably backfired upon Voldemort, when the latter attacked a one-year-old Harry, after Lily Potter had died protecting her son. But the deadly Curse has left a mark upon the boy: the lightening bolt-shaped scar on his forehead easily identifies him as "The Boy Who Lived." All over the country, witches and wizards praise Harry for getting rid of Lord Voldemort, whom everyone seems to refer to as "You-Know-Who" or "He Who Must Not Be Named."

Apparently, the Dark Lord was so evil and powerful that he could not be killed; his own Killing Curse merely reduced him to a malignant spirit-like force which still roams the earth, hoping to regain a body and return to full power. Before arriving at Hogwarts, Harry also learns (from the wandmaker Ollivander) that his chosen wand has the same core as Voldemort's wand. Both magic wands contain a feather from the tail of the same Phoenix.

During his first year at Hogwarts, the hero is sorted into Gryffindor, one of four houses named after the founders of the school: Godric Gryffindor, Helga Hufflepuff, Rowena Ravenclaw and Salazar Slytherin. He makes friends with Ron Weasley, the youngest son of Arthur and Molly Weasley, and Hermione Granger, the brightest student in their year. The protagonist also acquires two enemies in the form of Draco Malfoy, a fellow student, and Severus Snape, a teacher who appears to loathe Harry. But just before the end of the school year, the hero must face his ultimate adversary: the wizard who murdered his parents. He barely survives the struggle; but in the end the Dark Lord is defeated again, as Harry stops him from obtaining the coveted Philosopher's Stone. The stone produces a substance called "the Elixir of Life," which could help Voldemort to regain a body and return to full power. And so, once again, Harry gains fame, celebrity and gratitude from his peers and his mentor Dumbledore for defying the Dark Lord a second time.

Prejudice-Related Subplots in *Philosopher's Stone*

I. The subplots most relevant to our discussion on prejudice concern not only the plight of the orphaned Harry—who is mistreated and abused by the Dursleys simply because he is magical—but also the snobbery displayed by his schoolboy enemy Draco Malfoy. Draco's socio-economic superiority and prejudice are constantly highlighted throughout the series, but it all starts in *Philosopher's Stone*, where he first expresses disdain for the Weasleys' poverty: "My father told me all the Weasleys have red hair, freckles and more children than they can afford" (p. 81).

Even before coming to Hogwarts, Harry had got a glimpse of Draco's snobbery; and he instantly disliked him for it. While both boys were being fitted for their school robes during the summer, upon spotting Hagrid and discovering his identity through Harry, Draco ridicules the gamekeeper: "He's a sort of servant, isn't he? ... I heard he's a sort of *savage*—lives in a hut in the school grounds, and every now and then he gets drunk, tries to do magic and ends up setting fire to his bed" (p. 60). Also, at this stage, Malfoy remains unaware that he is talking to the famous Harry Potter, whose mother was a Muggle-born witch. And so, he unreservedly declares his allegiance to Slytherin House, insisting that attendance at Hogwarts should be reserved for "the old wizarding families" (p. 61). But the subplot relating to anti Muggle-born prejudice is not fully developed until the second book...

Book 2: *Harry Potter and the Chamber of Secrets*

In the second installment of *Harry Potter*, the boy wizard almost fails to return to Hogwarts, thanks to the efforts of Dobby the house-elf. Dobby belongs to a race of slaves; and he himself is bound to serve the Malfoy family for the rest of his life. Upon overhearing his masters discussing a plot to re-open the legendary "Chamber of Secrets," he takes it upon himself to warn and protect his idol, Harry Potter.

Legend has it that the Chamber was originally built by Salazar Slytherin many centuries ago, when the school was just founded, and that a student died when it was last opened—about fifty years ago. And so, after uncovering the plot to re-open it and release a terrifying monster upon the school to purge it of unwanted elements, Dobby visits Harry during the summer (at the Dursleys) and warns him not to return to Hogwarts.

But the boy remains defiant. Dobby therefore performs magic, and sabotages an important Dursley dinner party. As a result, a letter arrives immediately from the Ministry of Magic, warning Harry that he will be expelled from Hogwarts if he uses magic again outside of school. The Dursleys also lock him away indefinitely. And so, he and his beloved owl Hedwig are left to despair and starve inside his bedroom.

But they are soon rescued—with the aid of a flying car—by Ron and his twin brothers, Fred and George Weasley. The flying car proves useful again, when Ron and Harry find themselves shut out—also through Dobby's interference—at the barrier at King's Cross Station, where they normally board the train to go to Hogwarts.

Meanwhile, the plot to re-open the Chamber proceeds, as Lucius Malfoy has managed to plant a mysterious diary on Ginny, the youngest Weasley child. Over the summer, while doing the back-to-school shopping with their children, Malfoy and Arthur Weasley had a very public altercation, after Lucius made disparaging remarks about the Weasleys' poverty and poor taste in friends (Hermione and her Muggle parents); and Lucius slipped the diary into one of Ginny's books shortly after the scuffle. The girl confides everything—including her infatuation with Harry Potter—into the book. Apparently, the diary makes ink invisible and also converses with its writer. Eventually, Ginny becomes possessed and controlled by a strange spirit encased inside the book. The malignant force causes her to kill all of Hagrid's roosters, to write threatening messages in blood on the school walls and to re-open the Chamber of Secrets, thus allowing the mysterious monster to roam the school.

In the meantime, Harry keeps hearing strange voices threatening to kill. And amidst fearsome rumors that the heir of Slytherin has returned, most students now suspect him of being the culprit behind the mysterious attacks that have left a cat and two Muggle-borns "petrified"—frozen in a stony but living state. Harry's ability to speak to snakes marks him as a potential Dark wizard; and this frightens his peers.

Nevertheless, when the Minister of Magic, Cornelius Fudge, arrives at Hogwarts accompanied by Lucius Malfoy, it is Hagrid whom they arrest on suspicion of opening the Chamber. They also inform Dumbledore that, due to his inability to stop the attacks on Muggle-borns, the council of school governors has suspended him as Headmaster. But the Muggle-born attacks continue after Dumbledore's departure.

Meanwhile, Hermione helps the trio to solve parts of the mystery with the aid of a substance called the "Polyjuice Potion," which causes the drinker to temporarily take on the appearance of another person. They take on disguises in order to interrogate Draco Malfoy; but they are unable to discover the true identity of Slytherin's heir before Hermione, too, is petrified. Nevertheless, she uncovers a vital clue before the attack: The monster is a Basilisk—a snake that has a murderous gaze, and which can be killed by a rooster's crow.

The attacks cease for a short while, as Ginny finally fights off the diary's possessive influence and tries to discard it by flushing it down a toilette. Unfortunately, however, the book finds its way back into the school and into the hands of none other than Harry Potter. He unravels its secrets and discovers that it had once belonged to a former student called Tom Riddle. Riddle's living memory of the last time the Chamber was opened is encased inside the book; and it shows Harry a young Hagrid being accused and expelled for opening the Chamber fifty years ago.

But Ginny soon notices Harry with the diary, and she steals it back from him. Riddle's memory possesses her completely this time, and leads her into the bowels of the Chamber, where Harry must go to rescue her. Here, he discovers that Tom Riddle is Voldemort's birth name, and that it was he who had opened the Chamber fifty years ago and framed Hagrid. Through sheer bravery, luck and his unwavering loyalty to Dumbledore, Harry succeeds in destroying the diary, along with the ghost of Riddle's memory. He also kills the Basilisk with Godric Gryffindor's sword. Thus, the Dark Lord is defied yet again by The Boy Who

Lived; Dumbledore is immediately reinstated as Headmaster; and Dobby the house-elf is set free.

Prejudice-Related Subplots in *Chamber of Secrets*

I. We see some important pejorative terms being used for the first time in *Chamber of Secrets*, most notably when Draco Malfoy calls Hermione a "filthy little Mudblood" (p. 86). An outraged Ron gallantly defends Hermione; but neither she nor Harry understands why the term is so offensive. Hagrid and Ron later explain that "Mudblood" denotes "dirty blood," and that there are wizards who believe that people like Hermione should not be allowed access to the wizarding world (pp. 89-90). In Chapter 5 of this volume, I will discuss the use of the "Mudblood" pejorative in greater detail.

II. We also learn that prejudice against "Squibs" (wizard offspring who have no magical powers) is a dominant feature in the wizarding world. The school caretaker, Argus Filch, finally admits that he is a Squib, but only because he feels targeted when his cat (Mrs. Norris) is petrified. Ron's reaction to the revelation of Filch's Squib status is not at all sympathetic. But perhaps this is simply due to the fact that the caretaker has always been unkind to the students. I will discuss the Squib issue in greater detail in Chapter 4 of this volume.

III. Finally, Harry is also a victim of prejudice in *Chamber of Secrets*. The fact that he, like Voldemort, can speak snake language (or Parseltongue) makes him the object of immense suspicion and fear. Apparently, it is widely believed that "parselmouths" are Dark wizards. And so, as a result of his ability, plus the fact that he has had such an awful relationship with the Dursleys, Harry is deemed a hater of Muggles and, by extension, Muggle-borns. This subplot will be briefly re-visited in Chapters 2 and 7 of this volume.

Book 3: *Harry Potter and the Prisoner of Azkaban*

With the introduction of the "Dementors," the third book is much darker than the previous two. Dementors are dark creatures that guard the wizard prison Azkaban. They bring dense fog and extreme cold, as they suck all the happiness out of any place they inhabit. They also torture their victims to insanity by inflicting their own worst memories upon them; and they are particularly attracted to Harry because of the extreme horrors in his past. Whenever they approach him, Harry can hear his mother screaming and pleading with Voldemort to spare his life. Furthermore, the ultimate punishment that the Ministry of Magic can inflict upon convicted criminals is to subject them to the Dementor's kiss: the foul creature sucks out a human's soul via the mouth.

After running away from the Dursleys' home, Harry learns about the wizard prison and the Dementors through Stan Shunpike, the conductor on the "Knight Bus"—"emergency transport for the stranded witch or wizard" (p. 30). When he accidentally blows up (inflates) Uncle Vernon's sister (Aunt Marge), after she grossly insulted his parents, Harry is almost certain that he will be expelled from Hogwarts this time for performing magic outside school. But instead, he finds a very congenial and forgiving Minister for Magic (Cornelius Fudge) awaiting him at the Leaky Cauldron.[1] Harry later discovers that the Minister and nearly all the adults in his life are trying to protect him from his infamous godfather, Sirius Black. A recent escapee from Azkaban, Black had allegedly betrayed James and Lily Potter to Voldemort, and then murdered thirteen people with a single curse. Harry is overcome with anger and grief when he hears about Black's betrayal.

The boy is additionally frustrated by several unfortunate circumstances: First, the Dursleys had not signed his permission slip to go into Hogsmeade Village with the other third-year students on weekends. As a result, he is left behind at Hogwarts while Ron and Hermione are out sight-seeing. Second, the Dementors keep attacking him every chance they

---

[1] The Leaky Cauldron is a famous wizard inn which is said to be situated somewhere near Tottenham Court Road in London (*Deathly Hallows*, p. 135). It provides the only stealth entrance to the hidden Diagon Alley—an enchanted street, lined with wizard shops.

get, even while he is playing Quidditch.[2] Third, his two best friends are constantly bickering because Ron is convinced that Hermione's cat Crookshanks has eaten his pet rat Scabbers. And finally, Hagrid is having a terrible first year as the new Care of Magical Creatures teacher: When a pet Hippogriff called Buckbeak injures an exaggerating Draco Malfoy, the boy's father (Lucius) embarks on a ruthless campaign at the Ministry to get Hagrid fired. In the end, Hagrid keeps his job and adjusts his lesson plans; but the Hippogriff is sentenced to death.

Buckbeak's sentencing plus the sudden reappearance of Scabbers the rat, are among several strange events that lead Harry to cross Sirius Black's path. The trio stick together, as Ron and Hermione tell Sirius that he will have to kill them, too, if he means to kill Harry (p. 249). But they later learn that Sirius is innocent, before witnessing the transformation of the real traitor: Peter Pettigrew was another old friend of the Potters. After framing Sirius, he disguised himself as the rat Scabbers and has been hiding for the past thirteen years.

The trio also discover that Harry's father (James), Sirius and Peter had been friends with the werewolf Remus Lupin, the latest Defense Against the Dark Arts teacher. Apparently, while they were students at Hogwarts, they called themselves the "Marauders." Sirius, James and Peter had all learned to become "Animagi"[3] so that they could keep Lupin's company at the full moon. Nicknaming themselves Moony (Lupin), Wormtail (Pettigrew), Padfoot (Sirius) and Prongs (James), the Marauders gained extensive knowledge of the Hogwarts grounds through their monthly adventures. And they wrote

---

[2] Quidditch is a wizard game played on broomsticks high in the air. There are three different types of balls, and seven players on each team: Three "Chasers" use the "Quaffle" to score goals through hoops suspended in mid-air; two "Beaters" bat the "Bludgers" towards the other team to prevent them from advancing or scoring; a Goalkeeper protects the hoops; and a Seeker searches for the golden "Snitch," which ends the game and is worth a hundred and fifty points when captured. Harry becomes the youngest Seeker in a century when he is picked to play for the Gryffindor team during his first year at Hogwarts (See *Philosopher's Stone*, pp. 113-114 & pp. 124-125).

[3] An Animagus is a witch or wizard who can transform into an animal at will. We learn that, by law, an Animagus must be registered with the Ministry of Magic (*Prisoner of Azkaban*, pp. 257-258); and so, James Potter and his friends were all illegal Animagi.

the "Marauder's Map," which shows the location of everyone on the school grounds.

Harry is deeply enthralled by all these discoveries; and both he and his godfather are excited at the prospect of living together after Sirius' name is cleared. But a series of misfortunes robs them of their hopes of becoming a family. First, a rancorous Snape, intent on getting revenge on Sirius for having teased him while they were at school together, interferes with the plans to capture Pettigrew and hand the real traitor over to the Ministry. Then the sudden appearance of a full moon causes Lupin's untimely transformation. Pettigrew then re-transforms and escapes into the night.

Afterwards, Cornelius Fudge—encouraged by Snape—sentences Sirius to the Dementor's Kiss. However, with the aid of an instrument called a Time Turner (which Hermione has been secretly using all year to go back in time so that she could take several classes during the same hour) they manage to help both Sirius and Buckbeak to escape. The following day, an outraged Snape informs his Slytherin students that Remus Lupin is a werewolf. The rumor spreads quickly, causing fear and outrage amongst students and parents alike. And so, the man who had taught Harry to conjure a Patronus—the only protective charm that wards off Dementors—is forced to resign.

Prejudice-Related Subplots in *Prisoner of Azkaban*

I. Continuing with some of the themes from *Chamber of Secrets*, the third story emphasizes the dangers of allowing mere perception to influence decisions that affect people's quality of life. In the same way that parselmouths are stigmatized as Dark wizards, werewolves are deemed to be dark creatures (and are therefore rejected and isolated) because of their condition. We are told that Lupin's garments are shabby and that he looks impoverished (p. 59). And this is obviously due to the fact that werewolves are virtually unemployable in the wizarding world. Prejudice and institutional discrimination against werewolves will be examined more closely in Chapter 4 of this volume.

II. The third story also reverberates with a sense of the gross injustices inflicted upon the wrongly accused (Sirius). In fact, from the very first page, where Rowling makes reference to medieval witch hunts and witch burnings, to the very last chapter , where we see Sirius wrongfully condemned and Lupin walking away from his job with the proverbial tail between the legs, Book 3 teems with injustice and prejudice. And yet, it is perhaps the most subtly written of all the seven books in the series.

Book 4: *Harry Potter and the Goblet of Fire*

First, we learn the fate of Wormtail: Having returned to his master's side, he assists the Dark Lord in his plan to regain a body and rise to power again. By the end of the first chapter, they have already killed two people. And, somehow, Harry has severe scar pains and visions of real events through Voldemort's eyes whenever the Dark Lord is about to commit murder. Not wanting to alarm his friends, Harry writes to his godfather Sirius, who is now in hiding abroad, to tell him about his scar hurting. Sirius is greatly concerned for Harry's safety and decides to return to Britain.

Other departures from the content and structure of previous books include the Quidditch World Cup, which Harry attends with Hermione and the Weasley family during the summer. There is also a "Tri-wizard" tournament at Hogwarts. This ancient competition involves three difficult tasks (one each term) and three selected "Champions" from their respective schools. The competing schools are Hogwarts, a French school called Beauxbatons Academy, and another European school called Durmstrang. The competition also involves a Yule Ball, which, to Ron's dismay, Hermione attends with famous Quidditch player and Durmstrang Champion Victor Krum. Harry is turned down by Cho Chang, a pretty Ravenclaw girl with whom he has been infatuated since his third year. But Chang only refuses him because she has already been asked by handsome Hufflepuff student and Hogwarts Champion Cedric Diggory.

Somehow, the underage Harry becomes the fourth Champion in the Triwizard tournament. This severely tests his friendship with a jealous Ron, who believes his best friend found a way to enter the competition and decided to keep it a secret. But later we discover that the boy's name had been entered into the Goblet of Fire by Barty Crouch Junior, Voldemort's so-called "most faithful servant" (p. 15 & p. 565). With the aid of Polyjuice Potion, Crouch has been posing all year as Mad-Eye Moody. The real Mad-Eye is a trusted friend whom Dumbledore has appointed to become Remus Lupin's successor (as the new Defense Against the Dark Arts teacher). But the impostor proves to be rather useful, as he gives the students first-hand experience with all three Unforgivable Curses: The Imperius Curse (which forces the victim to act on the will of his attacker), the Cruciatus Curse (for torturing) and the Avada Kedavra (or Killing Curse).

Believed to be dead by everyone except his father and their house-elf Winky, Crouch has worked all year to secure a Harry Potter victory in the Triwizard tournament. He turns the Triwizard trophy into a Portkey[4] that will instantly transport the first person who touches it to a graveyard, where Voldemort and Wormtail await. Unfortunately, however, Harry shares his victory with Cedric, who is instantly killed when they reach the graveyard. Wormtail then proceeds with a hair-raising ritual to restore Voldemort to a body. The restorative potion must include bone from the father (taken from Tom Riddle Senior's grave), blood from the enemy (Harry) and flesh willingly given by a servant. And for the latter, Wormtail literally gives his right hand. After regaining a body, Voldemort fashions a replacement silver hand for Wormtail. He then presses the "Dark Mark" on Wormtail's forearm and summons his "Death Eaters"—a group of pure-blood wizards who had served him while he was at the height of his power.

After reprimanding them all for not trying to find him sooner, Voldemort entertains the Death Eaters by taunting and torturing Harry. But the spectacle is ruined when the boy

[4] A Portkey is an item that can be used as a transportation device. We are told that Portkeys are usually "unobtrusive things" that look like garbage, so that Muggles don't pick them up (*Goblet of Fire*, p. 66).

suddenly fights back. Unaware that they share brother wands, Voldemort is shocked when Harry shows extraordinary resistance, somehow summoning the spirits of the Dark Lord's last victims in reverse order. These include Harry's parents (James and Lily), as well as Cedric. And so, through the "Priori Incantatem" or "reverse-spell effect," Harry buys himself enough time to escape and take Cedric's body back to Hogwarts.

Dumbledore instantly believes Harry's gruesome tale about the Dark Lord being restored to a body and murdering Cedric. He uncovers the full plot by questioning the impostor Crouch, using Veritaserum—a potion which forces the drinker to speak the truth. The headmaster also discovers the real Mad-Eye Moody, barely alive and hidden in a compartment of his own magical trunk.

But the Minister of Magic (Cornelius Fudge) refuses to believe that Voldemort has indeed returned. He suggests that it is all part of the imagination of an attention-seeking, mentally disturbed Harry. Fudge forcibly distances himself from Dumbledore, submitting Barty Crouch Junior to the Dementor's Kiss—thus making it impossible for the criminal to give testimony of Voldemort's return, or to publicly confess to his crimes, which include working for Voldemort all year, and murdering his own father.

The story ends with a defiant Dumbledore rallying his troops: Molly and Arthur Weasley, Hagrid, Snape, McGonagall and Sirius, who finally comes out of hiding in front of this select group. Later, a severely traumatized Harry gives all his Triwizard winnings (one thousand gold Galleons) to the Weasley twins, who can now pursue their ambitions of setting up a joke shop.

Prejudice-Related Subplots in *Goblet of Fire*

I. Picking up on subplots from previous books, Book 4 sees the return of the house-elf Dobby, who still worships Harry Potter and—unlike other house-elves—treasures his own freedom. We also discover that there is a large group of elves working in the Hogwarts kitchens. Naturally, out of concern and indignation that there are slaves at Hogwarts, Hermione founds the Society for the Promotion of

Elfish Welfare (S.P.E.W.). But much of the resistance she encounters comes from the elves themselves. Are they "uneducated and brainwashed" (p. 211), as Hermione suggests? Or is it simply in their nature to be subservient? In Chapter 3 of this volume, I will discuss the house-elf situation in greater detail.

II. Prejudice themes become even more prominent in Book 4 with the discovery that Hagrid is half-giant. Ron's reaction to the news is very telling: giant blood is simply not allowed in wizarding society. The giant issue will be briefly addressed in Chapters 1 and 2.

III. Cornelius Fudge's judgmental attitude towards Harry is also quite telling. Thanks to the defamatory journalist Rita Skeeter, the boy has become a social outcast, and is suspected of being mentally disturbed. Surprisingly, Harry is stigmatized for the very same reason he became famous in the first place: the attack that has left him scarred since infancy. And, like most readers of the *Daily Prophet*, Fudge believes all the rumors. Wizarding society's intolerant views and treatment of the mentally Disabled can be likened to attitudes in our own world. This issue will be briefly re-visited in Chapter 4 of this volume.

Book 5: *Harry Potter and the Order of the Phoenix*

During the summer holidays, Harry is expelled from Hogwarts for using magic to ward off Dementors sent to attack him and his cousin, Dudley. He is later moved from the Dursleys' home by a group that calls themselves "the Order of the Phoenix." James and Lily were once members of the Order—a group of wizards who used to fight alongside Dumbledore when Voldemort was at the height of his power. Now the group is comprised of a few Aurors,[5] which includes the real Mad-Eye Moody, his young apprentice Nymphadora Tonks and the talented Kingsley Shacklebolt. The Order also

---

[5] Aurors are an elite force of dark wizard catchers working for the Ministry.

includes Remus Lupin, Sirius Black, Severus Snape, the Weasley parents and other long-time friends of Dumbledore.

Harry is escorted to Order Headquarters, located at 12 Grimmauld Place—a house which was once home to the prestigious Black family. Here, while he awaits his Ministry hearing, he meets Kreacher the elf and learns a great deal about his godfather's ancient pure-blood family. Sadly, however, Sirius is restless and often distant. He is still on the run from the Ministry; and, on Dumbledore's insistence, he has to remain locked away in a house that he has hated all his life. Also, the ever malicious Severus Snape never misses a chance to taunt him about not having to risk his life or do anything important for the Order. As a result, Sirius takes out his frustrations on his mutinous, foul-mouthed elf slave (Kreacher), who constantly calls Hermione a "Mudblood." But the group has far more important things to worry about than the demented house-elf...

To everyone's surprise, Harry does not get a hearing, but rather a full criminal trial by a Wizengamot[6] jury, from which Dumbledore has been recently expelled. Apparently, both Dumbledore and Harry are now outcasts in the wizarding world, stigmatized by Cornelius Fudge and the Ministry-controlled press for trying to spread the word about Voldemort's return. Nevertheless, against enormous odds, such as last minute changes to the time and location of the hearing, Dumbledore saves the day. He convinces the Wizengamot that Harry had indeed performed magic in a life-threatening situation. And the boy is not expelled.

But Fudge compensates for this setback by installing his Senior Undersecretary, Dolores Umbridge, at Hogwarts as the new Defense Against the Dark Arts teacher. Umbridge

---

[6] The term "Wizengamot" seems to be drawn from a pre-medieval Anglo-Saxon political institution called the 'Witenagemot,' a term whose meaning in Old English translates as "meeting of wise men." Similarly, the Wizengamot of the *Harry Potter* series is comprised of the oldest and the wisest wizards of the day. They act as judges in the most serious criminal trials, which take place in large courtrooms deep in the basement of the Ministry of Magic.

employs a very non-practical approach to teaching Defense,[7] subjects the staff to extreme scrutiny and tries to silence Harry. But the boy stages an effective resistance, establishing an illegal Defense group nicknamed "Dumbledore's Army," or the "DA." He uses this medium to prepare his peers for Voldemort's return by teaching them to fight the Dark Arts.

In the meantime, without any explanation whatsoever, Dumbledore refuses to speak to Harry or to even look at him. We later discover that he is simply trying to protect the boy from Voldemort. At this point, the Dark Lord has not yet realized that he and Harry share a rather dangerous mind-link. And even though the connection proves useful when Harry is able to raise the alarm following an attack on Arthur Weasley by Voldemort's pet snake Nagini, Dumbledore fears for the boy's safety. Voledemort could possess Harry's mind and force him to harm himself or others.

And so, the headmaster schedules Occlumency lessons for Harry with Professor Snape, who tries to teach the boy how to close his mind. But it all goes horribly wrong when the ever curious Harry invades Snape's privacy, exploring painful childhood memories that the teacher never wanted him to see. He discovers why Snape hated his father (James Potter) so much: Sirius and James had ruthlessly taunted the awkward young Severus while they were at school together. And so, feeling violated, Snape decides that there is too much of James in Harry, and he discontinues their private lessons.

Voldemort eventually discovers the link and plants an image of Sirius being tortured at the Ministry inside Harry's mind. And so, accompanied by Hermione, Ron and other members of the DA, Harry rushes off to rescue his godfather. He has clearly walked into a trap, but there is a slight twist...

Apparently, in his bid to protect Harry, Dumbledore had chosen not to tell him about the Prophecy hidden in the Department of Mysteries at the Ministry. This is the ultimate weapon which Voldemort needs in order to learn how to overcome Harry Potter. But he can only get it by going into the Ministry himself—thus exposing himself to the wizarding

---

[7] Fudge fears that Dumbledore might try to overthrow him by forming a student army at Hogwarts; and so, he instructs Umbridge to remove all practical training elements from the teaching syllabus.

world—or by getting Harry to retrieve it for him. And so, after Harry removes the Prophecy from its shelf, a battle with the Death Eaters ensues. The Order of the Phoenix, including Sirius, arrives just in time to help. But the Prophecy (encased in a glass sphere) is destroyed. And, tragically, Sirius is killed while fighting his cousin Bellatrix Lestrange.

Dumbledore arrives during the fight and captures several Death Eaters. And so, realizing that his servants are in trouble, Voldemort joins the battle. But he can neither defeat Dumbledore nor succeed in possessing Harry, whose emotions are far too powerful for the Dark Lord: Harry's love and grief for Sirius are so strong that it is sheer torture for the cold, conscience-less Voldemort to take hold of his mind for long. Nevertheless, Voldemort and Bellatrix manage to escape capture, but not before Fudge and other Ministry officials arrive to witness their presence.

Later, Dumbledore takes the blame for Sirius's death, and allows a grief-struck, enraged Harry to express his own feelings. But the boy nearly destroys the headmaster's office in the process. Soon afterwards, the headmaster reveals that Kreacher betrayed Sirius. It appears that the elf informed the Death Eaters about Sirius's devotion to his godson and of Harry's love for him in return—thus allowing the Dark Lord to use Sirius as bait to capture the boy and obtain the Prophecy. We also learn that the original Prophecy had been made to Dumbledore by Sybill Trelawney, the troubled Divination teacher. And according to the prediction, Harry is the only one who can destroy the Dark Lord, "for neither can live while the other survives" (p. 741).

Prejudice-Related Subplots in *Order of the Phoenix*

I. On the journey to Hogwarts, Harry shares a train carriage with the quirky Luna Lovegood and the exceedingly clumsy Neville Longbottom. And when the pretty and popular Cho Chang stops by to greet him, we see him wishing he were seen with much 'cooler' people. However, by the end of the story, Harry comes to recognize his own shallowness, and values the faithful friends that have stood by him through hard times, regardless of their appearance.

Harry's emotional development will be discussed in Chapter 7 of this volume.

II. The giant issue re-emerges in this novel. Hagrid gets back from an important secret mission with information about a major giant settlement in France, where there is now a raging contest going on between Dumbledore and the Death Eaters: Though the giants are feared and shunned, each side wants them as allies—presumably to exploit their power—in the upcoming war. We also discover that people who (like Hagrid) have giant blood are impervious to wand spells—which partly explains why wizards fear the giants so much. Issues concerning the giant race will be briefly discussed in Chapters 1 and 2.

III. We also discover that Harry's cat-loving neighbor in the Muggle world, Mrs. Figg, is a Squib. Dumbledore calls her as a witness in Harry's trial; but Cornelius Fudge ridicules the old woman because of her Squib status. This will be discussed further in Chapter 4.

IV. Harry is also a social outcast throughout most of this book: Almost the entire wizarding world believes he is insane. He endures severe ridiculing in the press and also from his peers. Social stigmas concerning mental illness will be briefly discussed in Chapter 4.

V. Finally, the house-elf enslavement issue is another important recurring theme. Harry and Dumbledore differ on the matter of Kreacher's responsibility for Sirius's death. Dumbledore maintains that the elf is the true victim because "Kreacher is what he has been made by wizards" (p. 733). This issue will be discussed at length in Chapter 3 of this volume.

Book 6: *Harry Potter and the Half-blood Prince*

The sixth book starts with Cornelius Fudge—now playing an advisory role to his successor, Rufus Scrimgeour—giving the muggle Prime Minister the bad news that Voldemort has returned to full power. Random disasters are happening all over the country; and people are dying—both muggle and magical. In a desperate bid to convince the public that they are in control of the situation, the Ministry arrests several people—such as Stan Shunpike—with very little proof of guilt. But persecuting the innocent only puts them further out of favour with Dumbledore and Harry Potter, whom they desperately want on their side—at least in appearance. Still, the new Minister refuses to release Stan. Meanwhile, the real Death Eaters escape from Azkaban and the Dementors have abandoned their post to rejoin Voldemort.

At Hogwarts...Harry is suddenly popular again. He is now the boy every girl wants to date. He captains the Gryffindor Quidditch team, romances the highly desired Ginny Weasley, and has private lessons with the headmaster. With the aid of an instrument called a "Pensieve," which allows them to explore the past through other people's memories, Dumbledore teaches Harry everything he knows or has guessed about Voldemort. He believes the Dark Lord has a fragmented soul—split into seven pieces, or "Horcuxes." And a Horcux is usually made after murdering someone.

Dumbledore believes that two of Voldemort's Horcruxes have already been found: the diary that opened the Chamber of Secrets and an ancient ring that was last owned by the Gaunts, the Dark Lord's relatives on his mother's side. Apparently the Gaunts were also the last remaining descendants of Salazar Slytherin. Along with the ring, they last owned Slytherin's locket—another of the four Horcuxes which must be found and destroyed before the seventh piece of Voldemort's soul (that which resides in his body) can be destroyed. Dumbledore has already destroyed the ring; but the effort it took nearly killed him: The Horcrux had been protected by a very powerful curse.

Meanwhile, Harry is doing relatively well in the rest of his classes. Momentarily overjoyed after discovering that his nemesis is no longer the Potions master, he is miserable again when Snape becomes the new Defense Against the Dark Arts teacher. Still, his grades in Potions improve significantly. This is partly due to the new teacher, Horace Slughorn, who had also taught the popular Lily (Evans) Potter when she was at Hogwarts. Also, Harry discovers some highly instructive scribbles in a second-hand Potions textbook which apparently once belonged to a mysterious "Half-blood Prince."

But the Prince seems to have had a dark side: Harry earns himself what seems like a lifetime of detentions with Snape when he uses one of the Prince's inventions—a flesh-splitting curse ("Sectumsempra")—during a fight with Draco Malfoy. Since the beginning of the school year, Harry has suspected Draco of being a newly inducted Death Eater. But no one else seems to share his concerns. Unfortunately, though, Harry is proved right when Death Eaters infiltrate the school while he and Dumbledore are out hunting Horcruxes.

Dumbledore orders Harry to remain hidden under his Invisibility Cloak, and he puts a Body-Bind Spell on the boy just before Draco and several Death Eaters ambush them at the top of the Astronomy Tower. Disarmed by Draco, Dumbledore speaks calmly to the boy, who finally confesses that Voldemort had set him the task of assassinating the headmaster. But Dumbledore continues to speak kindly and reassuringly to Draco, telling him that he is not a killer. But just as Draco lowers his wand, Snape—later revealed to be *the* Half-blood Prince—storms in and blasts Dumbledore with a Killing Curse.

Harry watches helplessly and in silence as his mentor falls to his death. And shortly after the funeral, he nobly ends his relationship with Ginny Weasley. This is a precaution he feels he must take in order to prevent Ginny from being exploited by Voldemort, just as the Dark Lord had once used Sirius (with fatal consequences) to lure him into a trap. Harry also decides to go in search of the remaining Horcruxes instead of returning to Hogwarts for his final year of school. And, of course, Ron and Hermione pledge to stay by his side.

Prejudice-Related Subplots in *Half-blood Prince*

I. Although it is not one of the themes that I intend to develop in this book, it is worth noting that, despite the lessons learned from the tragedy of Sirius's death the year before, Dumbledore has yet to overcome his *old man's prejudice*[8] towards younger people. And this flaw is what ultimately causes his demise. He knew all along that Voldemort had set Draco the task of killing him; and he was trying to protect the boy. But he did not know that Draco had discovered a way to give the Death Eaters direct access to the school. This caught the headmaster completely by surprise and could have been prevented if he had heeded Harry's warnings about Draco's activities in the Room of Requirement. The headmaster's unwillingness to listen lead to catastrophic consequences; and his mistake is a good example of when adults fail to listen to the young, and suffer for it.

II. Other prejudice-related subplots include the "Squib," anti-Muggle and "Mudblood" issues, which all recur in this story, particularly with the introduction of Voldemort's relatives. Although she was not a very powerful witch, Voldemort's mother, Merope Gaunt, had magical powers. But she was often intimidated by her tyrannical father, who was obsessed with his wizarding lineage. We see him calling her a "dirty Squib" (p. 195). We also discover that Muggle-torture was not always against wizarding laws, as Marvolo Gaunt fully condoned his son's crimes against Voldemort's Muggle father, Tom Riddle Senior: "[Morfin] taught a filthy Muggle a lesson, that's illegal now, is it?" (p. 195). And finally, we learn that there is a form of physical stereotyping involved in recognizing Muggle-borns, as we see Marvolo getting aggressive with a Ministry official for having the wrong-shaped nose: "Are you pure-blood?... Now I come to think about it, I've seen noses like yours down the village." (p. 193). All of these issues will be revisited in the fourth and fifth chapters of this volume.

---

[8] Shortly after Sirius's death in Book 5, Dumbledore had said to Harry: "Youth cannot know how age thinks and feels. But old men are guilty if they forget what it is to be young…and I seem to have forgotten lately." (*Order of the Phoenix*, p. 728)

Book 7: *Harry Potter and the Deathly Hallows*

As soon as Harry turns 17, on July 31st, the protective charms that have kept him safe while he lived with the Dursleys will break. The boy intends to embark on the Horcrux quest, but his relatives must also go into hiding. Before parting ways with Harry, Dudley and Petunia Dursley come as close as they can to apologizing to him for 16 years of torment; but Vernon Dursley remains unrepentant. Dudley expresses gratitude to Harry for having saved him from the Dementors two years ago. With Hermione's help, Harry also eventually reconciles with Kreacher; and the elf helps them to locate Slytherin's locket, one of the four remaining Horcruxes.

The wizarding world is now in a state of open warfare: Voldemort's forces have taken over the Ministry of Magic; and even Stan Shunpike is now a full Death Eater. But Harry suspects that Stan might be acting under the Imperius Curse; and he spares his life during a heated showdown with Voldemort and the Death Eaters, in which Mad-Eye Moody dies and George Weasley loses an ear. Meanwhile, the wizarding press mounts posters of Harry Potter, labeled "Undesirable Number One." And Dolores Umbridge joins forces with the Death Eaters, putting Muggle-born witches and wizards on trial for "stealing" magical powers. Attendance at Hogwarts is now mandatory for all children born in wizarding families; but most Muggle-born students are now on the run from the Ministry. Many Pure-bloods, too, (usually referred to as blood traitors[9]) are fleeing. The Weasleys, for example, are forced into hiding when a Death Eater raid interrupts the wedding ceremony of the eldest son, Bill.

Amidst all this chaos, Rita Skeeter has published a scandalous biography on the late Albus Dumbledore; and Harry struggles to come to terms with some of its revelations...

Still, Dumbledore has left clues for Harry, Hermione and Ron in his will. And the trio eventually discover the existence of the "Deathly Hallows"—three objects that will allow the bearer to become "Master of Death." These are: the Elder

---

[9] "Bloodtraitor" is a derogatory name for a pure-blood wizard who sympathizes with Muggles and Muggle-borns, and who treats other magical races with equality. The entire Weasley family are deemed to be bloodtraitors.

Wand, the Resurrection Stone and the Cloak of Invisibility. And through the mind-link he shares with Voldemort, Harry finds out that the Dark Lord is already in pursuit of one of the Hallows—the Elder Wand. Harry thinks he himself already owns one Hallow—the Invisibility Cloak which he inherited from his father. But he remains unaware that the Resurrection Stone is hidden inside the golden Snitch that Dumbledore left him in his will. Naturally, the boy becomes obsessed with the idea of possessing all three objects. Hermione, however, refuses to believe in the Hallows legend. Nevertheless, she accompanies Harry on a quest which leads them to Godric's Hollow, where his parents died 16 years ago. But a trap awaits them there: Voldemort's snake Nagini attacks them; they barely manage to escape; and Harry's wand is broken during the scuffle.

Other unforeseen hardships such as the presence of a powerful Horcrux (the locket) in their midst, plus Ron's growing insecurities about Hermione's feelings, lead to strained relationships amongst the trio. Ron abandons the group but later returns to redeem himself by saving Harry's life and destroying the Horcrux with Gryffindor's sword. He also returns with crucial information about what is happening in the outside world: Apparently it is now "taboo" to say Voldemort's name out loud. Any utterance of "Voldemort" breaks protective charms instantly, allowing the culprits to be found and arrested by Death Eaters and "Snatchers."[10]

Meanwhile, Harry is becoming increasingly disillusioned with his former mentor, as Rita Skeeter's new book and the *Daily Prophet* newspaper reveal that Dumbledore had some significant skeletons in his closet: Apparently Dumbledore had befriended the infamous Dark wizard Gellert Grindelwald during their youth; and they both shared adolescent aspirations of bringing wizardkind out of hiding and ruling over Muggles "*for the greater good*." Also, the book claims that Dumbledore and his mother had allegedly suppressed and imprisoned his Squib sister.

---

[10] These are gangs who are "trying to earn gold by rounding up Muggle-borns and blood traitors." (*Deathly Hallows*, p. 311).

Some of these rumors are later contradicted by Dumbledore's brother Aberforth. But it is clear that the younger brother still harbors deep resentment towards Albus for the friendship with Grindelwald; and he blames them both for their sister Ariana's untimely death. Aberforth pleads with Harry not to follow Dumbledore's orders anymore, to forget about "the greater good" and save himself. But the hero's resolve is unmoved: he must complete his mission, regardless of his mentor's imperfections or youthful errors in judgment...

A heated argument with Hermione (over the existence of the Deathly Hallows) leads Harry to mistakenly break taboo. The trio are then captured by a group of Snatchers and taken to Malfoy Manor. There, Bellatrix Lestrange tortures Hermione almost to the point of death; but the girl's resolve holds and she does not disclose any of the trio's secrets.

Other prisoners at the Manor include their schoolmates Luna Lovegood and Dean Thomas, the wandmaker Ollivander and a goblin called Griphook. Wormtail is also there, but he is later throttled by his own silver hand when Harry stirs his conscience. Desperate for help, Harry then uses a keepsake that Sirius had given him. Miraculously, the house-elf Dobby (sent by Aberforth) arrives and helps them to escape. Then Harry and Ron overpower Draco and Disarm the Death Eaters before rescuing Hermione. But unfortunately, Dobby does not survive this last fight: Bellatrix throws a deadly knife, piercing him in the chest just before they escape.

Harry's grief over Dobby's death impels him to prioritize finding and destroying the other Horcruxes above the Hallows quest. And with Griphook's help, they stage a successful attack on Gringotts and retrieve Hufflepuff's cup (another Horcrux) from the Lestranges' vault. They then return to Hogwarts to find another Horcrux—Ravenclaw's diadem. Here, they are joined by members of the Order of the Phoenix and Dumbledore's Army, all of whom have decided to fight the Dark Lord alongside Harry.

Following the attack on Gringotts, Voldemort finally realizes that his Horcruxes are in danger; and he stages a bloody battle at Hogwarts. Several beloved characters die, including Remus Lupin, Nymphadora Tonks and Fred, one of the Weasley twins. He then commands Nagini to kill Severus Snape, assuming that Snape had become the Elder Wand's master after having killed Dumbledore. But, in fact, according to wandlore, since it had been Draco Malfoy who Disarmed[11] Dumbledore just before his death, it was Draco and not Snape who was the wand's master. And when Harry overpowered Draco and took his wand during the recent scuffle at Malfoy Manor, he then became the true master of the Elder Wand.

The hero obtains crucial memories from Snape just before he dies; and he uses the Pensieve inside Dumbledore's office to explore them. Here, he discovers that his own death had always been a part of the plan, as he witnesses Dumbledore telling Snape that Voldemort had unintentionally made Harry a Horcrux when he attacked the boy sixteen years ago and left him with a curse scar. And as a result, Harry will have to let the Dark Lord kill him.

And so, unaware that he is now in command of all three Hallows, Harry faces the Dark Lord and accepts his own death. At the same time, unaware that he had made Harry a Horcrux, Voldemort tries to kill the boy again. This time, they both collapse; and Harry enters a sort of limbo between life and death, where he speaks with Dumbledore and sees Voldemort's tattered, mutilated soul. Later, both he and the Dark Lord return to the mortal world to fight one last battle. Neville Longbottom destroys the snake Nagini, Voldemort's last remaining Horcrux. And, in their final showdown, Voldemort's Killing Curse backfires once again; and Harry Potter finally triumphs over the Dark Lord for good.

Prejudice-Related Subplots in *Deathly Hallows*

I. Extreme violence against Muggle-borns finally becomes institutional in this book, when Voldemort's forces finally take over the Ministry. It is not clear whether the aim is to exterminate them or to turn them into a subordinated class of depraved beggars: Perhaps it is both. The matter of anti-Muggle-born legislation will be briefly re-visited in Chapter 5 of this volume.

---

[11] See *Half-blood Prince*, p. 545. The incantation for the "Disarming Charm" is "Expelliarmus."

II. Also, through Dumbledore's family history and the intense suspicions that Skeeter's biography raises, we get a better insight into how Squibs used to be treated in the wizarding world. When rumors emerge that Dumbledore had a Squib sister who had been locked away, certain characters (such as Ron's Auntie Muriel) do not seem as surprised nor as revolted as Harry clearly is. Squib exclusion will be further discussed in Chapter 4 of this volume.

III. All in all, *Deathly Hallows* is about the role that appearance and misperceptions play in forming prejudiced opinions. None of Rowling's characters is perfectly good or purely evil (with the possible exception of Dolores Umbridge). The series finalc constantly calls the reader's love-prejudice and hate-prejudice into question, as seemingly one-dimensional characters such as Kreacher and Dudley Dursley suddenly acquire layers. Dudley is a kind, sensitive boy, after all; Kreacher is perfectly loyal and loveable; and even the vile Snape is capable of the noblest of actions and the deepest love, having endured many great dangers to protect Lily Potter's son. And, of course, we see that the luminescent, wise Dumbledore did not have a 'squeaky clean' past. Therefore, Rowling's message is quite clear: The human character is complex; and people are much more than what they seem to be on the surface.

Chapter 1

Social Hierarchy and the Nature of Wizarding World Prejudice

Figure 1.1 [1]

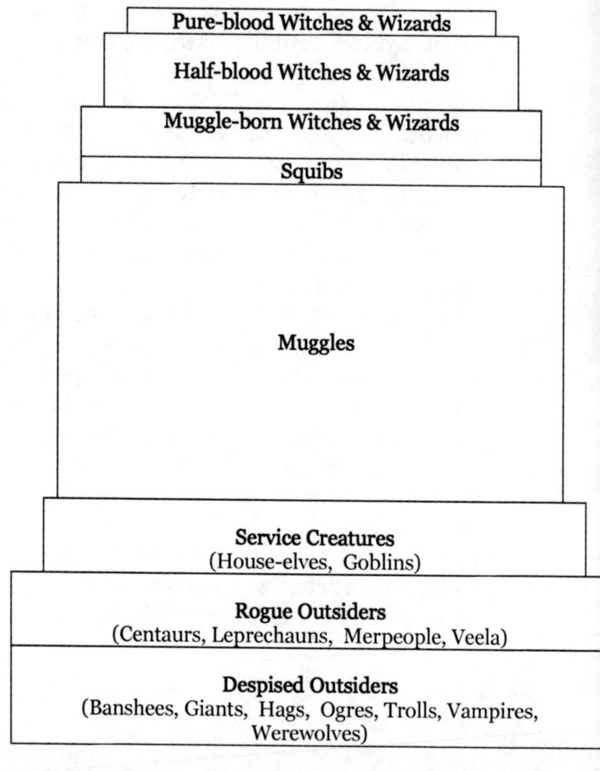

The social hierarchy outlined in the diagram above (Figure 1.1) raises the important question of what constitutes 'humanity' in the context of J.K. Rowling's wizarding world.

---

[1] Items in the diagram are first classified according to groups; then, they are arranged in alphabetical order within their respective groups. However, later in the chapter, when their status is described in greater detail, they will be listed only according to where they stand in the pecking order of the wizarding world.

In the *Harry Potter* novels, we see the so-called 'humanity' of magical creatures continuously being called into question simply because they are not part of the dominant group–wizards. Notions of 'humanity' play a crucial role in the wizarding world's political ideology, which determines not only the magical community's social (and to an extent, racial) hierarchy, but also the right to govern, the right to free speech, access to basic social privileges such as education or employment, and the right to freedom from enslavement.

In the most rudimentary sense, 'humanity' denotes 'the human race,' or 'humankind.' But another important denotation of the word relates to an individual's ability to feel solidarity or to empathize with other beings. As far as wizarding world politics go, where the first denotation of the word is concerned, 'humanity' includes wizardkind only. This, in turn, creates problems for other magical beings, who are not regarded with empathy or solidarity, simply because they do not belong to the dominant group.

Hence, much of wizarding prejudice is borne out of the conviction that only humans (wizards) are entitled to social rights within the magical community. Presumably, they alone are worthy of sympathy because they 'feel' things far more acutely than other magical beings. Muggles are included here, in the wizarding world's hierarchical set-up, because they share in *the* distinguishing trait that assures wizard superiority over other magical beings: they are *human.* Also, the fact that they constitute the largest part of the human race ranks them above so-called "sub-human" magical creatures, but below the Squibs and Muggle-borns, who have direct access to the wizarding world.

Wizards discriminate against other magical beings by, first, excluding them from the status marker of being considered 'human' or 'fully human.' And this is the underlying principle used to support the rigid social hierarchy outlined above, and also to justify most instances of inhumanity against social Others (werewolves, house-elves, giants, and so forth). And yet, as will be discussed in later chapters, a distorted sense of superiority has led some wizards to also persecute Muggles and those directly connected with the muggle world.

Naturally, the privileging of certain groups over others creates social unrest and discontentment. And so, the series culminates in a costly wizard war, after Muggle-borns become excluded from privileges that are now reserved for Pure-bloods and Half-bloods only. Also, we discover in the fourth book that wizard law prohibits certain "non-human" or "sub-human" groups from using wands. When the house-elf called Winky is caught carrying Harry's wand, a Ministry official makes reference to "clause three of the Code of Wand Use," which states that "no non-human creature is permitted to carry or use a wand" (*Goblet of Fire*, p. 119). Also, the fifth book (*Order of the Phoenix*) reveals that, years ago, the Ministry of Magic passed anti-werewolf legislation that made it virtually impossible for wizards like Remus Lupin to get a job (p. 271). These are just a few examples of the sort of institutional discrimination that exists in the magical community.

However, the author has suggested in a recent interview (given shortly after the release of *Deathly Hallows*) that the Ministry of Magic eventually becomes purged of its propensity for prejudice and discrimination. After the last war against Voldemort, Harry, Hermione and Ron essentially help to create a better world and an improved—or we might say "revolutionized"—Ministry: "the discrimination that was always latent there is eradicated."[2]

***

The pyramid above (Figure 1.1) outlines the social hierarchy of the pre-revolution wizarding world. It is based on a combination of factors, including the role that the so-called "sub-human" or "non-human" creatures played in wizarding society, as well as their proximity to wizards in general. It is also worth noting that the construction of this hierarchy is based on the viewpoint of those to whom the pecking order matters most: i.e. wizards.[3] Therefore, all evidence to support the accuracy of the diagram comes from the books—in the form of interaction between individual characters as well as

[2] J.K. Rowling Live Chat, Bloomsbury.com. July 30, 2007 (2.00-3.00pm BST).

[3] It matters most to them because they stand to gain the most from it.

groups, and also information given by the author (on wizarding laws, customs and so forth).

Also, a staggered pyramid is used here in order to portray the estimated population size of the groups, in relation to each other. Though there is no clear statement in the books regarding the total wizard population, nor that of the entire magical community in Great Britain (where the novels are set), the books provide certain clues about population size. For instance, in *Chamber of Secrets*, Ron informs Harry and Hermione that "most wizards these days are half-blood," because if wizards had not inter-married with Muggles they would have died out (p. 89). And so, wizards are clearly a minority group amongst humans.

In fact, considering that there is only one wizard school in all of Great Britain, this suggests that the wizard population is relatively minuscule. Also, we discover in *Order of the Phoenix* that Harry's godfather, Sirius Black, belonged to one of the few remaining pure-blood families. Sirius informs his godson that "the pure-blood families are all interrelated" because there are so few of them. And they tend to marry each other to preserve the purity of their lineage (p. 105).

***

All non-wizard groups, with the exception of Squibs and Muggles, are classified as either "sub-humans" (which is used inter-changeably with "non-humans" in the books) or "part-humans." Centaurs and werewolves are examples of "part-humans"—that is to say, their physical forms incorporate both animal and human features. "Sub-humans" are creatures that are humanlike in appearance and have the gift of speech: giants, elves, goblins and perhaps hags and vampires are categorized as such. As the diagram shows, some of these creatures have been placed in the "feared and despised" category because they are perceived to be "dark creatures."

For example, we discover in *Chamber of Secrets* (p. 38) and *Prisoner of Azkaban* (p. 128) that there are special chapters reserved for creatures such as hags, vampires and werewolves in Defense Against the Dark Arts textbooks. Werewolves are considered as "half-breeds" or "part-humans"[4] even though they are fully human in the absence of the full moon.

Also, in the pre-revolution wizarding world, no species considered to be sub-human or part-human is entitled to the same rights as "normal" witches and wizards. For example, the young Remus Lupin was only admitted to Hogwarts because an open-minded and empowered Wizengamot official—Albus Dumbledore—was headmaster of the school at that time. While previous headmasters would not have taken the risk or invested the required time and effort, Dumbledore was willing to facilitate what we could describe as Lupin's "disability." This matter will be discussed in far greater detail in Chapter 4 of this volume.

The "part-human" or "sub-human" factor is instantly called into question when we consider that wizards have been known to mate and produce off-spring with other kinds of magical beings: Mating and reproduction are good indicators of not only biological compatibility, but also equality. And so, the author (Rowling) appears to be suggesting that what really separated the privileged from the non-privileged in the wizarding world were merely artificial distinctions that had been created and sustained by wizards for centuries. Among those categorized as "human," "part-human" and "sub-human" magical beings, there is no difference substantial enough to justify wizard superiority.

The rest of this chapter describes the status and roles of each group mentioned in Figure 1.1. And in Chapter 2, I will discuss the elements of wizarding society, and human nature in general, that help to preserve this social hierarchy.

***

---

[4] *Order of the Phoenix*, p. 271.

A Description of the Social Hierarchy in the Wizarding World

1. Pure-blood Witches and Wizards

Pure-bloods are right at the top of the social pyramid. Naturally, the oldest wizarding families are the ones with the strongest ties to the elite and most prestigious organizations such as Hogwarts, Gringotts and the Ministry of Magic. In the series finale, the author reveals that the wealthy pure-blood families have access to the most well-protected high-security vaults at Gringotts.[5] And among the wealthiest families are the Malfoys, Lestranges, the Blacks, the Selwyns and the Smiths. Some enjoy unrivalled prestige and privilege within the magical community, while others are particularly noted for their pure-blood pride.

However, not all pure-bloods embrace bigotry; nor do they all possess great wealth. The Weasleys are also quite prominent, perhaps because of the sheer size of that family. Arthur Weasley has good connections at the Ministry, but it has been suggested throughout the novels that he has been held back in his Ministry career because of his open acceptance of Muggle-borns and sympathy towards Muggles.[6]

Other pure-blood families mentioned in the series include the Gaunts, Voldemort's last living wizard relatives—the Dark Lord himself being the last remaining descendant of Salazar Slytherin—, the Longbottoms, the Macmillans, the Prewetts and the Selwyns.

2. Half-blood Witches and Wizards

As I mentioned earlier, the author reveals in the second book that most wizards nowadays are Half-bloods (p. 89). Wizardkind was once a race in decline; and so, witches and wizards were obliged to inter-marry with Muggles in order to prolong the survival of their species. And yet, in wizarding terms, one is not necessarily a Pure-blood even if he or she should have two magical parents. A Muggle-born witch or

---

[5] See *Deathly Hallows*, p. 411.

[6] See *Goblet of Fire*, p. 617.

wizard will invariably produce "half-blood" off-spring if they mate with pure-blood or half-blood partners.

Half-blood lineage seems to be a common thread linking many of the major characters in the series. Interestingly, although there are several pure-blood families mentioned in the books, the series protagonist, Harry, is a half-blood. And even more intriguingly, so is his arch-nemesis, Voldemort. What is even more ironic is the fact that, while Harry has two magical parents, Voldemort's father is a Muggle. Hence, the main perpetrator of hate-ridden sentiments and pure-blood ideals is a product of the very thing he purports to hate.

We also discover in the seventh book that Dumbledore, Harry's mentor and guide throughout the series, might have been a Half-blood.[7]

3. Muggle-born Witches and Wizards

Muggle-borns are witches and wizards born to two Muggle parents. Rowling admitted in a recent interview that the Muggle-born concept is not one borne out of mere coincidence: "Muggle-borns will have a witch or wizard somewhere on their family tree, in some cases many, many generations back. The gene resurfaces in some unexpected places."[8] One could argue whether or not Muggle-borns should be higher up in the social hierarchy than Squibs, especially since "wizard blood" is of the essence for those to whom the hierarchy really matters.

Squibs might just be the unfortunate bi-products of centuries of inbreeding amongst Pure-bloods. However, because they have very little or no magical powers, and since magical ability—particularly the ability to use wands—is such an important signifier of empowerment within the magical community, Muggle-borns must occupy a higher place in this hierarchical set-up. And moreover, for proof of the Muggle-born's perceived superiority to Squibs, we need look no

[7] The notoriously gossipy Muriel, Ron's pure-blood great-aunt, suggests that Dumbledore's mother, Kendra, might have been a Muggle-born, and that, presumably out of shame, "she pretended otherwise" (*Deathly Hallows*, p. 129).

[8] J.K. Rowling Live Chat, Bloomsbury.com. July 30, 2007 (2.00-3.00pm BST).

further than Hogwarts, where there are no Squib children enrolled, but plenty of Muggle-borns.

In *Philosopher's Stone*, Neville Longbottom talks about his earlier childhood fears that he might not be admitted to Hogwarts: Everyone in his family had thought that he was a Squib, until one day when he fell out of a window and produced life-saving magic by accident (p. 93). The series finale reveals that young magical children often show signs of uncontrolled magic at around age six.[9] But according to Neville, he did not display any magical ability at all until he was about eight.[10]

Also, judging by Neville's fears about not being "magic enough" to come to Hogwarts, we may deduce that some Squibs have a limited amount of magical ability, but not enough to give them access to formal magical education. Muggle-borns, on the other hand, are fully-fledged magical beings who, as we see in Hermione's case, can perform magic to the highest standard.

4. Squibs

Squibs are the first truly disadvantaged group that we see in the series. In *Philosopher's Stone*, during their first trip aboard the Hogwarts Express, Harry asks Ron if his entire family is comprised of witches and wizards. And Ron replies: "I think Mum's got a second cousin who's an accountant, but we never talk about him" (p. 75). The statement encapsulates the very nature of anti-Squib prejudice: In most cases they are simply excluded or ignored because of their lack of magical ability. Basically, they are an embarrassment to their families: It is perceived as a shameful thing for a witch or wizard to produce non-magical offspring.

The actual term "Squib" is used for the first time in *Chamber of Secrets*, where the trio discover that Argus Filch, the school caretaker, has no magical powers. Apparently, the caretaker thinks he can learn to do magic through something called a "Kwikspell course" (pp. 97-98 & p. 111). But this may

[9] *Deathly Hallows*, p. 454.

[10] *Philosopher's Stone*, p. 93.

just be a sort of wizarding-world business scam designed to give people like Filch false hopes and exploit them financially:

> 'And what on earth is a Squib?' said Harry.
> To his surprise, Ron stifled a snigger.
> 'Well—it's not funny really—but as it's Filch...' he said. A Squib is someone who was born into a wizarding family but hasn't got any magic powers. Kind of the opposite of Muggle-born wizards, but Squibs are quite unusual. If Filch's trying to learn magic from a Kwikspell course, I reckon he must be a Squib. It would explain a lot. Like why he hates students to much.'
> Ron gave a satisfied smile. 'He's bitter'
> (*Chamber of Secrets*, pp. 110-111).

The Squib's affliction seems to be a sort of wizarding *disability*; but whether or not it is insurmountable remains unclear. Ron's amusement at Filch's expense shows a noticeable lack of sympathy for the caretaker's disability. But perhaps the boy's insensitivity is indeed only targeted towards Filch rather than at Squibs in general.

Still, one may hazard a good guess that Squibs are generally ridiculed in the wider wizarding world. Rowling gives certain hints of this in the series finale, when Rita Skeeter starts a rumor that Dumbledore's ill sister, Ariana, had been locked away because she was a Squib. The rumor is quite believable because imposed isolation is precisely what one would normally do with Squib offspring in those days:

> "Squibs were often hushed up ... [They] were usually shipped off to Muggle schools and encouraged to integrate into the Muggle community."
> [Aunt Muriel quote] (*Deathly Hallows*, pp. 129-130).

Of course, later in the story, through Aberforth Dumbledore's narrative, we learn that Ariana was definitely magical. But she had an illness which made her unable to control her powers, and she ended up killing her mother as a result.

5. Muggles

Presumably, the "International Statute of Secrecy" is a treaty that was established centuries ago between Muggle governments and wizarding communities across the world. Its purpose was to keep the non-magical population separate and unaware of the existence of a magical community, though some Muggles remained linked to the magical world through their "Muggle-born" witch or wizard offspring. On the surface, it is hard to tell whether the treaty was designed to protect wizards from Muggles, or vice-versa: Although magical ability provides wizards with a unique empowerment, Muggles greatly outnumber wizards.

Also, Rowling occasionally makes reference to the persecution of witches during medieval times.[11] But later in the series we see that the persecution went both ways: In *Half-blood Prince*, Harry goes back several decades in time (through someone else's memory) to meet Marvolo Gaunt. When informed that his son, Morfin, had abused a Muggle, Marvolo suggested that wizard law had not always prohibited Muggle torture: "He taught a filthy Muggle a lesson, that's illegal now, is it?" (p. 195). And in *Deathly Hallows*, we discover that a teenage Dumbledore, during his brief friendship with the Dark wizard (and fellow teenager) Grindelwald, had once entertained hopes of leading wizards out of hiding to rule over the Muggle population.

6. Goblins

It seems that goblins are indeed the highest ranked among the "sub-human" magical species. There are a few bits of evidence from the texts which justify this claim. First and foremost is the fact that wizarding history is littered with goblin wars and rebellions—a topic which features most frequently in Professor Binns' History of Magic lessons. Of all the sub-human species, goblins have the most documented cases of contesting wizard superiority. Hermione points this out to Ron in the fourth book, when he ridicules her sympathy

[11] See *Prisoner of Azkaban*, p. 7.

for goblins by citing her futile attempts to advocate for elfish rights:[12]

> 'Worrying about poor 'ickle goblins, now, are you?' Ron asked Hermione.
>
> 'Thinking of starting up S.P.U.G. or something? Society for the Protection of Ugly goblins?'
>
> 'Ha, ha, ha,' said Hermione sarcastically. 'Goblins don't need protection. Haven't you been listening to what Professor Binns has been telling us about goblin rebellions?'
>
> 'No,' said Harry and Ron together.
>
> 'Well, they are quite capable of dealing with wizards...They're very clever. They're not like house elves, who never stick up for themselves.'
>
> (*Goblet of Fire*, p. 390)

The second indicator of the goblins' relatively superior status is the mere fact they run the wizard bank Gringotts. They also manufacture and control the money, or the gold, which wizards depend on for trade and day-to-day sustenance.

In *Order of the Phoenix*, we learn that wizard money carries serial numbers "referring to the goblin who cast the coin" (p. 353). And in *Deathly Hallows*, one of Voldemort's Death Eaters rues wizard dependence on goblin-made gold: "Gold, filthy gold! We cannot live without it, yet I confess I deplore the necessity of consorting with our long-fingered friends" (p. 426).

Finally, goblins possess magical abilities that wizards do not; and they can do magic without the use of wands. The same can be said of house-elves; but the main difference with the elves, as Hermione suggests, is that they have a subservient attitude towards wizards and never use their powers against them. And moreover, as they are slaves, the elves' powers are owned and controlled by wizards; so there is no need for wizards to covet them as much as they have coveted goblin knowledge and skill in metal work[13]—for which

---

[12] Hermione had just founded the Society for the Promotion of Elfish Welfare, or S.P.E.W.

[13] *Deathly Hallows*, p. 395.

they must pay dearly. In contrast, house-elves are merely exploited, and very little value is placed on their unique skills and magical knowledge.

***

One of the first goblins whom we meet in the series is Griphook, who accompanies Harry to his Gringotts vault in *Philosopher's Stone*, and reappears briefly in *Deathly Hallows*. Described as clever-faced, short, swarthy, long-fingered and long-footed,[14] goblins have very strange views on the matter of possessing goblin-made goods; and Griphook is the perfect embodiment of the stereotypical goblin. According to him, all goblin-made armor and jewelry continue to belong to the maker even after the purchase of the goods, which should be returned to the goblin race after the death of the purchaser.[15]

The idea of passing on goblin-made family heirlooms to posterity is mere thievery, from a goblin's point of view. And presumably, this disparity in trade-related views is just one of the reasons why the relationship between wizards and goblins became strained, and remains acrimonious after centuries of quelled rebellions and even the establishment of a "Goblin Liaison Office" at the Ministry of Magic.

Griphook also refers to wizards as "wand carriers," as he informs the trio that "the right to carry a wand ... has long been contested between wizards and goblins."[16] Evidently, the only perceived distinction between their races—from the goblin's standpoint—is that wizards are allowed to carry wands and goblins are not. And so, while wizards govern and make laws, goblins are forced into the role of a working underclass.

As was previously mentioned, goblins do not recognize wizard superiority the way house-elves do. Therefore, when Griphook complains that the wizard race remains "still more firmly above" his own, as the Dark Lord ascends to power and

---

[14] *Philosopher's Stone*, p. 56,

[15] *Deathly Hallows*, pp. 408-409.

[16] *Deathly Hallows*, pp. 394-395.

war breaks out within the magical community,[17] one gets a sense of immense defiance and an unyielding belief in his own superiority.

7. House-elves

Other *Harry Potter* readers may have an entirely different opinion on this placement of the house-elves within a wizarding world social hierarchy. After all, they are slaves and, as Dobby surmises in *Chamber of Secrets*, the "dregs of the magical world" (p. 133). My justification for ranking them above rogue outsider part-humans like centaurs and merpeople is the intimacy they share with wizards. No doubt, the closeness that house-elves share with their wizard families (as carers, child-minders, cooks, house-keepers, nannies, butlers and secret keepers) is perceived as a coveted privilege—even if only among themselves and the wizards whom they serve.

Once again, for those individuals to whom the social hierarchy matters most, access to the innermost circles of wizarding society must count for a great deal—although it obviously does not carry the same weight as having wizard blood. But more important is the fact that, although the house-elves are controlled, abused and exploited, they are neither as despised nor as shunned as creatures like werewolves clearly are.

Described as smaller than goblins, with long, bat-like ears and toga-draped tea-towels or pillowcases as their sole garments,[18] house-elves are by far the most disturbing group within the magical community. They are essentially a race of slaves trained to serve wizard families with unequivocal deference and unwavering loyalty. And in the event of disobedience or disloyalty—whether intentional or not—the elf is obliged to punish himself physically until his master is satisfied.

Ironically, although goblins consider themselves to be in many ways superior to wizards, and by extension, house-elves, the latter see themselves as far superior to goblins: In

---

[17] Ibid.

[18] See *Chamber of Secrets*, p. 15 & *Goblet of Fire*, p. 88.

Goblet of Fire the elf Winky berates Dobby for accepting his freedom so wholeheartedly. Winky is concerned that, by demanding wages and being so happy to be free, Dobby is exhibiting behavior that might land him "in front of the Department for the Regulation and Control of Magical Creatures *like some common goblin*" (p. 90).[19]

And so, in the same book, when Hermione establishes the Society for the Promotion of Elfish Welfare (S.P.E.W.), she encounters as much resistance from the elves themselves as she does from her peers. Pure-blood wizard children like Fred, George and Ron Weasley show a disturbing uniformity of opinion, insisting that the elves "*like* being enslaved" (p. 198); and Hagrid firmly maintains that it would be doing them "an unkindness" to free them (p. 233). The wizards remain indifferent, if not defiant in their belief that the house-elves are "happy" with their lot. And the elves do not, in any way, contradict this view. In fact, they are appalled by the mere suggestion that they—like Dobby—should pursue freedom (pp. 327-330 & pp. 466-468).

But Hermione is right to persist in her belief that the house-elves only accept their lot in life "because they're uneducated and brainwashed."[20] In *Order of the Phoenix*, Dumbledore finally confirms her convictions when he tells Harry that Kreacher, the house-elf who betrays his master Sirius Black to Voldemort, "is what he has been made by wizards" (p. 733). In other words, house-elves at one point were forced—and then conditioned—to serve wizards in this subservient manner. And the enchantments cast upon their kind—spells which presumably have bound them to slavery for centuries—are mostly psychological barriers that can be broken, where there is courage and the strength of will to endeavor it.

8. Centaurs

Half man and half horse, the Centaur species in the *Harry Potter* novels has been drawn directly from Greek mythology, and are a popular feature in modern fantasy

---

[19] Emphasis added.

[20] *Goblet of Fire* p. 211.

literature. Other prominent Centaur characters feature in C.S. Lewis's *Chronicles of Narnia*, as well as the *Xanth* series by Piers Anthony. Sprung from a wise and ancient race, the Centaurs in the *Harry Potter* series are gifted with the ability to read the future in the stars. But, as we are told in *Philosopher's Stone* (pp. 184-189) and *Order of the Phoenix* (pp. 530-532), they set themselves apart from the wizard race and do not share their divination secrets.

In the fifth book, Dumbledore recruits the Centaur Firenze to teach Divination, after Umbridge had just unceremoniously dismissed Sybill Trelawney. But Firenze is banished from his so-called "herd" because the fact that he takes the job is seen as "a betrayal of our kind'" (p. 530). Like goblins, Centaurs harbor great resentment for wizards' arrogance, as well as the presumed superiority of the so-called "wand carriers." But rather unlike goblins, they do not engage in trade or any kind of exchange with the wizard race, insisting that:

> "We are an ancient people who will not stand wizard invasions and insults! We do not recognize your laws. We do not acknowledge your superiority...'"
> (*Order of the Phoenix*, p. 667).

Furthermore, Centaurs truly believe that they possess knowledge far superior to that of humans; and so, Firenze often ridicules Professor Trelawney for what he regards as human foolishness, or "fortune-telling" (p. 531).

***

The first sign of discord within a sub-human group takes place among the Centaurs in *Philosopher's Stone*. It is here that Harry meets Firenze for the first time, when the Centaur helps him to escape from a weakened but no less malevolent Voldemort in the Forbidden Forest. Another Centaur called Bane, who has strong isolationist ideals and anti-human feelings, attacks Firenze when he sees him carrying the injured Harry on his back:

> "Remember, Firenze, we are sworn not to set ourselves against the heavens...It is not our business to run around like donkeys after stray humans in our Forest'" (*Philosopher's Stone*, pp. 187-188).

It is clear that other Centaurs share Bane's beliefs (that they should never interfere in human affairs). Nevertheless, the Centaurs do play a part in the final battle against the Dark Lord in *Deathly Hallows*, after finally realizing that the fate of humankind does concern them.

9. Merpeople

Part human and part fish, the beings who are called "merpeople" in the *Harry Potter* books are simply another variation of the mermaid myth, which dates back to the sirens and water nymphs of Greek mythology. Curiously, they are almost equally mythical in Rowling's magical community: We only discover in the fourth book (*Goblet of Fire*) that there are merpeople living under the lake in the Hogwarts grounds. In addition, wizards do not seem to know much about them: There is a portrait of a beautiful blonde mermaid in the Prefect's bathroom at Hogwarts;[21] and she looks nothing like the real creatures Harry later meets during his second Triwizard task. Here, they are described as having "greyish skin and long, wild, dark green hair," along with yellow eyes and broken teeth (p. 432).

Like Centaurs, merpeople live apart from wizardkind and are quite isolated. They also have very unusual tastes in pets: water creatures known as "Grindylows," which are considered to be minor dark creatures,[22] are tied to stakes outside merhomes (p. 432). And yet, considering that there are wizards, like Dumbledore, who can speak their language (mermish), there must be some level of communication between wizards and merpeople. Unlike the centaur race (who seem to communicate in English), the merpeople have not mastered the language of wizards. And the fact that only a few

---

[21] *Goblet of Fire*, p. 399.

[22] See *Prisoner of Azkaban*, p. 116, where Professor Lupin shows Harry a Grindylow trapped in a tank.

humans speak mermish suggests that linguistic factors play a major role in the merpeople's isolation from the rest of the magical community.

In *Order of the Phoenix*, Sirius informs the trio that Dolores Umbridge once "campaigned to have merpeople rounded up and tagged" (p. 271). From this evidence, one may hazard a good guess that the merpeople are not quite as hostile towards wizards as the Centaurs clearly are. Although there is no suggestion anywhere in the texts that they would allow wizards to enter their territory and serialize them, there is a marked difference in the way merpeople perceive themselves in relation to wizards. This issue will be briefly re-visited in the next chapter.

10. Leprechauns

In Irish mythology a 'Leprechaun' is a type of male fairy that inhabits the island of Ireland. Leprechauns appear only briefly in the fourth *Harry Potter* book, as they perform as mascots at the Quidditch World Cup (for the Irish national team). The extent of their involvement in Rowling's wizarding world remains unknown. All we know of these creatures is that they can produce fake gold, which disappears after a few hours (*Goblet of Fire*, p. 472). They are ranked here as rogue outsiders, partly because they are Irish, and partly because they do not seem to be exploited or despised in the same way as elves or goblins.

11. Veela

These mythical Eastern European beings are also known as Slavic fairies; but in some myths, they are quite sinister. They appear very briefly in *Goblet of Fire* as mascots for the Bulgarian Quidditch team at the World Cup. And, also like the Leprechauns, they are regarded as foreign magical "creatures" that are not typical to Great Britain. Rowling has readapted the Eastern European myth to portray the Veela as beautiful, self-transfiguring women who transform into vulture-like creatures when angered (p. 101). Finally, from what we know about the beautiful Fleur Delacour, who first appears in the fourth book, it is clear that wizards have mated with the

Veela: Fleur's wand has at its core a hair from the head of her Veela grandmother (p. 270). This also suggests that the Veela have significant magical qualities, and that they are more regarded as "creatures" rather than as "beings."

12. Ogres

In many traditional Anglo-Saxon fairytales, ogres are depicted as large, green-skinned humanoid creatures with bad breath and a temperament to match. Like hags, they sometimes appear in children's stories as people-eating monsters. There is only one mention of an ogre in the *Harry Potter* series: In *Prisoner of Azkaban*, Ron reports to Harry that he and Hermione might have spotted one in the Three Broomsticks[23] (p. 119). The fact that the ogre was spotted at such a popular location is a good indicator that, while they are definitely rogue outsiders, ogres are not necessarily severely despised in Rowling's wizarding world.

13. Hags

There are very few mentions of hags throughout the entire series. However, in terms of traditional witch myths, a humanoid, crooked-eyed, bent-back, wrinkle-skinned, hook-nosed female is universally acknowledged as bearing some resemblance to a "hag." Perhaps this is why, on the few occasions when Rowling mentions hags, she does not bother to describe them. In some witch myths, the hag is portrayed as an evil, one-eyed and very dangerous old woman who eats little children. It is not clear whether or not the hag race in Rowling's series has the same level of notoriety.

Intriguingly though, there is one subtle suggestion that wizards have mated with hags: In *Chamber of Secrets*, the facial features of Millicent Bullstrode—a Slytherin girl who wrestles with Hermione at the Dueling Club— "reminded Harry of a picture he'd seen in *Holidays with Hags*" (p. 143). That book just happens to be one of Gilderoy Lockhart's many

---

[23] The Three Broomsticks is a well-known pub in the village of Hogsmeade, which is the only remaining all-magical settlement in Great Britain. Hogwarts students usually frequent the pub during their weekend outings to the village.

Defense Against the Dark Arts textbooks, which suggests that hags are classified as "dangerous dark creatures" in Rowling's magical community. But it remains unclear whether they inspire the same level of fear as werewolves.

14. Miscellaneous "Dark Creatures": Banshees, Trolls and Vampires

Once again, Rowling appeals to her readers' passive knowledge of fairy-tale myths, as she does not bother to describe many of her so-called "dark creatures" in detail. Banshees, trolls and vampires are all "sub-human" species that are only briefly mentioned in the series.

Invariably female, the Banshee is drawn directly from Irish mythology, where she is usually depicted as an omen of death. The Banshee is only mentioned a few times in the series: Among Professor Gilderoy Lockhart's many Defense Against the Dark Arts text books, listed in *Chamber of Secrets*, is one called *Break with a Banshee* (p. 38). And in a long list of gloats, including one about winning *Witch Weekly*'s Most-Charming-Smile Award, Lockhart claims he "didn't get rid of the Bandon Banshee by *smiling* at her" (p. 77). Finally, in *Goblet of Fire*, Irish student Seamus Finnigan thinks he recognizes the sound of a banshee wailing when Harry opens his golden egg, the clue for the second Triwizard task (p. 319)—the Banshee myth being as typically Irish as the Loch Ness Monster is Scottish.

Trolls receive slightly more attention in the series, but they are of no real importance to the plot, except in *Philosopher's Stone*, where Professor Quirrel—possessed by Lord Voldemort—releases a troll into the school at Halloween. Harry and Ron barely manage to rescue Hermione from the monster after accidentally locking her in the girls' toilette with it (pp. 127-132). Their heroics seal a loyal friendship with Hermione. And the trio later discover that another larger troll is one of the enchantments protecting the Philosopher's Stone (p. 206).

There is one subtle suggestion of mating between trolls and wizards. In *Philosopher's Stone*, Marcus Flint, Captain of the Slytherin Quidditch team, is said to look "as if he had some troll blood in him" (p. 136).

Along with a reputation for being large, brutish and armed with clubs, trolls are generally regarded as stupid. In fact, the troll's stupidity is an institutional standard in Rowling's wizarding world: The lowest grade that one can receive in an exam is a T, which stands for Troll.[24] Other mentions of trolls in the series include the "security trolls" protecting the portrait of the Fat Lady in *Prisoner of Azkaban* (p. 199). Another portrait shows Barnabas the Barmy trying to teach a group of trolls how to ballet (*Half-blood Prince*, p. 428) and being mercilessly clubbed for his efforts (*Order of the Phoenix*, p. 344).

Finally, vampires complete the list of briefly-mentioned dark creatures; and, once again, there are only a few mentions of vampires throughout the entire series. Many variations of the vampire legend are scattered throughout literary history; but most notable is Brahm Stoker's Transylvanian villain in *Dracula*. The term 'vampire' invariably corresponds to the blood-drinking 'Undead' from Eastern European myths, except when used metaphorically to denote cruel or parasitic tendencies in a person.

There are no vampire characters with significant roles in the *Harry Potter* novels; and, rather unlike werewolves and giants, they do not seem to have participated in either of the wars against Voldemort. Of course, with them being dark creatures, Professor Lockhart is bound to have written a book about them: *Voyages with Vampires*.[25] The next mention of vampires takes place in *Prisoner of Azkaban* (p. 313), where Dean Thomas hopes that the next Defense Against the Dark Arts teacher might be a vampire, after the werewolf Remus Lupin is forced to resign.

And finally, in *Half-blood Prince*, Professor Slughorn invites a motley crew of old friends to his Christmas party. A former colleague named Worple brings along his vampire assistant—appropriately named Sanguini. This vampire's brief presence at Hogwarts suggests that, as long as he or she can be controlled, a vampire's company might be tolerable. But there is a rather hungry look in Sanguini's eyes when he sees

---

[24] See *Order of the Phoenix*, p. 278. Other marks include 'O' (Outstanding), 'E' (Exceeds Expectations), 'A' (Acceptable), 'P' (Poor) and 'D' (Dreadful).

[25] *Chamber of Secrets*, p. 38.

the female students; and Worple has to rein him in with a blood-flavored pasty (p. 296).

15. Werewolves

In Anglo-Saxon folklore the werewolf is a shape-shifting man who can transform into a wolf either purposefully or as a result of being put under a curse. However, werewolf legend can be traced back to Greek mythology; and it was in the writings of Petronius that werewolf transformation was first associated with the full moon. Popular culture and literature have transformed the myth even further: Legend now has it that a werewolf's transformation at the full moon is involuntary; and that werewolves can only be killed with a silver bullet. However, J. K. Rowling seems to have mostly adhered to the Greek myth: Werewolf characters transform at the full moon in the *Harry Potter* series. They also die in battle, but there is no suggestion of silver being involved in their deaths.

Next only to giants at the bottom of the wizarding world's totem pole, werewolves are among the most feared and despised creatures in the magical community. Prior to the introduction of Remus Lupin in *Prisoner of Azkaban*, werewolves are only mentioned in the context of "dark creatures": In *Philosopher's Stone* (p. 182), a terrified Draco Malfoy wonders if there might be werewolves in the Forbidden Forest when he, Harry, Hermione and Neville have to enter the woods at night to do their detentions. And in *Chamber of Secrets* (p. 38), we learn that self-proclaimed Dark Arts expert Gilderoy Lockhart has also written a book called *Wanderings with Werewolves*. He later entertains the students with an incredulous story about how he "performed the immensely complex Homorphus Charm" to transform the Wagga Wagga werewolf back into a man (p. 122).

Werewolves are mostly feared because they are hostile towards other wizards; and furthermore, they can easily disguise themselves in the absence of the full moon, which makes them even more dangerous if their intent is to harm or kill when they transform. In *Half-blood Prince*, when Dumbledore sends Remus Lupin on a mission to recruit and spy among his kind, we discover that most of the werewolf population is on Voldemort's side. According to Lupin, werewolves like Fenrir Greyback purposefully set out to bite and contaminate as many wizards as possible. Greyback had even bitten Lupin, who bitterly recalls growing up with sympathetic feelings for the werewolf who had bitten him when he was a boy. Until he met Greyback, Lupin had always believed that the attack was a random act of insanity. But in reality, it had been planned: Greyback sought revenge on Lupin's father, who had offended him (pp. 313-314).

Although such premeditated violence is intolerable and unpardonable, evidence from the books suggests that werewolf animosity towards wizardkind is, to a certain degree, justified. Not only are they shunned from wizarding society, but also, little or no effort is made on the part of the Ministry of Magic to facilitate their needs. In fact, by limiting their ability to access jobs, the Ministry has made it virtually impossible for werewolves to live with dignity. This issue will be discussed further in Chapter 4 of this volume.

16. Giants

A race teetering on the brink of extinction, the giants are the most feared and despised creatures in the magical community. Evidence to support this view appears in *Goblet of Fire*, where the diabolical journalist Rita Skeeter disgraces Hagrid by exposing his giant heritage in the press (pp. 380-382). Hagrid had kept his mother Fridwulfa's racial identity a secret for many years, discussing it for the first time with the only person he has ever met who bore physical features similar to his own—Madame Olympe Maxime, Headmistress of Beauxbatons Academy. But Hagrid was not aware that Skeeter—an illegal Animagus who can disguise herself as a beetle—was lurking in the bushes during his romantic chat with Olympe.

Naturally, he attempts to establish solidarity with his love interest by citing the one thing that they have in common—both being "half-breeds" (part wizard and part giant). But Madame Maxime does not take too kindly to the suggestion that she might be half-giant. In fact, her reaction is almost violent:

> 'Ow dare you!' [she shrieked] ... 'Alf-giant? Moi? I 'ave—I 'ave big bones!' (p. 373).

Clearly, it is not acceptable to have giant blood and live among wizards; Ron's reaction to Hagrid's revelation confirms this. Even though he has known Hagrid for years, Ron finds the news of his giant blood extremely unpalatable (pp. 373-377).

In contrast, Harry and Hermione display their ignorance of wizarding customs by not being surprised or perturbed at all about Hagrid's racial background: "So what?" asks Harry (p. 373), while Hermione surmises the unthinkable:

> 'Well, I thought he must be...I knew he couldn't be pure giant, because they are about twenty feet tall.'
> (*Goblet of Fire*, p. 377)

Ron is shocked at his friends' lack of concern, having come to the same conclusion as Draco Malfoy, upon meeting Hagrid for the first time—that Hagrid must have been the victim of some kind of Engorgement Charm (p. 374) or "just swallowed a bottle of Skele-Gro when he was young" (p. 382). The difference in the way Ron and Draco react to the discovery, when compared with Harry and Hermione's reaction, supports the argument that environment and upbringing profoundly influence attitudes, beliefs and behavior towards out-groups.

Conclusion

In sum, notions about "humanity" (versus *non*-humanity) amongst the magical creatures in Rowling's wizarding world are not meant to be taken at face value. Rather, they are to be challenged and questioned by the reader—especially considering the irony that magical humans (witches and wizards) are regarded as "abnormal" [26] (hence social outcasts) in the Muggle world. And so, the recurrence of the humanity issue throughout the series emphasizes its purpose as a metaphor of bigotry and the irrational nature of

---

[26] See *Philosopher's Stone*, p. 44, where Petunia Dursley berates Harry and his mother for being magical.

social hierarchies in general—whether in the fictional magical community or in our own world.

There is great irony in the segregation of magical beings based on factors such as blood lineage, socio-economics, transmittable diseases or social exploitability. This is highly reminiscent of our own world, where some social groups are either left out or targeted due to a general perception that they are fundamentally 'different' or 'dangerous.' Similarly, based on erroneous beliefs among wizards, the so-called "lesser creatures" in the magical community are not attributed with the same level of humanity. Likewise, it goes without saying that some groups command far greater sympathy and consideration than others in the real world.

Our own world has a history of depriving some groups of inalienable rights. And 'cultural difference' is often cited as justification for ignoring human rights violations currently taking place in some parts of the globe. Also, the Trans-Atlantic Slave Trade was once justified on the basis that the African was "sub-human." Therefore, one could argue that the notion of "humanity" has been continuously called into question by our own history. And for this reason, the term is more unstable and susceptible to change than it is normally perceived to be.

Another important issue which Rowling raises is the matter of solidarity and co-operation between oppressed groups. Unfortunately, a common feature in any society, whether in the real or magical world, is the lack of unity amongst marginalized groups. In Great Britain, for example, far too often have I heard Black children using the pejorative term "paki" to refer to their peers of South East Asian origin. The reverse is also true with the use of the term "nigger" or "blackie." Other disturbing trends include the fact that every Arab-looking person or Muslim is now presumed to be a potential terrorist, and every Italian related to the Mafia. It is most worrisome when the persecution and generalizations emanate from people who are themselves marginalized for some reason or other. Minority groups often fail to realize that, in persecuting each other, they are merely embracing the same bigotry and ignorance that have victimized their own kind for decades in Western societies.

Likewise, in Rowling's fictional wizarding world, there is a disturbing lack of unity and respect between persecuted groups of magical creatures. Instead of uniting and protecting each other's rights, each group seems determined to prove either that it can resist the hierarchical set-up by isolating itself, or that its status or intrinsic worth is greater than that of other marginalized or exploited groups. For example, we see the Centaurs turning their backs on wizardkind until they are forced to act. For many centuries they have failed to realize that, although they can read the stars, they still have to live on the earth. And the outcome of a wizard war could alter their own quality of life for the worse, whether or not they recognize or accept their designated place in wizarding society.

Contempt for social Others is also rife among house-elves and goblins, who are far too busy casting aspersions on each other's worth and dignity, to make any unified attempt to secure better working and living conditions for themselves and their posterity. For example, in *Goblet of Fire*, we see a subserviently obedient Winky, and others like her, chastising Dobby for having "ideas above his station" (p. 89), just because he values his freedom and demands wages for his work. And in *Deathly Hallows*, we witness the full extent of the animosity between house-elves and goblins: They cast aspersions against each other even in times of crisis, when they should rather unite.

Griphook's reaction to Harry's grief following Dobby's death is quite telling. The goblin loathes the fact that Harry actually does Dobby the honor of digging a grave—even though the elf had just died saving all their lives—including his own (Griphook's). Despite the gratitude and honor he owes to Dobby, the goblin clearly considers the act of digging a grave for an elf to be beneath him (and Harry). And so, many of the so-called "sub-human" and "part-human" groups fail to realize how much they stand to gain by standing united and preserving each other's rights and dignities. And, perhaps, this is the main social circumstance which sustains the wizarding world's rigidly hierarchical structure. In the next chapter, I will list and discuss four other factors that have helped to foster unjust social systems in Rowling's wizarding world, as well as in our own.

Chapter 2

How the Hierarchy is Maintained: The Four I's

There are four undeniable factors which cause humans to act in a prejudiced manner towards social Others. These are:

1. a lack of knowledge regarding the social Other,
2. a lack of concern for the social Other,
3. fear of the social Other, and
4. irrational, negative prejudgments, which then lead to negative attitudes and behavior towards the social Other.

Therefore, I have summarized the causes of prejudice and discrimination according to what we could call 'the *Four I*'s': *ignorance*, *indifference*, *insecurity and intolerance*. The *Harry Potter* novels contain many examples of the sort of prejudice which results from these four factors. And so, in this chapter, I will highlight examples from Rowling's work to demonstrate how *the Four I's* have helped to maintain the social hierarchy within the magical community, as well discuss their relevance to social and political trends in our own world.

Ignorance

Conventional definitions of ignorance denote "not knowing" something. But the word has an entirely different meaning in Jamaican Creole. When one is described as "ignorant" in Jamaican *Patois*, it means that the person is being rude or ill-tempered. Although this denotation is wildly different from the traditional meaning of the word, somehow it makes sense when we consider that "not knowing" the facts can sometimes affect a person's simplest rational judgments.[1]

In the Harry Potter series there are many examples of marginalized people being treated "ignorantly"—in both senses of the word. One example of this appears in *Chamber of Secrets*, where Harry becomes the subject of wild rumors that he might be a Dark wizard, simply because of his ability to speak to snakes. Apparently, in the wizarding world, most people believe that "parselmouths"—witches or wizards who

[1] Allport, 1954/1979, p. 190.

can speak "Parseltongue," or snake language—are evil. And so, even if Harry uses this gift to save lives, as he does repeatedly throughout the series, the mere fact that he can speak Parseltongue incriminates him.

Harry encounters undue hostility particularly from Hufflepuff students, when he uses his ability to call off Draco Malfoy's snake from attacking one of their classmates. And matters worsen for the protagonist when the same student is later petrified by Slytherin's monster. Interestingly, Harry finds that his schoolmates have already anticipated his counter-arguments—in the event that he should defend himself by pointing out that one of his best friends and his deceased mother were both Muggle-borns:

> 'And in case you're getting ideas,' [Ernie] added hastily, 'I might tell you that you can trace my family back through nine generations of witches and warlocks and my blood's as pure as anyone's, so—'
>
> 'I don't care what sort of blood you've got!' said Harry fiercely. 'Why would I want to attack Muggle-borns?'
>
> 'I've heard you hate those Muggles you live with,' said Ernie swiftly.
>
> 'It's not possible to live with the Dursleys and not hate them,' said Harry. 'I'd like to see you try it.' (*Chamber of Secrets*, p. 150).

Clearly, Ernie has carefully thought through all the evidence in the case mounted against Harry: It all starts with the fact that Harry is a parselmouth, because "everyone knows that's the mark of a Dark wizard." (p. 148).

Dumbledore later explains to Harry that Parseltongue is a gift that has nothing at all to do with dark magic, and that his peers are referring to something that is a mere perception amongst wizards. And furthermore, it is a wizard's choices in life that matter, rather than his abilities (p. 245).

The Parseltongue issue is a good example of the power of stereotypes and the privileging of perceptions over facts in an individual's day-to-day interaction with others.

Allport believed that stereotypes played an important part in creating prejudice. He described stereotypes as

> "primarily images within a category invoked by the individual to justify either love-prejudice or hate-prejudice."
> (Allport, 1954/1979, p. 189).

As with Harry and his Parseltongue abilities, the stereotypes associated with most minority groups in our own world tend to be attributed to individuals on a day-to-day basis, thus depriving them of the opportunity to prove themselves to be otherwise.

Furthermore, although some stereotypes may have a shade of truth in them, as Allport explained, others have "no ascertainable basis in fact":

> A verifiable assessment of a group is not the same as the selecting, sharpening, and fictionizing of a stereotype. It is possible for a stereotype to grow in defiance of *all* evidence.
>
> For example, in Fresno County, California, at one time the prevailing stereotype of Armenians held them to be "dishonest, lying, deceitful." La Piere made a study to determine whether there was objective evidence to justify the belief. He found that the records of the Merchant's Association gave Armenians as good credit ratings as those received by the other groups. Moreover, Armenians applied less often for charity and appeared less frequently in legal cases. [2]
>
> One wonders how, with all evidence so contradictory, the stereotype of "dishonest, lying, deceitful" could have arisen.
>
> (Allport, 1954/1979, pp. 189-190).

The above (Armenian) example does not easily apply to the parselmouth issue because evidence suggests that, throughout wizarding history, various Dark wizards (including Voldemort and Salazar Slytherin) had the gift of Parseltongue. But we

[2] Allport quotes La Piere's essay, entitled "Type-rationalizations of group antipathy" (1936).

can certainly make a pertinent example of the Muggle-born issue here...

The general perception of Muggle-borns in the wizarding world seems to contradict all evidence thus far. For example, in *Half-blood Prince*, where we meet the character Horace Slughorn for the first time, we can see that it is common to "expect less" from Muggle-borns and more from Pure-bloods in terms of academic achievement. Slughorn does not conceal his shock at the discovery that Lily Potter—the brightest and most popular witch in her year—was a Muggle-born:

> "Couldn't believe it when I found out. Thought she must have been pure-blood, she was so good."
> (*Half-blood Prince*, p. 71).

The Professor's open admission brings to mind Allport's notion of "inner conflict", which Devine re-terms as "*defensive rationalization*," whereby people who hold negative preconceptions about others continue to do so, despite glaring evidence contradicting their views. Devine summarizes the theory thus:

> Defensive rationalizations do not truly resolve the conflict, but rather allow people to make sense of inconsistencies by marshalling evidence to justify negative views of outgroup members. People can, for example, selectively cite examples to support negative views of outgroup members, while simultaneously ignoring or distorting contrary evidence. [This] enables people to maintain the illusion that they are objective and fair-minded. For example, evidence of a highly-accomplished Black person who contradicts the stereotype of Blacks as lazy is easily handled by viewing that individual as the "exception that proves the rule." Contemporary authors refer to this process as subtyping (Rothbart & John, 1985). Once subtyped, the person no longer threatens the validity of stereotypic thinking. Allport recognized that this strategy enables people to

> recognize their negative beliefs but to view them as valid rather than prejudiced.[3]

Likewise, we can see that Professor Slughorn genuinely believes that his views are perfectly normal and in no way discriminatory. This speaks not only of the stereotype's dominance over verifiable fact, but also of humanity's failure to recognize some of the most deep-seated forms of bigotry. As Slughorn's example demonstrates, stereotypes have a way of "normalizing" harmful untruths and half-truths until they have become so tightly woven into the fabric of society that they are nearly impossible to cut out.

Moreover, ignorance resulting from stereotypes often helps in the justification of the proclaimed superiority of one group over all others. This is not only evident in the Pure-bloods' perceived superiority over Muggle-borns, but also in the "moral upper-hand" that wizards seem to have over goblins. For example, in *Deathly Hallows*, Ron's dislike for Griphook, and goblins in general, is quite clear. His feelings are perhaps justified, as Griphook does not appear to be a likeable character at all; and, in the end, the goblin double-crosses the trio. However, in Griphook's defense, Harry had been planning to double-cross him, too, by delaying payment for his work.

And so, what remains clear is that wizarding history—in Hermione's words—"often skates over what the wizards have done to other magical races" (p. 409). The biased history textbooks, which Hermione constantly berates, have facilitated universal ignorance, stereotyping and one-sided views that have largely contributed to the demonization of goblins and other marginalized magical beings. But where Griphook's anti-wizard feelings and old grudges are concerned, Ron can hardly contain his indifference—which brings the discussion to the second of *the Four I's*...

[3] From Devine's essay entitled "Breaking the Prejudice Habit..." in *On the Nature of Prejudice*. (Edited by Dovidio et al., 2005, pp. 330-331)

Indifference

Of the three main characters in the *Harry Potter* books, Ron is perhaps the one with whom most readers can identify: Both Harry and Hermione are extraordinary[4] in their own way; and so, one could argue that Ron is the most "normal" of the trio—in terms of being an average, non-traumatized teenager who has been raised in a decent home. And so, it is important that the author uses Ron's character so effectively in order to demonstrate exactly how prejudice works, and how common it is amongst humans in general.

Whereas Hermione displays an extremely alert social conscience and awareness—which probably stems from the fact that she belongs to one of the wizarding world's most severely persecuted groups (Muggle-borns)—Ron is largely unconcerned by social issues. He also takes many of his day-to-day comforts for granted: He simply does not realize how lucky he is to be born in the home in which he was born, or to have the parents he has. Nor does he realize how privileged he is to be a part of the dominant group in the wizarding world.

Ron is a good-hearted, compassionate and caring person, especially with those close to him, and he is as open-minded as anyone his age can be under normal circumstances. But until he gets first-hand experience of the hardships other groups face—after being forced to step outside of his comfort zone in *Deathly Hallows*—he simply does not understand what it means to suffer, to be excluded, to be patronized or to be hunted and persecuted. Ron never fully understands the price of wizard superiority and indifference towards other groups, until he himself is forced to live as an outcast.

And so, Ron's character serves to show how *ignorance* sometimes fosters *indifference*. And, of course, eventually he does change his social outlook. He also comes to realize that ignorance is not an excuse for indifference and inhumanity towards social Others.

***

[4] As "The Boy Who Lived," Harry has endured enough hardships to last ten lifetimes. And as for Hermione, she is an extraordinarily bright girl who outperforms her peers in almost every subject. She also goes above and beyond the required effort in everything that she does.

General wizard indifference manifests itself in various ways, but the most obvious is the manner in which they tend to rationalize their way out of feeling guilty about how they treat other magical groups. As Allport explained, sometimes people handle guilt feelings in benign and wholesome ways, but at other times, guilt can lead to intense prejudice. The three unwholesome guilt-purging mechanisms highlighted by Allport are:

1. denial,
2. justification of conditions, and
3. projection.

Denial is by far the most common guilt-evading tactic. Individuals tend to deny guilt by insisting that there is absolutely no reason or cause for it. Allport used the example of discrimination against Blacks in the pre-Civil War United States. "They are happier by themselves" was the most common justification for the segregation of the black underclass from the dominant white population.[5]

Likewise, in the *Harry Potter* novels, we see Hermione founding the Society for the Promotion of Elfish Welfare in protest against the house-elves' enslavement; and she encounters similar justification from wizards' for the brutal conditions in which house-elves perform their roles. Also, S.P.E.W. is a poignantly amusing acronym because Hermione takes every opportunity to rant—as in "spewing (or spilling) her guts"—about the "*very* raw deal"[6] that the house-elves get. But she does so to no avail because, like Ron, most people are highly indifferent towards matters concerning elves.

Although Ron changes his social outlook in the series finale—after Dobby dies saving his and his friends' lives—, at this earlier stage (in *Goblet of Fire*), we see him joining the rest of the student body in rolling their eyes every time Hermione mentions elf rights. Initially, Hermione only manages to sell two S.P.E.W. badges (and Ron and Harry only bought them, partly to silence her impassioned speeches and partly because they were terrified of angering her further).

As this example demonstrates, it is far too much of a deep-seated belief amongst wizards that house-elves "love"

---

[5] Allport, 1954/1979, p. 379.

[6] See *Goblet of Fire*, p. 112.

their jobs, "like" being enslaved, and are "happy" with their lot.[7] And Hermione has to accept that, as long as wizards and elves embraced this rhetoric, nothing would ever change. Therefore, we could say that, in the pre-revolution wizarding world, most groups remained largely indifferent to the conditions in which house-elves lived and worked. And this was partly because they did not attribute full humanity to the elves, and partly because—unlike Hermione—they had never bothered to research how the elves came to be slaves in the first place. The matter of elf slavery will be examined more closely in the next chapter.

***

The next guilt-evading mechanism is justification of conditions: "The simplest evasion of all is to say that the hated person is wholly to blame," explained Allport. He continued:

> ...many people who are prejudiced take this path. This is prejudice without compunction. "Who could tolerate them? Look, they are dirty, lazy, sexually libertine." The fact that these qualities may be the very ones we have to fight in ourselves, makes it all the easier to see them in others. In any case [it] ... avoids the necessity of guilt. (Allport, 1954/1979, p. 380)

We can certainly see examples of this in J.K. Rowling's magical community. Most notable is the issue of werewolf and giant exclusion. As with many of the incurably ill in our own world, particularly with people who are known to carry transmittable diseases such as the HIV virus, werewolves are perceived as posing a physical threat or a major health risk. There is no antidote to the werewolf's bite; and, of course, this is used as a justification for stigmatizing and shunning them.

Giants undergo even more extreme persecution, as Ron explains that many of them were killed by Aurors after the first war against Voldemort. The entire Giant race was presumed to be in league with the dark side. Hence, we can see why there is such a harsh reaction from Ron, upon

[7] See *Goblet of Fire*, Chapters 14, 16 & 21.

discovering Hagrid's lineage. While Hermione expresses no surprise at all, and Harry says that he has no problem with Hagrid having a giantess mother, Ron insists:

> 'Well ... no one who knows him will care, 'cos they'll know he's not dangerous ... But ... Harry, they're just vicious, giants ... it's in their natures, they're like trolls ... they just like killing, everyone knows that...'
> (*Goblet of Fire*, p. 374)

Almost everything that Ron says about giants is proved to be true when we first get to see a giant community in *Order of the Phoenix*. But we also learn that their violence is largely a result of the social condition that has been enforced upon them by wizards. As Hagrid informs the trio, giants were forced out of the magical community and into smaller, secluded groups, by themselves. And this was not their natural way of living:

> 'Yep...eighty left, an' there was loads once, musta bin a hundred diff'rent tribes from all over the world. Bu' they've bin dyin' out fer ages. Wizards killed a few, o' course, bu' mostly they killed each other, an' now they're dyin' out faster than ever. They're not made ter live bunched up together like tha'. Dumbledore says it's our fault, it was the wizards who forced 'em to go an' made 'em live a good long way from us an' they had no choice bu' ter stick together fer their own protection.'
> (*Order of the Phoenix*, pp. 377-378).

In the same way that Ron needs to justify his own prejudices, Hagrid sounds almost as though he needs to justify the giants' violence against each other. But it is worth noting that he uses personal pronouns ("we" and "our") when referring to the wizard race. Although Hagrid is half-giant, he fully counts himself among the empowered wizard group because, on some level, he recognizes that being an 'insider' is crucial.

In fact, being biologically linked to both worlds, Hagrid more than anyone else knows how much it matters to be counted among the empowered. But he also has a degree of sympathy for giants that he knows most wizards will never attain: "mos' wizards aren' bothered where they are, 's'long as it's a good long way away."[8]

Later, in the same book, through the development of Hagrid's relationship with his half-brother Grawp, we can see why it would take much more than a mere passing interest in giants to overcome wizarding indifference to the Giant race—or to quell the giants' fear and dislike for wizards, especially after what wizards did to them in the past. It takes an extraordinary amount of bravery, patience and unconditional love for his half brother, in order for Hagrid to bridge the gap between them. And the family ties binding him to the Giant race turn out to be a fortunate twist of fate for those fighting against Voldemort: The Dark Lord had managed to procure two very large giants to fight in the war, and if it were not for Grawp, Hogwarts might have been totally destroyed.

Furthermore, as we see in Grawp's development over the three years after Hagrid found him, it is clear that, with open-mindedness and the right motivations, giants can adapt quite easily to wizarding society. And moreover, contrary to what most wizards believe, giants have very little in common with trolls. Grawps is proven to have excellent memory, intelligence and a very deep sense of loyalty to the people who have looked after him.[9] And so, through Grawp's character, Rowling proves rather effectively how the general wizarding perception of giants—though not entirely unfounded—remains unjust and harmfully stereotypical. These perceptions also encouraged wizarding indifference to the near-extermination of an entire race of magical beings.

***

Finally, projection is one of the more complex forms of guilt-evasion because it includes a partial admission of wrong-doing. The previous (giant) example is also applicable here:

---

[8] *Order of the Phoenix*, p. 376.

[9] To Hermione's surprise, Grawp recognizes her and Harry, and he remembers their names after their first meeting. He also learns English rather quickly; and he chases off an entire herd of centaurs to protect Hermione and Harry. (See *Order of the Phoenix*, Chapter 33, "Fight and Flight").

Note the way that Ron justifies wizard violence against giants, after admitting that Aurors have killed some of them:

> "But ... Harry, they're just vicious, giants ... it's in their natures, they're like trolls ... they just like killing, everyone knows that..."
> (*Goblet of Fire*, p. 374)

Clearly, Ron needs Harry to understand that, whatever wizards might have done to the giants,

1. it has nothing to do with him—Ron—holding personal prejudices because "everyone knows" that giants are violent and vicious; and
2. the giants must have deserved it anyway because their very "nature" is evil and prone to cruelty ("they just like killing").

Allport effectively summed up this (projection) strategy of guilt-evasion thus:

> "There is guilt somewhere, yes, but it is not *my* guilt."
> (Allport, 1954/1979, p. 380)

He also used the example of a Gentile businessman who was guilty of unethical practices that forced a Jewish competitor into bankruptcy, and who consoled himself, saying:

> "Well, they are always trying to run Christians out of business, and so I had to get him first."
> (Allport, 1954/1979, p. 378)

We see Ron using the same tactic with Griphook in the series finale, when he says:

> "Goblins aren't exactly fluffy little bunnies, though, are they? ... They've killed plenty of us. They've fought dirty too."
> (*Deathly Hallows*, p. 409)

And while Hermione has deep reservations about Harry's plan to double-cross Griphook, Ron thinks the plan is simply "genius" (p. 411)—perhaps because he genuinely believes that this is exactly the sort of thing that any goblin would do.

Insecurity

The third of the *Four I's* is a multi-faceted concept: Denotations of "insecurity" can relate to a person's economic or financial wellbeing, his sense of personal worth, or his sense of physical safety. As far as it relates to prejudice in the wizarding world, insecurity encompasses all of these things. And what all types or expressions of insecurity have in common is fear...It may be the fear of loss (of status, loved ones, dignity, financial security and so forth) or the fear of attack from outside forces.

Whether in the fictional wizarding world or the real world, financial security profoundly influences all other forms of security. Hence, in the social hierarchy outlined in Chapter 1, goblins were ranked the highest among all "sub-human" magical beings because they are a self-sufficient race. And, as previously stated, goblins manufacture the gold that wizards depend on for sustenance and trade. Also, as we may deduce from Griphook's refusal of Harry's gold in *Deathly Hallows* (p. 408), the Gringotts goblins are all fairly wealthy. Why then, do they still undergo such persecution from wizards?

Apparently, the goblins' wealth not only affects their social status but also provokes wizard envy. In fact, both sides seem to envy each other's special knowledge—in wandlore and metalwork respectively. Clearly, each side has power that remains inaccessible to the other, but they both perceive the need to have more, either to maintain their status (as is the case with wizards) or to gain equality with the other (as is clearly the case with goblins). I believe this is what Allport spoke of when he elaborated on "envy" and its role in the development of prejudice.

> Economic worries have their origins in hunger and the need to survive. But they continue to exist long after this rational function has been fulfilled. They ramify into the need for status, prestige and self-esteem. Food is no longer the issue, nor is money—excepting so far as it can buy that one thing in life that is always short in supply: *differential status.*

> Not everyone can be "on top." Not everyone wants to be. But most people want to be higher on the status ladder than they are.
> (Allport, 1954/1979, p. 371)

But the status war is not only between goblins and wizards. Perpetually marginalized groups envy each other, too. For instance, goblins and house-elves have their own brand of magic, but due to ancient wizarding laws, both groups are prohibited from carrying wands. And yet, rather than standing as a unified force, each group seeks its own means of exerting superiority over the other. As was mentioned in the previous chapter, the resentment that elves and goblins feel towards each other is apparent in Winky's warning to Dobby about behaving like a "common goblin,"[10] as well as Griphook's disparagement of Harry for making the effort to give his elf friend a proper burial.[11]

Allport used several fitting metaphors to explain the phenomenon of envy between marginalized groups:

> The philosopher Hume once pointed out that envy seems to appear only when the distance between ourselves and those more fortunate than ourselves is small enough so that we can reasonably compare ourselves with them—"the narcissism of small differences." A schoolboy does not envy Aristotle, but he may envy his neighbor whose 'A' in a course of study makes his own grades seem intolerably low. Slaves probably did not envy their rich masters—the gap was too great—but they may well have envied other slaves who had positions of favor.
> (Allport, 1954/1979, p. 371)

By the same token, many people who adulate their favorite celebrities or royalty would never harbor resentment for the wealth and privilege of these idolized figures; but they would loathe the idea of their neighbor driving a Mercedes Benz, if they themselves can only afford a Ford Taurus. And while

[10] *Goblet of Fire*, p. 90.

[11] See *Deathly Hallows*, p. 393.

goblins—who resemble house-elves somewhat—are entrusted with guarding wizard gold and treasures, wizards do not usually socialize with them. They are somewhat despised because of their reputation for being "blood-thirsty";[12] and they are also considered to be "ugly"[13] and disagreeable. Elves, on the contrary, are very close to their wizard families; and this is essentially a status marker that remains as inaccessible to the goblins as the coveted wandlore.

One could go as far as saying that elves influence their masters' decisions, despite their slave status. For example, prior to being so unceremoniously dismissed, Winky had been rather close to the Crouches. She even managed to convince Barty Crouch Senior to allow his son to go outside and take in fresh air. The father despised the boy and wanted to keep him locked away for good; but Winky pleaded with him and softened his heart—something that Crouch Junior would never have been able to do.[14] Also, in *Deathly Hallows*, we discover that Regulus Black had sacrificed his life to protect his family and also to save Kreacher.[15] It is no wonder, therefore, that goblins harbor such immense resentment for house-elves. The influence that the elves have over the so-called "wand carriers" gives them a special status, which the goblins crave. And perhaps, they even feel that their wealth should enable them to purchase the elves' privileged position.

***

Winky's aforementioned warning to Dobby could also be interpreted as another kind of insecurity: i.e., the fear of loss of status. Her statement implies that elves are not usually called in front of the Department for the Regulation and Control of Magical Creatures, because they do not usually disobey their masters or leave their families. And so, Winky might be concerned that, if Dobby continues to resist the hierarchy and fails to 'toe the line,' he may risk losing what—in her view—is not only a highly privileged status, but also the

[12] *Deathly Hallows*, p. 412.

[13] *Goblet of Fire*, p. 390.

[14] See *Goblet of Fire*, pp. 594-596.

[15] See *Deathly Hallows*, Chapter 10 ("Kreacher's Tale).

only status to which an elf is entitled. House-elves like Winky do not possess a sense of self-worth that is independent of their designated place in the social hierarchy. Nor do they understand—as Dobby does to a certain degree—that they have the power to define their own self-worth.

Self-worth not only plays a vital role in the way society treats people, it also affects what they aspire for, how they treat others, and what they are prepared to accept from society in general. A school bully would think twice about picking on the new student who is confident and who knows how to defend himself; but he will not hesitate to physically or verbally abuse another student, who seems insecure or who doesn't know how to stand up for himself. In the same way, wizards would think twice about enslaving goblins. And so, the contrast between goblin defiance and the eager subservience of the house-elves is quite striking.

On a similar note, the dominant wizard race would not lightly consider rounding up centaurs and tagging them; and yet, it seems plausible enough for them to achieve this with merpeople.[16] Here, we can see that the main difference between centaurs and merpeople lies in their respective self-images. The author alludes to the merpeople's self-perceived inferiority in the fourth book, where we discover that they are terrified of wands: When Harry goes to retrieve Ron from the mervillage as part of the second Triwizard task, he refuses to leave another human behind; and so, he attempts to rescue Fleur Delacour's sister Gabrielle. Armed with spears and sharp rocks, the merpeople try to stop him; but he is able to scare them all off by simply raising his wand threateningly.[17]

When we compare the above to the centaurs' reaction to Dolores Umbridge's taunts in *Order of the Phoenix*, we can see a marked difference. The centaurs are neither intimidated by Umbridge's wand nor by her office as "Senior Undersecretary to the Minister for Magic" (pp. 664-667). And so, the great disparity between the way these two out-groups are viewed is entirely based on the fact that Centaurs do not fear wizards, whereas Merpeople do. Therefore, we may argue

---

[16] Here, once again, I make reference to Dolores Umbridge's proposal to round up the merpeople and tag them. (See *Order of the Phoenix*, p. 271).
[17] See *Goblet of Fire*, p. 435.

that it is mostly the merpeople's insecurity (or their lack of self-esteem and their fear of wizards) that sustains their lower placement in the wizarding world's social hierarchy.

***

Sometimes a lack of security—whether it is self-esteem, financial or other forms of security—may cause an individual or a group to conform to social situations that they would normally resist, provided that their circumstances were different. An extreme impulse or 'need' to conform sometimes leads to marginalized individuals or groups persecuting each other even more cruelly than their superiors would do. For example, the Dolores Umbridge we see in *Deathly Hallows* is equally cruel and fanatic as herself in *Order of the Phoenix*. And, in both situations, I believe that what drives this character is paranoia about her place in society, or her status. Hence, she conforms in an extreme manner in order to ensure at all costs that her position remains safe.

In the series finale, we see Dolores alongside the Death Eaters, subjecting Muggle-borns working at the Ministry to fiercely unjust trials before handing them over to the Dementors. It is no surprise that Umbridge lies about her own blood status, claiming that the golden locket that she has bribed off a petty criminal is a family heirloom:

> "The 'S' stands for Selwyn ... I am related to the Selwyns ... indeed, there are few pure-blood families to whom I am not related..."
> (*Deathly Hallows*, p. 215).

Here, we see the character telling a blatant lie in order to protect her status among the empowered. She is clearly afraid of something; and I believe it is no coincidence that the author often mentions her alongside Squib characters: She is probably not a very powerful witch.

Despite her "wands away" policy in Defense classes, we do know that Dolores can do some magic. For instance, she admits to summoning the Dementors that attacked Harry and his cousin in *Order of the Phoenix* (p. 658); and she also conjures a small Patronus in *Deathly Hallows* (p. 214).

However, even during her most fearsome hour as High Inquisitor at Hogwarts, she never challenges anyone to a duel; and we never see her engaged in a fight that does not involve three or four attackers against one defender. Also, it cannot be mere coincidence that she has so much in common with the Squib characters in the series.

For instance, we discover in *Order of the Phoenix* that Umbridge is an obsessive cat-lover, very much like Filch, the Squib caretaker at Hogwarts, and Mrs. Figg, Harry's Squib neighbor in the Muggle world.[18] Also, in *Deathly Hallows*, Harry is reminded of Filch's filing cabinets when he searches Dolores's office for the Horcrux (p. 207). If it is indeed the case that Dolores is not very powerful or talented as a witch, then we may deduce that the terror she inflicts upon her victims is nothing more than the product of her own fears.

This brings to mind situations in our own history, where individuals or nations may have tried to disguise their fears and flaws by violently persecuting social Others. The following quotation from Jean-Paul Sartre—also cited by Gordon Allport in *The Nature of Prejudice*—makes particular reference to Jewish persecution during the Nazi regime; but there are also other examples which come to mind.

> We are now in a position to understand the anti-Semite. He is a man who is afraid. Not of the Jews, to be sure, but of himself, of his own consciousness, of his liberty, of his instincts, of his responsibilities, of his solitariness, of change, of society, and of the world—of everything except the Jews.[19]

In the same way, in *Order of the Phoenix*, Dolores is not afraid of Harry, per se; but she is afraid of what it would mean for her, personally, if people should start accepting the idea that Voldemort has returned: It might be a loss of status (her Ministry job, for instance), a loss of control of the situation, and so forth. And in *Deathly Hallows*, we may also surmise that she is not necessarily afraid of Muggle-borns usurping

---

[18] See *Order of the Phoenix*, Chapter 13 ("Detention with Dolores").

[19] Allport quotes Sartre—Source unidentified; (1954 / 1979, p. 367).

wizard power (or whatever other ludicrous charges the Death Eaters have mounted against the Muggle-born '*race*'). Instead, she is afraid of what it might mean for her if anyone ever finds out that she is a second-rate witch, who is probably far less powerful than the average Muggle-born.

And so, in both cases, it was *not* the object of her persecution that she feared, but rather public opinion, loss of authority and power, and the changes that would unavoidably come about for her, personally. In essence, all of Umbridge's acts of cruelty are fear-related and conformity-inspired. And it is also worth noting that, in the last two novels, even though Cornelius Fudge is no longer the Minister for Magic, Umbridge is still at the helm of power in the Ministry. Essentially, she is a survivor. She maintains her safe status and privilege regardless of the cost to her conscience—assuming, of course, that she has a conscience.

This is by no means a defense of a character that the author herself has described as "a very nasty piece of work,"[20] but rather an explanation of how fear and insecurity influence people's behavior in extreme situations: The greater the fear, the greater the extremity of violence and persecution.

***

This brings us to the final denotation of the term "insecurity" that I will discuss in this section: the fear of attack from outside forces. It is worth noting that wizards fear giants for almost the same reasons that Muggles fear wizardkind: The striking imbalances in power cause intense feelings of insecurity in the group that perceives the other as a physical threat. For example, in *Order of the Phoenix* we see that although Hagrid is only half-giant, his giant blood makes him impervious to even the most powerful wizard spells; and this makes it impossible for the repressive Umbridge and her mob of Aurors to contain him (pp. 635-637). Not surprisingly, therefore, wizards are very wary of giants and people with giant blood: They would have clearly lost the upper-hand in such a confrontation.

[20] J.K. Rowling Live Chat, Bloomsbury.com. July 30, 2007 (2.00-3.00pm BST).

Curiously, in the series finale the author seems to justify wizards' fear of goblin empowerment (through the right to use or carry wands). Rowling apparently subscribes to traditional Anglo-Saxon literary myths which portray goblins as mysteriously powerful but morally reprehensible beings.[21] And so, we see Harry—who had never harbored prejudice towards goblins before— increasingly disliking Griphook as he spends more time in the goblin's company. Nevertheless, Harry's gradual discovery of Griphook's flaws is subtly contrasted with Ron's pre-judgments about goblins in general.

But we also see Harry finding Griphook to be "unexpectedly bloodthirsty," as the goblin "laughed at the idea of pain in lesser creatures and seemed to relish the possibility that they might have to hurt other wizards to reach the Lestranges' vault" (p. 412). While the main character's perception of one goblin should not be used to make generalized statements about goblins in general, Bill Weasley—having lived and worked amongst goblins for a long time—seems to express the author's own sentiments: Bill warns Harry to be careful with Griphook because, "'it would be less dangerous to break into Gringotts than to renege on a promise to a goblin'" (p. 418).

Later, we also see that Griphook is quite knowledgeable of the use and effects of the Unforgivable Curses, as he encourages Harry to use the Imperius Curse on others, during the heist (p. 428). We may deduce from these events that wizards had originally taken away the right for other magical beings to carry wands, partly out of fear that this power would have been used against wizardkind, and partly out of a belief—perhaps justified in the case of goblins—in their own moral superiority and ability to bear the responsibility of power.

Issues concerning power-related responsibility and the moral superiority of certain groups (nations, religions, races, and so forth) over others are currently echoed in our own world, through concerns over the right to develop nuclear technology and weaponry. The concern, simply put, is that some weapons are far too dangerous 'in the wrong hands.' And some may perceive this as 'justifiable discrimination.' Still, it all depends on which side of the fence one is sitting...

---

[21] J.R.R. Tolkien's writings are good examples of this tradition.

Nevertheless, there are many other instances in the books, where we see fear-related discrimination that could never be considered justifiable under any circumstance. For example, from the end of Harry's fourth year at Hogwarts and throughout his fifth, Cornelius Fudge exhibits severe prejudicial behavior towards both Dumbledore and Harry. And it is all because of the Minister's fear of admitting the truth: the wizarding world is in grave danger because Voldemort has returned. More specifically, Fudge is afraid of what Voldemort's return might mean for himself and the Ministry: Presumably, millions of Galleons will have to be spent on extra security measures; people will have to be on their guard, and this might cause wide-spread panic; the population will look to their leader to protect them against unknown dark magic; and inevitably, people will die. Simply put, Fudge is afraid of the truth; and he is also afraid of facing his own personal insecurities: As a leader, does he have what it takes to protect the wizarding world from Voldemort?

And so, in accordance with the above Sartre quote, I conclude this section by stating that the defining feature of insecurity-related prejudice is not necessarily the fear of the social Other, but rather the fear of the unknown, the fear of change, and perhaps even fear of the effort it will take to bring about change.

Intolerance

Expressions of intolerance include making negative statements about a person's intrinsic worth, or communicating the feeling that someone's presence is not to be borne—probably because of some distinguishing feature, obvious physical traits, personality type, or some other characteristic. Similar to the sort of stereotyping that I discussed earlier in the chapter (relating to ignorance), expressions of intolerance constantly evoke perceived group characteristics as unassailable boundaries which separate the minority (or the 'outsider') from the majority (or the 'insider' or 'mainstream').

Intolerance can sometimes be an understated *non*-acceptance of the outsider's humanity in relation to our own. In other words: "They are not like us so they are not entitled to the same treatment." As blatant as this may seem, intolerance has a clever way of disguising itself—usually with humor. Most people who make racist jokes do not perceive this as an expression of intolerance. But a racist joke plays precisely upon the prevailing negative stereotypes normally used to emphasize the 'outsider' status of the subject of the joke. Also, there are different levels of intolerance—ranging from expressing mildly intolerant views (such as racist jokes) to embracing extreme and violent fanaticism (such as the sort of extermination regimes that lead to genocides). And, in the *Harry Potter* novels, there are several examples of every level of intolerance; but I will only highlight a few here.

Even the great champion of elf rights, Hermione Granger, occasionally expresses intolerant views about other magical beings. For example, in *Order of the Phoenix*, she does not react favorably to Grawp's presence, especially since the giant is living so close to Hogwarts (in the Forbidden Forest). Harry is far more understanding of Hagrid's need to care for his half brother. And so, he remains far more optimistic about the whole situation than Hermione, who clearly cannot fathom the idea of having to look after a giant—or having one living among wizards:

> 'We haven't got to do anything yet!' Harry tried to reassure her...'He's not asking us to do anything unless he gets chucked out and that might not even happen.'
>
> 'Oh, come off it, Harry!' said Hermione angrily ... 'Of course he's going to be chucked out and, to be perfectly honest, after what we've seen, who can blame Umbridge?'
>
> There was a pause in which Harry glared at her, and her eyes filled slowly with tears.
>
> 'You didn't mean that,' said Harry quietly.
>
> 'No ... well ... all right ... I didn't,' she said, wiping her eyes. 'But why does he have to make life so difficult for himself—for *us*?'
>
> (*Order of the Phoenix*, pp. 617-618).

Even though Hagrid had just explained to her and Harry that he had to bring Grawp back with him because the other giants had been beating him to death, Hermione cannot think of anything else but how "difficult" life will be for her and others like her, with Grawp now among them.

Harry is better able to relate to Hagrid's crisis because he is also an orphan who has no family in the wizarding world. In addition, Harry has a strong impulse to save and protect others, regardless of who they are. Hermione displays similar traits, but not to the same extent as Harry.[22] The apparent mess that Hagrid has got himself into—even for the sake of a half-brother—is far too much for her to tolerate. And besides, it seems impossible that Hagrid will succeed in helping Grawp to adapt. Therefore, as far as Hermione can see, it is not worth the effort. Perhaps she has also embraced certain wizarding perceptions about giants: For example, she, like Ron, has obviously stereotyped giants as being "as stupid as trolls."[23] In fact, when Hermione later realizes that Grawp remembers their names and is swiftly picking up English, she is literally shocked...

There is another important instance, from the fifth book, where Hermione displays mild intolerance towards another species. In the following, her classmates tease her about having abandoned Professor Trelawney's Divination course years before, suggesting that she probably regrets her decision now that the subject is being taught by a fascinating centaur. Hermione's response to the jibe is rather interesting:

> 'I'll bet you wish you hadn't given up Divination now, don't you, Hermione?' asked Parvati, smirking.
>
> 'Not really,' said Hermione indifferently. ... 'I've never really liked horses.'
>
> 'He's not a horse, he's a centaur!' said Lavender, sounding shocked.
>
> 'A *gorgeous* centaur...' sighed Parvati.
>
> 'Either way, he's still got four legs,' said Hermione coolly...
>
> (*Order of the Phoenix*, p. 528).

---

[22] In *Order of the Phoenix*, p. 646, Hermione points out Harry's "*saving-people thing*" as a character flaw.

[23] See *Goblet of Fire*, p. 374, where Ron tells Harry that giants are like trolls.

Here, we can see a few of the previously discussed factors that foster prejudice, namely ignorance and insecurity. Expressing such an insensitive viewpoint is highly untypical for our heroine, Hermione. (But she is, after all, only human).

To say that Firenze is merely a horse is the sort of ignorant, swiping, dismissive remark that has caused such grave animosity between wizards and the centaur race.[24] But the remark mostly reveals Hermione's insecurities, and a denial of her true feelings. First of all, she is afraid of being proved wrong: Two years prior to the above conversation, in *Prisoner of Azkaban*, she had fervently agreed with Professor McGonagall that "Divination is one of the most imprecise branches of magic" (p. 84), before walking out on Trelawney.

And now, her classmates are getting a coveted once-in-a-lifetime opportunity to study the subject with a true authority: a centaur—a magical being who, no doubt, fascinates Hermione. But instead of acknowledging her true feelings, she responds to her classmate's one-upmanship by dismissing Firenze, and by extension his entire race, as mere "horses." And by emphasizing Firenze's animal features over his human ones, she effectively dehumanizes him.

Still, Hermione's jibe is a relatively harmless expression of intolerance when compared with what Hagrid and Lupin experience when word gets out about their respective half-giant and werewolf statuses. In both cases, angry letters from parents arrive, saying they do not wish for their children to be taught by such people, and calling for their immediate dismissals.

Hermione herself also comes in for a dose of overt intolerance in the fourth book, when the Malfoys see her sitting in the Top Box at the Quidditch World Cup with Harry and the Weasleys:

> Mr. Malfoy's eyes had returned to Hermione, who went slightly pink, but stared determinedly back at him. Harry knew exactly what was making Mr. Malfoy's lip curl ... they considered anyone of Muggle descent, like

[24] For example, Umbridge is severely roughed up in the Forbidden Forest, after referring to a group of centaurs as "Beasts," "Filthy half-breeds" and "Uncontrolled animals." (See *Order of the Phoenix*, p. 665)

> Hermione, second-class. However, under the gaze of the Minister for Magic, Mr. Malfoy didn't dare say anything. He nodded sneeringly to Mr. Weasley, and continued down the line to his seats. Draco shot Harry, Ron and Hermione one contemptuous look, then settled himself between his mother and father
> (*Goblet of Fire*, p. 92)

Later in the same book, Hermione receives a mountain of hate mail—some with harmful curses enclosed in them—after Rita Skeeter publishes an absurd story about her being Harry's girlfriend whilst playing him false with Quidditch superstar Viktor Krum. One letter reads:

> "Harry Potter deserves better. Go back where you came from Muggle."
> (*Goblet of Fire*, p. 470)

Once again, emphasis is placed on the one dominant trait—her blood status or Muggle heritage—that the general wizarding public has stereotyped in people like Hermione.

Later in the series, we witness the highest level of intolerance—extreme violence and fanaticism—as the Death Eaters and Snatchers target Muggle-borns in *Deathly Hallows*. Many of the so-called Snatchers are ordinary and sometimes uneducated boys who suddenly find themselves with extraordinary amounts of power. For example, Ron tells Harry that the Snatchers who caught him "weren't the brightest" (p. 311).

We may assume that some of them are ordinary young people who become caught up in the sudden waves of euphoria which often culminate in severe persecution and violence towards marginalized groups. Some might have been placed under the Imperius Curse. And others perhaps participate because of a survival instinct—knowing that they themselves will be targeted if they do otherwise. The minor character called Stan Shunpike might fall into any of the aforementioned categories ... Or perhaps he was simply caught in the wrong place at the wrong time. In *Half-blood Prince*, we learn that an innocent Stan has been sent to Azkaban for consorting with Death Eaters. He is forced to remain there just because the corrupt Ministry had to be seen to be doing something to stop Voldemort from returning to full power (pp. 208-209).

Later in the series, there is a mass breakout from Azkaban, as the Dementors turn against the Ministry and join Voldemort. Stan is then recruited as a Death Eater and placed under the Imperius Curse. The last we hear of the character, in *Deathly Hallows*, is that he is helping the Snatchers by giving them leads on Muggle-borns and blood traitors who are on the run (p. 363).

One gets the impression that Harry sympathizes with Stan: He is convinced that the former Knight Bus conductor is simply conforming to wizarding society's violent intolerance, out of fear for his life or because of the influence of the Imperius Curse. We may never know the answer; but as far as metaphors go, the Imperius Curse certainly functions as an appropriate, (though somewhat 'metaphysical') symbol of physical coercion in the real world.

***

To conclude this chapter, it is worth noting that the pre-revolution wizarding world was highly susceptible to another wizard war, because it had all the elements of a society on the brink of upheaval. The prevailing wizard stance on relations with other magical beings left much to be desired; and although wizarding laws were not necessarily discriminatory towards Muggle-borns, there remained intense undercurrents of inequality and superiority feelings lurking beneath the surface. And so, although the wizarding world's vast majority of citizens were against Voldemort and his Death Eaters—and although they opposed the Dark Arts in general—as a society, they made it easy for the Dark Lord and his agents to infiltrate their governmental system and disguise themselves among the masses. Without realizing it, the wider wizarding world embraced some of Voldemort's most intolerant views, propagating racist ideologies in mild and seemingly unthreatening forms, thus enabling the Dark Lord to return among them without detection.

Chapter 3

Extreme Measures: Examining the Mindset of the House-elf

If a domestic worker from an ethnic minority group—say, Hispanic or African-American—trains up her daughter to be a maid, too, and insists that the child not aim for higher education or seek more high-profile jobs, is she displaying prejudice against her own offspring? Is she 'conditioning' the young girl to think of herself as inferior to her Caucasian peers, or perhaps less deserving of success and economic prosperity? Does the mother intentionally restrict her child's social or educational advancement; and does she do so out of fear, or perhaps out of envy or jealousy? In other words, does she harbor resentment for the fact that, during her youth, she herself lacked the opportunities that her daughter now has?

Perhaps she is just being protective? In other words, is she 'holding back' her daughter because of a genuine belief that society will never allow her to be on equal terms with those who belong to the dominant race, and that the child's efforts will inevitably lead to frustration and disappointment?

All of the above questions are related to the mindset of inferiority, which is inextricably linked to the 'psychologies of enslavement.' And so, one of my aims for this chapter is to show how self-perceived inferiority becomes an integral part of the slave's mindset and personality—as is aptly demonstrated in the *Harry Potter* novels through the house-elf subplot. Also, I will discuss the importance of the parent-child (but more specifically, the mother-son/mother-daughter) dynamic in transmitting the psychologies of enslavement to future generations. My other aims include showing how J.K. Rowling's house-elf subplot can be read on many levels, and also how certain insidious, debilitating prejudices can easily develop into societal norms.

***

For this chapter, I interviewed thirty *Harry Potter* readers and asked for their opinions on the house-elf subplot.

Seven readers equated the house-elf's fixed status (particularly his lack of social mobility and complete devotion to his job and master) to the lower working classes in most societies today. The most frequent explanation given for this interpretation is that, "most people within that socio-economic class fail to move up the social ladder." And this tendency was deemed to be partly due to low wages and a lack of education, and partly due to a certain "mentality" which keeps the lower classes fixed in their social situations.

Nine readers surmised that the house-elf's situation is a representation of female subordination in male-dominated societies. One reader's interpretation involved comparisons with the extremely devout, who remain "unwaveringly devoted to their religious groups because of blind faith." Another reader compared the house-elves' low self-esteem to individuals who find themselves in one-sided relationships, where "their opinions are never heard or acknowledged—as though they are not entitled to having feelings at all and the other [dominant] person in the relationship owns you and is always right." And another reader compared the house-elves' adulation and service impulses to motherhood:

'The daily demands of being a mother are a kind of slavery,' she said. 'We are always slaving away in the kitchen, too; and mothers are compelled to care for their offspring and love them unconditionally—almost like a house-elf is compelled to serve his masters.'

And finally, eleven of my interviewees chose the most literal interpretation, equating the house-elf's situation to modern forms slavery—from the recent victims of human trafficking and the illegal sex trades currently thriving in some Western countries, or the roaring Arab trade of Nuba Slaves in the Sudan, to the Trans-Atlantic Slave Trade centuries ago.

All of the above interpretations are important and relevant: It goes without saying that there is no one way of reading a text. Also, one may surmise from all of these readings that, contrary to popular opinion, slavery is not just a shunned taboo subject; rather, it is very much a modern reality and a societal feature of our times. As these diverse interpretations suggest, there are many social situations nowadays—some of them seemingly non-injurious—that can be likened to slavery. And there are still places in the world where human enslavement continues to be an institutional practice to this day.

Slavery being the controversial subject that it is, I believe that, in creating the house-elf subplot, J.K. Rowling wished to provoke her readership into asking the following questions: What exactly goes into "making" a slave? And what causes society to turn a blind eye to the kind of slavery in which the house-elves find themselves? After all, it would take a frighteningly high level of societal *indifference*[1] to overlook the subordination and systematic abuse of an entire race of beings.

As Allport explained, by the time slavery has become a social norm in any society, "a *modus vivendi*" or "way of living" has been firmly established and embraced by the enslaved class, as well as the dominant majority.[2] In other words, the inferiority of the slave has become such a widely accepted 'fact' that it is very seldom or never questioned—neither by the master class nor by the slave class. By then, most people simply abide by the rules without questioning how or why they came into being.

And so, slavery is not just a social condition; it is a mindset that is acquired and normalized over long periods of time by both the oppressed and the oppressor. Allport also surmised that such severe group power disparities "may result from a deliberate (and even from an unconscious) exploitation" of the minority group, because those belonging to the dominant class/group "stand to win the most advantage."[3] Then, after a while, it becomes *un*noticeable as a form of social injustice: The oppressed simply know their place, and the oppressors know theirs.[4]

Occasionally, some among the oppressed who still have the presence of mind and the strength of will to rebel against the system will do so. But, more than likely, their efforts will

---

[1] See Chapter 2 of this volume (pp. 66-72) for the definition and discussion of prejudice-related indifference.

[2] Allport, 1954/1979, pp. 11-14.

[3] Ibid, p. 234.

[4] Allport uses the example of segregated Black-White communities in early 20th Century America: "Since they merely follow the folk ways they deny that they are prejudiced. The Negro simply knows his place, and white people know theirs." (Ibid, p. 11)

be ridiculed or thwarted by members of their own group. We can certainly see this trend in the *Harry Potter* novels, particularly in the way Winky (the Crouch family's elf) and the Hogwarts elves relate to Dobby—an elf who had the audacity to aspire to freedom.

Sometimes there are also individuals among the empowered group—those with sharp social consciences and/or a vested interest in bringing about social change—, who recognize the injustice and feel it more acutely than the oppressed themselves do. The following quote provides one such example. Here, we see Hermione taking up the charge to campaign for basic rights for the Hogwarts house-elves, only to have her efforts firmly disdained and rejected by the elves themselves:

> 'Oh, for heaven's sake!' said Hermione ... 'You've got the right to wages and holidays and proper clothes, you don't have to do everything you're told—look at Dobby!'
>
> 'Miss will please leave Dobby out of this,' Dobby mumbled, looking scared. The cheery smiles had vanished from the faces of the house-elves around the kitchen. They were suddenly looking at Hermione as though she was mad and dangerous.
>
> 'We has your extra food!' squeaked an elf ...'Goodbye!'
>
> The house-elves crowded around Harry, Ron and Hermione, and began shunting them out of the kitchen, many little hands pushing in the smalls of their backs. (*Goblet of Fire*, p. 468).

As the above quotation demonstrates, Hermione feels rather passionately about elf rights and wants to incite a revolution or some form of resistance. But the elves are alarmed at the very idea that they should accept wages or proper clothing. They simply cannot understand why anyone would want to disturb the 'natural order of things' and start treating them like humans.

Nevertheless, from the little that we know of wizarding history, we can deduce two important, incontrovertible facts regarding house-elves:

i. They were not always enslaved.
ii. Contrary to popular wizarding beliefs, it is not in their "nature" to be as subservient as they are now.

Therefore, there must have been a grueling 'method' to enslaving the elves. And, obviously, after a long period of compliance, it became unnecessary to use that method to 'form' later generations of slaves (or to instill in them the sort of mentality required to keep them enslaved). And those born into the system, centuries later, simply accepted it as a way of life without questioning its legitimacy or fairness.

In our own world, sociologists have come up with various theories to explain the mindset of inferiority, which evidently 'normalizes' during the enslavement process. That which is most relevant to the house-elf situation is what Jost and Banaji have termed "System Justification Theory." Esses et al. have summarized it thus:

> [The theory] discusses the processes that ensure that members of both privileged and disadvantaged groups believe that the hierarchically structured society in which they live is legitimate and fair. In particular, the theory proposes that stereotypes justify the positive outcomes of dominant groups, the negative outcomes of subordinate groups, and the exploitation of subordinate groups by dominant groups. For example, dominant group members may be stereotyped as intelligent and hard-working, whereas subordinate group members may be stereotyped as unintelligent and lazy...Threats to the *status quo* may lead to heightened endorsement of these stereotypes in an attempt to defend and strengthen the system.[5]

The above theory applies to Rowling's house-elves because they appear to have embraced slavery completely, as a social condition which suits their skills and intrinsic worth. They

---

[5] See essay entitled "Instrumental Relations Among Groups: Group Competition, Conflict and Prejudice" in *On the Nature of Prejudice*. (Edited by Dovidio et al., 2005, p. 231)

have also passed on the lifestyle and the mindset of enslavement from generation to generation for many centuries, and now perform the slave's role without any strict enforcement from wizards.

Wizards, in turn, have accepted the house-elves' enslavement as a way of life, to the point where they fully embrace the notion that the house-elf has certain intrinsic qualities that make him slavery-bound: Not only does he "like" being enslaved, but he is also *only* suited for enslavement.

For the rest of this chapter, I will first postulate my own theory on the sort of 'conditioning' that got the house-elves to submit to slavery in the first place. Then, I will show how the elves maintain their own status (through the principle of System Justification Theory, as explained in the last quote).

The Language of Violence: The Physical & Social Conditioning of the House-elves

Even after the completion of the *Harry Potter* series, a few questions are purposefully left unanswered, particularly where the house-elves are concerned. In *Goblet of Fire*, we learn that "Elf enslavement goes back centuries" (p. 198): Hermione wanted to call her pro-elf rights society "Stop the Outrageous Abuse of Our Fellow Magical Creatures and Campaign for a Change in Their Legal Status," which suggests that the creation of the elf's "legal status"—as a socio-political institution—took place at around the same time wizards targeted them to be used as an enslaved class. The books also inform us that wizards have "made"[6] the elves what they are by casting "enchantments"[7] upon them, but leave the reader to speculate on the 'method' or the processes involved in slave-making...

---

[6] As was mentioned in the Book Summaries section of the Introduction to this volume (pp. 26-27), Dumbledore sympathizes with the treacherous Kreacher following Sirius's death (See also *Order of the Phoenix*, p. 733).

[7] Dumbledore asks Harry to summon an unwilling and resentful Kreacher. The elf is obliged to obey because of what Dumbledore calls "the enchantments of his kind." Sirius had bequeathed everything to Harry before his death; therefore, Kreacher also now belongs to the boy. (See *Half-blood Prince* [pp. 54-55])

What caused the house-elves to become slaves? And what were the methods used to "enchant" them into submission? I believe that Rowling leaves these questions unanswered in the spirit of open interpretation. But whatever methods were used to turn the house-elves into slaves, we can be sure that they involved some form of physical, verbal or psychological violence—or perhaps all of the above.

At first, violence—and/or the threat of violence—must have been used to break the elves' will and to teach them to respect and fear wizards, and also to employ 'intropunitive' means (as in self-directed violence) whenever they disobeyed. And in *Chamber of Secrets*, Dobby informs Harry that the house-elf's situation used to be a lot worse than it is now:

> 'Ah, if Harry Potter only knew!' Dobby groaned, more tears dripping into his ragged pillowcase. 'If he knew what he means to us, to the lowly, the enslaved, us dregs of the magical world! Dobby remembers how it was when He Who Must Not Be Named was at the height of his powers, sir! We house-elves were treated like vermin, sir! Of course, Dobby is still treated like that, sir...But mostly, sir, life has improved for my kind since you triumphed over He Who Must Not Be Named. Harry Potter survived, and the Dark Lord's power was broken, and it was a new dawn, sir, and Harry Potter shone like a beacon of hope for those of us who thought the dark days would never end, sir...'
> (*Chamber of Secrets*, pp. 133-134).

From what we know about the Malfoys, it is safe to assume that they would have gladly stuck to the "old ways" of mistreating house-elves, long after Voldemort's first fall—when it suddenly became 'politically incorrect' to physically abuse elves. In the same text, Harry discovers that the Malfoys supported Voldemort's bid to return to the "old ways," when he overhears a conversation between Lucius Malfoy and Dark Artifacts salesman Mr. Borgin. When the shop owner bemoans the fact that "wizard blood is counting for less everywhere," Lucius, on the other hand, insists "Not with me" (p. 44), stressing his determination to keep up the ancient wizarding customs.

Dobby also explains to Harry that he receives constant death threats at home ("five times a day" [p. 133]). And death threats are obviously an effective tool for breaking a person's will. Even in our own world, death threats are often used to ensure that some types of servants 'toe the line'—a theme constantly portrayed in gangster films and television dramas. And the same practice thrives under tyrannical political regimes, where oppressed citizens live in constant fear of retribution from repressive governments. And so, death threats are vital to the slave-making process, and instilling the psychologies of enslavement in the future slave's mind.

For instance, in an autobiography where she gives graphic details of her own enslavement in the Sudan, Mende Nazer recounts stories of rape, severe beatings and death threats (for herself and her family), after she was kidnapped and forced to live as a slave in the Khartoum during the 1990s. But a far more controversial document of one tried and proven method of slave-making appears in "The Willie Lynch Letter," a speech delivered to slave owners in Virginia in 1712, where the speaker (himself a slave-owner) instructed his audience to be careful not to kill the slave during the will-breaking process, but to "put the fear of God in him..."[8] According to Lynch, violence is crucial not only in breaking the slave's will, but also in taking full control of his mind through fear: "Keep the body take the mind! ... In other words, break the will to resist."[9] After a while, the slave comes to think of himself as "deserving" unkindness and violence: he understands that he is not fully human, therefore *only* worthy of being treated like an animal or even less.

As a result, the most basic displays of courtesy shown to the slave—especially by anyone from the master class—are viewed as overwhelming acts of kindness. Likewise, in *Chamber of Secrets*, we see a shocked Dobby reduced to tears when Harry apologizes for having *possibly* offended him, and invites him to sit down—"like an *equal*" (p. 16). And later, in *Goblet of Fire*, the elf is simply overjoyed when Ron gives him an unwanted jumper and a pair of socks for Christmas (p.

[8] The full Willie Lynch document can be found on several internet sites. See the Works Cited page for one source in PDF format.
[9] Ibid.

356). Dobby showers Ron with the highest praise; and he does so sincerely, because he genuinely believes that house-elves do not deserve such attention from wizards. Similarly, in her autobiography, Mende Nazer speaks of feeling "overcome" when treated with kindness by Arabs other than her masters: "I wanted to go and hide in the kitchen" she says.[10]

Nazer probably felt that the kitchen was her 'rightful place.' And here, we see violence being used alongside language to keep the slave within a designated space—physically, socially and psychologically. Through language, the slave recognizes certain *words* connected to *places*, as her 'rightful place.' And so, under normal circumstances, a slave like Nazer would not dare to breach these social boundaries because she 'knows her place.'

Furthermore, as we can see with Dobby, the slave comes to associate violence and the language of violence with its everyday existence, and so he is no longer alarmed by it:

> 'You nearly got Ron and me expelled,' [Harry] said fiercely. 'You'd better clear off before my bones come back, Dobby, or I might strangle you.'
>
> Dobby smiled weakly.
>
> 'Dobby is used to death threats, sir. Dobby gets them five times a day at home.'
>
> (*Chamber of Secrets*, p. 133)

Dobby knows his place so well that he no longer needs the Malfoys to punish him: he does it entirely by himself. He even punishes himself for "almost" speaking ill of his wizard family. And he continues to do so long after he gains his freedom.

Self-inflicted violence is such a frequent recurrence in this house-elf's life that his masters take no notice of his injuries: In any event, it is the slave's duty to self-punish, so they probably assume that he must have committed some minor mistake, and therefore fully deserves his punishment:

> '... Dobby will have to shut his ears in the oven door for this. If they ever knew, sir—'

[10] Nazer, *Slave*, p. 274.

> 'But wont they notice if you shut your ears in the oven door?'
>
> 'Dobby doubts it, sir. Dobby is always having to punish himself for something, sir. They lets Dobby get on with it, sir. Sometimes they reminds me to do extra punishments ...'
> (*Chamber of Secrets*, p. 16).

Here, we see that both slave and master take the self-punishing act as a given. As cruel and inhumane as this might seem to an outsider, the master and slave are no longer perturbed by the practice. In the slave's mind, the act of angering, disobeying or upsetting his master, even in the slightest way, is invariably associated with physical suffering. Hence, the fear of being punished evolves into the fear of disobedience—until the slave starts punishing himself for simply *thinking* of disobeying. And so, Dobby's impulses are the result of centuries of physical and mental conditioning through violence and the threat of violence.

Still, the fact that Dobby is complaining suggests that some part of him is aware of the unfairness of his situation. The uneducated elf might not be aware of the constraints of System Justification Theory; and although certain dominant wizarding customs are compelling him to act so self-deprecatingly, we can see that a vibrant, self-affirming sense of personal worth still lurks beneath the surface...

***

The house-elves' condition could also be read as an indictment of the manner in which some children are brought up: Sometimes child members of a dominant group, class or race are socialized to disparage social Others whom parents, peers or guardians have taught them to regard as inferior.

Conversely, the subplot might also be interpreted as an example of how people (children as well as adults) tend to embrace whatever esteem society—through parents, teachers, employers or peers—projects upon them or forces them to accept. For instance, after a while, a person no longer needs to be told that he is worthless, if he already believes in his own worthlessness as a result of a lifetime of neglect, abuse (verbal, physical or otherwise), abandonment or general indifference. In the same way, wizards no longer need to physically punish house-elves because the latter already '*know*' that they deserve to be punished when they disobey or assert their free will.

And so, an important aspect of conditioning slaves is the minimization of the effort required to 'form' future generations of slaves. During Lynch's era, this was usually accomplished through specifically targeting the females, so that they, in turn, would raise future generations to be slaves. During the 17th century, the manipulation of the female slave's mind became crucial to the slave-making process. The Lynch method included torturing the adult male in front of the female, sometimes to the point of death, so that, "for fear of the young male's life, she will psychologically train him to be mentally weak and dependent, but physically strong."[11]

Wizards may have employed similar techniques, in terms of targeting the female elves, for reasons similar to the ones Lynch cited. Once the breaking of the female psyche had taken place, the female elves would raise their offspring to think and act like slaves, as we can see in Winky's case:

> 'I is looking after the Crouches all my life, and my mother is doing it before me, and my grandmother is doing it before her ... oh, what is they saying if they knew Winky was freed? Oh, the shame, the shame!' She buried her face in her skirt again and bawled.
> (*Goblet of Fire*, p. 332-333)

Winky is severely distressed for failing to live up to her ancestors' expectations: She has failed to die in the service of the Crouches. And as far as she is concerned, she has missed out on the highest office that an elf can attain. This is why Dobby's quest for self-enhancement (on human/wizarding terms) is such an affront to her: By refusing to follow in his ancestors' footsteps, Dobby is going against the 'natural' order of things—but only as far as the typical slave's mentality goes.

We also see an example of the mother-son dynamic in *Order of the Phoenix*, where we learn that Kreacher had been

---

[11] See Works Cited for "Willie Lynch Letter" document URL reference.

raised by his mother to be a good and efficient servant, and a house-elf who aspired to nothing more or less than the same gruesome fate as his forefathers:

> 'His life's ambition is to have his head cut off and stuck up on a plaque just like his mother.'
> (*Order of the Phoenix*, p. 72)

With such compulsion to carry on the tradition of enslaved ancestors, wizards would not have to do much to keep the house-elves and their descendants in their place.

In addition, there seems to be a single-parent dynamic going on with the elf race: Winky was raised by her mother, and so was Kreacher. There is no mention of a father figure in either case; and Dobby does not speak of either of his parents. It is almost as though elf marriages are non-existent. And while there is nothing immoral about being a single-parent, if the elves are indeed reproducing outside of marriage, this could be easily latched onto as further proof of the slave's inherent (moral) inferiority to the master class—even if it was the masters who had originally inflicted this social condition upon them in the first place.

This was widely practiced during the Trans-Atlantic slave trade, as families were broken up, and slaves were not encouraged to marry or settle down as nuclear families. Instead, the physically stronger male slaves were encouraged to reproduce with as many females as possible. Eventually, it became a requirement for the slave to adopt the masters' religion (Christianity); but in many cases, the slave's sexual morality remained a non-issue: He was to be bred like any other animal; and his breeding was partially controlled by the master. After all, the slave was considered to be only sub-human; so he did not have the same need for sexual chastity or salvation...

It could very well be that wizards encouraged or enforced the same single-parent dynamic as a definitive social condition amongst elves. This would be one of the more predictable strategies for compromising the elves' humanity in a social context that looked unfavorably upon procreation outside of marriage. At the same time, single-parenthood (with mothers performing as the main/only parent) helped to foster the development of the psychologically stronger and independent female, who would raise her male offspring to be "physically strong but psychologically weak," as Lynch instructed.

The aim was to 'castrate' the male psychologically, so that he was led by the female. Because, despite her independence from her social equal (the slave-class male), she remained totally dependent on the master. And so, ironically, although the female slaves were psychologically independent from their males, it was they (the females) who facilitated the perpetual mental enslavement of their kind, by raising their offspring to think and act as the master's servant and dependant. It was therefore absolutely crucial for the female slave to be conditioned as the dominant single-parent who led, instructed and protected the slave-class male.

Although the author only develops the character of one female house-elf (Winky), one can still identify significant differences between the mentality of the female elf and that of males like Dobby and Kreacher. Winky shows a sort of sisterly or maternal concern for Dobby, and is more worried about his fate than even *he* is. Her response to his sudden change of status demonstrates the fearful, protective instinct of the female slave towards her male counterpart or offspring. It is simply part of her role—as a female elf—to instruct and keep wayward males like Dobby 'in their place'; and she does so mostly out of fear for his safety.

Likewise, by embracing his freedom, Dobby does something that Winky would never do, because, as she informs Hermione, she is a "good house-elf," who "is properly ashamed of being freed!"[12] And her response to freedom is so different from that of the two male elves, that it cannot be mere coincidence...

***

The first noticeable difference between Winky and the male elves is how well she embodies *all* the psychologies of enslavement (which I will list and explain in the next section of this chapter). But there is a simple reason for Winky's

[12] *Goblet of Fire*, p. 331.

devotion to the Crouches, especially when compared with Dobby's contempt for the Malfoys and Kreacher's animosity towards Sirius. Simply put, the Crouches treated her much better than the Malfoys ever treated Dobby, or the way Sirius treated Kreacher.

And that, in itself, disproves the prevailing wizarding perception that house-elves simply "like" being slaves, or that their natures oblige them to love and serve their wizard masters unconditionally, or that the "enchantments" placed upon them are anything more than mental barriers whose roots have grown deeper after centuries of enforced conformity. Furthermore, as the following quote suggests, many wizards, like Sirius Black, continued to hold fast to erroneous beliefs about the house-elves' mental conditioning, or their sense of free will:

> 'Come to think of it,' said Sirius ... 'has anyone actually seen Kreacher lately?' ...
>
> 'He couldn't have left, could he?' said Harry. 'I mean, when you said "*out*," maybe he thought you meant get out of the house?'
>
> 'No, no, house-elves can't leave unless they are given clothes. They're tied to their family's house,' said Sirius.
>
> 'They can leave the house if they really want to,' Harry contradicted him. 'Dobby did, he left the Malfoys' to give me warnings three years ago. He had to punish himself afterwards, but he still managed it.'
>
> Sirius looked slightly disconcerted for a moment, then said 'I'll look for him later...'
>
> (*Order of the Phoenix*, p. 446).

Evidently, elves have as much control over their will as any other group of magical beings. They only need to recognize their power and embrace it. Also, it is clear that their continued suppression is facilitated not only by their own ignorance but also by that of modern wizards who take their services, subservience and loyalty for granted. People like Sirius fail to consider how or why the elves became slaves in the first place. Of course, wizards stand to lose a significant amount of privilege, as well as economic resources and time, if they are to eliminate some of the social barriers inflicted upon house-elves.

It is also worth noting how quickly Sirius dismisses Harry's suggestion (that Kreacher, like Dobby, can embrace his free will and leave the house if he wishes). Quite frankly, Sirius cannot be bothered to reconsider his assumptions: It simply takes too much effort. And as Allport surmised, "*effort, except in the area of our most intense interests, is disagreeable.*"[13]

Perhaps the average slave resists seeking freedom for the same reason: the effort it would take and the hardships and punishment that he will no doubt have to endure, are intimidating and bothersome. And furthermore, the outcome of a rebellion is uncertain; and there is no real *need* to change things, as long as he is being fed and has a roof over his head. Dobby, however, is willing to face any punishment—self-inflicted or otherwise—if it means that he can thwart the Malfoys in their bid to harm Harry. Dobby has an active interest in saving Harry's life because he is very much aware of how the wizarding world would change (for himself and other house-elves), if Voldemort were to rise to power again.[14] And so, although he still feels restricted by the prohibitive enchantments cast upon his kind, he does whatever he can to protect his idol, Harry Potter.

Likewise, Kreacher shows little loyalty to Sirius, although he is obliged to serve him as the last remaining member of the Black family. As soon the elf finds a loophole in the orders given to him, he leaves his master and goes to Narcissa Malfoy and Bellatrix Lestrange, Sirius's cousins. These are not only family members whom Kreacher respects because of their pure-blood ideals, but also (and most importantly), people who treat him well. However insignificant this may seem, it is a considerable contradiction to the prevailing belief amongst wizards that the house-elves' sense of selfhood and humanity, or their ability to choose who to love and serve, are either totally repressed or non-existent. Hermione has been trying to

---

[13] Allport, 1954/1979, p. 21.

[14] See *Chamber of Secrets* (pp. 133-134) or the citation on page 92 of this volume, where Dobby explains how house-elves used to be treated "like vermin."

explain this to Harry and Ron for years; and they finally get the message in *Deathly Hallows*:

> 'Sirius was horrible to Kreacher, Harry, and it's no good looking like that, you know it's true. Kreacher had been alone for a long time when Sirius came to live here, and he was probably starving for a bit of affection. I'm sure "Miss Cissy" and "Miss Bella" were perfectly lovely to Kreacher, when he turned up, so he did them a favor and told them everything they wanted to know. I've said all along that wizards would pay for how they treat house-elves. Well, Voldemort did ... and so did Sirius.'
>
> Harry had no retort. As he watched Kreacher sobbing on the floor, he remembered what Dumbledore had said to him, mere hours after Sirius's death: *I do not think Sirius ever saw Kreacher as a being with feelings as acute as a human's ...*
> (*Deathly Hallows*, p. 164)

Likewise, as I previously suggested, Winky was devoted to the Crouches because they treated her relatively[15] well. Barty Crouch Junior's recollections, of how she managed to soften his father's heart, denote a sense of kindness and esteem from masters to servant:

> 'Winky talked my father into it ... She spent months persuading him. I had not left the house for years. I had loved Quidditch. Let him go, she said. He will be in his Invisibility Cloak. He can watch. Let him smell fresh air for once. She said my mother would have wanted it. She told my father that my mother had died to give me freedom. She had not saved me for a life of imprisonment. He agreed in the end.'
> (*Goblet of Fire*, p. 595)

However, Winky would not recognize her complete dedication to the Crouches as mere reciprocation for the respectful

---

[15] By normal wizarding standards, they treated her fairly well. But they still abused her slave status by ordering her to climb high up in the stadium stands, when they knew she was afraid of heights, and also by dismissing her unfairly.

treatment she used to receive from them. She is more likely to insist that she behaved well because she was "a good house-elf" who simply did whatever her job required her to do. Hence, the character's proclaimed fear of heights[16] is also a subverted reference to her slave status, as well as her unwillingness to embrace her humanity or social equality with wizards. Winky's existence is so defined by the social condition of slavery that she fails to realize how and when she contradicts the psychologies of enslavement and embraces her humanity.

The Nearly-Unbreakable Bonds of Mental Slavery

There are three indispensable psychological traits that the slave must possess if he or she is to remain enslaved. First, and most important, is the psychology of denial of identity and humanity; second, the psychology of adulation (of the master), and finally, the psychology of dependence. Once a slave has incorporated these flawed mentalities into his being, and accepted that being enslaved is his 'rightful place' or status, it becomes almost impossible to free his mind.

We see all of these features (or characteristics of the enslaved mind) uniquely embodied in the character Winky. Nevertheless, even rebellious slaves like Kreacher and Dobby struggle to overcome their mental conditioning.

First, to a certain extent, all three house-elves deny their right to a personal identity; and they do so by continuously referring to themselves in the third person. Their inability to use the personal pronoun ('I') is a good example of how language has been used to condition the house-elves' minds. We see that Winky—confident and assured in her slave status while working for the Crouches—uses the personal pronouns "I" and "me" when speaking to Harry at the Quidditch World Cup about how she has been trying to get Dobby back on the right track. But after being dismissed by Barty Crouch Senior, she reverts to speaking of herself mostly in the third person:

> 'Winky is a disgraced elf, but Winky is not yet getting paid! ... Winky is not sunk so low as that!'[17]

---

[16] See *Goblet of Fire*, p. 332.

[17] *Goblet of Fire*, p. 331.

Her existence is only legitimate as the Crouches' faithful servant; and so, in Winky's mind, not only has her life now lost its purpose, but she herself has also lost her identity.

Both Kreacher and Dobby display similar habits, but to a far lesser degree. The male elves also continuously refer to themselves in the third person: "Dobby has come to tell you, sir...Dobby wonders where to begin...";[18] "Kreacher is cleaning...Kreacher lives to serve the Noble House of Black";[19] and so forth. Kreacher even speaks of himself in the third person when he is trying to assert his will—when trying to disobey a direct order ("Kreacher won't, won't, won't, WON'T!")[20]

However, unlike Winky, Kreacher does not plead for his master not to dismiss him ... When Sirius threatens him with clothes, a forlorn Kreacher merely responds: "Master must do as Master wishes."[21] And, as for Dobby, he practically revels in his new freedom: "Dobby likes work, but he wants to wear clothes and he wants to be paid, Harry Potter ... Dobby likes being free!"[22]

Still, it is clear that Dobby remains unable to completely liberate himself from the psychological bond of wizard ownership: Even after being free for more than a year, Harry has to stop him several times from punishing himself when he speaks ill of the Malfoys. In fact, all three elfin characters 'perform' the required deference towards their wizard families, whether they want to or not—or in Winky and Dobby's case, whether they are obliged to or not. Winky insists on keeping the Crouches' secrets long after she has been freed, and disparages Dobby for speaking ill of his former masters. And even Kreacher, who loathes Sirius, is compelled to obey direct orders and bow lowly to him—even though he only does so resentfully, whilst muttering aspersions under his breath.[23]

---

[18] *Chamber of Secrets*, p. 15.

[19] *Order of the Phoenix*, p. 102

[20] Kreacher passes to Harry's ownership rather unwillingly. (See *Half-blood Prince*, p. 55)

[21] *Order of the Phoenix*, p. 109

[22] *Goblet of Fire*, p. 330.

[23] See *Order of the Phoenix*, p. 102

Where denial of humanity is concerned, it is clear that house-elves generally accept that they are not entitled to human feelings. Unlike Winky, Dobby has started to acknowledge his humanity—first by complaining to Harry about how poorly he was being treated by the Malfoys, and then, by embracing his freedom. But the fact that he still feels compelled to hurt himself when he criticizes the Malfoys shows that he does not completely believe that he is entitled to free will or human feelings. As Harry tells him, he just "needs a bit of practice."[24]

In contrast, Winky and the Hogwarts elves are firmly in denial of their humanity. In the following, an exasperated Winky tries to explain the duties of a house-elf to Harry, whom she blames for Dobby's sudden unorthodox behavior:

> 'It's about time he had a bit of fun,' said Harry.
>
> 'House-elves is not supposed to have fun, Harry Potter,' said Winky firmly, from behind her hands. 'House-elves does what they is told. I is not liking heights at all Harry Potter ... But my master sends me to the Top Box and I comes, sir.'
>
> (*Goblet of Fire*, p. 90)

Later, we see the Hogwarts elves echoing Winky's sentiments when she herself overindulges in grief, as she descends into depression and debauchery after being freed:

> 'We is sorry you had to see that, sirs and miss!' squeaked a nearby elf, shaking his head and looking very ashamed. 'We is hoping you will not judge us all by Winky, sirs and miss!'
>
> 'She's unhappy!' said Hermione, exasperated. 'Why don't you try and cheer her up instead of covering her up?'
>
> 'Begging your pardon, miss,' said the house-elf, bowing deeply again, 'but house-elves has no right to be unhappy when there is work to be done and masters to be served.'
>
> (*Goblet of Fire*, p. 468)

---

[24] *Goblet of Fire*, p. 332.

Ironically, the Hogwarts elves are in total agreement with Winky's belief that house-elves are not entitled to portraying human feelings. As far as they are concerned, it is neither their business nor their place to feel abused, exploited or underpaid. And so, the grief-stricken Winky fails to see that, like Dobby, she is now an elf who has "ideas above her station." By her own standards and reasoning, she has no right to wallow in self-pity.

***

The second psychology of enslavement is manifested in the slave's unconditional adulation of the master. When the Headmaster tells the Hogwarts elves that they can call him "a barmy old codger" if they want to,[25] he is not only trying to get them to embrace their humanity and start exercising free will, but also to absolve them of the duty of unconditional adulation. But it is impossible for one man, even the great Albus Dumbledore, to reverse the effects of centuries of mental conditioning, or for the house-elves to take such a gigantic collective leap so soon.

Even in the matter of wages, we see that Dobby is incapable of accepting a reasonable salary. The mere fact that he is being paid is already such a significant change for him:

> 'And Professor Dumbledore says he will pay Dobby, sir, if Dobby wants paying! And so Dobby is a free elf, sir, and Dobby gets a Galleon a week and one day off a month!'
>
> 'That's not very much!' Hermione shouted indignantly...
>
> 'Professor Dumbledore offered Dobby ten Galleons a week, and weekends off,' said Dobby, suddenly giving a little shiver, as though the prospect of so much leisure and riches was frightening, 'but Dobby beat him down, miss ... Dobby likes freedom, miss, but he isn't wanting too much, miss, Dobby likes work better.'
>
> (*Goblet of Fire*, pp. 330-331)

---

[25] Ibid.

Dumbledore can only offer encouragement and support as Dobby gradually embraces his freedom, asserts his will and acknowledges his humanity. But he cannot force the elf to accept more than what he thinks he deserves; and he certainly cannot "free" Dobby's mind. Dobby has been well-trained in the arts of self-deprecation and loving a master more than he loves himself. And he continues with these habits until his death.

Nevertheless, he has taken the first step towards psychological freedom by *choosing* to love a master who values him, and who treats him well. And moreover, it takes several generations (of freedom) before the descendants of slaves accept that they are worthy of as much respect, as many rewards and as much adulation as the master class. Though Dobby remains somewhat inhibited by the mindset of slavery, he has fully embraced the idea that he deserves freedom, compassion and rewards for his work; and that, in itself, is quite extraordinary.

***

Lynch's slave-making method emphasized the need for the slave to "love, respect and trust" the master class unconditionally, and to "remain perpetually distrustful of each other." These traits were crucial in controlling the 17th century slave. The slave, in adulating the master class, neither valued himself nor others like him. Likewise, we can certainly see a lack of sympathy for Winky from the other house-elves. In the second-to-last quote above, the elves' reaction to Hermione's suggestion (of cheering up a depressed Winky) underscores the extent to which they deny their individual and collective humanity. And, as seen earlier, whenever Hermione mentions Dobby's freedom, the other house-elves become even more visibly hostile.

Their reaction is partly related to fear (of the uncertainty of what such radical changes in status and privilege might bring), and partly related to the 'group envy' concept discussed in Chapter 2 of this volume:

> "Slaves probably did not envy their rich masters—the gap was too great—but they may well have envied other slaves who had positions of favor."[26]

The Hogwarts elves clearly believe that it is perfectly alright for them to be inferior to wizards; but it is not at all acceptable for another house-elf, like Dobby, to aspire to partaking in wizard privileges such as salaries and clothes.

In addition, as we see in Dobby and Kreacher's cases, when the house-elf loses esteem for the designated master, he may transfer his adulation to other members of the master class, but rarely to others from his own class. The house-elf's adulation for the master is merely a duty. But as we see with all three house-elves, over time, the sense of duty becomes an impulse (which is a part of what forces the house-elf to self-punish whenever he expresses, or even experiences, feelings that contradict his sense of duty).

To add an aside here, it is worth noting that, of all the house-elves at Hogwarts, Dobby is the only one who actually takes the time to comfort Winky. This is probably due to the fact that they are now both outcasts (or "freed slaves"); but he should still be commended for being able to triumph over the centuries of emotional brutality which dictated that elves were not entitled to human feelings. It is also worth noting that one of the first points of departure for the newly freed Dobby (in terms of resisting the scripted existence of the slave) lies in his ability and his willingness to act compassionately towards someone of his own race and social status. In contrast, the other house-elves, secure in the safety of their jobs and their slave status, are not bothered at all by Winky's demise.

Also, in *Half-blood Prince*, we see Harry taking advantage of Kreacher and Dobby's animosity towards each other,[27] when he asks them both to spy on Draco Malfoy so that Dobby can keep an eye on the rebellious Kreacher. Of course, Kreacher does not hide his adulation for Pure-bloods like the Malfoys:

---

[26] See Allport, 1954/1979, p. 371 or page 73 of this volume.

[27] "Kreacher will not insult Harry Potter in front of Dobby, no he won't, or Dobby will shut Kreacher's mouth for him!" cried Dobby in a high-pitched voice. (*Half-blood Prince*, p. 393)

> 'Master Malfoy moves with a nobility that befits his pure blood,' croaked Kreacher at once. 'His features recall the fine bones of my mistress and his manners are those of...' (*Half-blood Prince*, p. 423)

Here we see Kreacher giving a speech that almost sounds rehearsed: The language of adulation is an integral part of the slave's scripted existence. Kreacher uses this language (the sort of words that a house-elf should use to speak of his own master) to speak of Draco, who comes from a wizarding family that he respects—even though the Malfoys are not his designated masters.

The latest quote also betrays the house-elf's deeply entrenched self-hatred: Kreacher clearly identifies most of all with the master class's value system, which dictates that social Others who do not possess "fine-bones" (or other physical features) like his mistress's are innately inferior. Kreacher's adulation for Draco is grounded in wizarding society's overriding valorization of everything that pertains to the master class: physical features, ideology, social customs, and so forth. As far as physical features go, in this particular case, it concerns bone structure (such as the shape of the nose and cheek bones), but it might also extend to hair type: For instance, when a group of Death Eaters torture a Muggle family at the Quidditch World Cup in *Goblet of Fire*, we see Draco warning Hermione to "keep that bushy head down" because Voldemort's supporters know how to "spot a Mudblood" (pp. 110-111).

This has raised an important question where Muggle-borns are concerned: Are there any distinguishing marks that can be used to identify a Muggle-born witch or wizard? Three of the Muggle-born characters in the series are all initially described as having curly hair;[28] but such limited evidence is hardly conclusive. Perhaps Rowling leaves these questions unanswered precisely to underline the insignificance of

[28] The other two characters (in addition to Hermione) are the "curly-haired" Justin Finch-Fletchley, the second Muggle-born to be petrified by Slytherin's monster in *Chamber of Secrets* (p. 73), and Penelope Clearwater, Percy Weasley's girlfriend, is also described as having "long curly hair" (p. 190).

physical features where humanity is concerned. And so, in *Half-blood Prince*, Kreacher's admiration for Draco's physicality further highlights the irrational distinctions that Pure-bloods have set up to differentiate themselves from other kinds of wizards.

Ironically, since Kreacher is *'just'* a house-elf, he himself will never meet the same physical requirements that he seems to be imposing on others. And so, this elfin character provides a good example of what Allport described as the "assimilationist strivings" which may sometimes lead an outsider to "lose himself totally in the dominant group as soon as his level of possessions, customs, and speech makes him indistinguishable from the majority" (1954/1979, p. 151). But the elf's/slave's position is peculiar because: In his current social circumstance, there is absolutely no hope for social equality with the master class—except perhaps in speech. And although Kreacher has mastered the English language much better than Winky and Dobby, who both speak some form of broken English, he is still compelled to speak of himself in the third person (e.g. "Kreacher is cleaning," etc). In other words, he is still a mere slave, with no right to free will, compassion or human feelings.

And yet, despite being "hopelessly barred from assimilation," this particular slave "mentally identifies himself with the practices, outlook and prejudices of the dominant group."[29] In other words, Kreacher accepts his inferior state so completely, that he is willing to adulate any member of the master class who possesses the physical traits and professes the same bigotry-ridden outlook as his former mistress. And, as we know, the Malfoys are quite suitable in this regard.

Nevertheless, the fact that Kreacher has made up his own mind about whom he prefers to admire—despite being bound to serve and adulate Sirius—speaks of the elf's unknowing belief in his own free will. Coincidentally, Dobby also exercises transference of adulation; but he does so for different reasons than Kreacher. Dobby quickly accepts Dumbledore as his new master because, unlike the Malfoys, Dumbledore is "a good master to a house-elf.[30]" And, of

[29] Allport, 1954/1979, p. 151.

[30] *Half-blood Prince*, p. 423.

course, he simply adores Harry, sacrificing his life in the end to protect the boy and his friends. And so, it is clear that although their values are quite different—and although they both continue to embody the psychologies of enslavement in their own way—both Dobby and Kreacher acknowledge their humanity by being resentful towards master class members who do not treat them well. Each elf asserts his individual will by *choosing* whom to admire and love, as opposed to unconditionally loving their designated masters.

Nonetheless, any formerly enslaved house-elf would continue to preserve some sense of duty-bound respect for the designated master. Once again, Winky's abilities in this regard exceed those of Dobby and Kreacher, as she refuses to turn against or to speak ill of her ungrateful former master and his Death Eater son—even after the latter confesses to heinous crimes which include murdering his own father.

***

Finally, the psychology of dependence is another form of mental bondage that binds the house-elves to their social status. Lynch emphasized the need to "break that natural string of independence from [the slaves] and thereby create a dependency status."[31] In reality, it was the masters who needed the slaves, as Lynch points out, for reasons of "economy"; and so, it was crucial to create a reversed sense of collective dependency in the slave class. Likewise, wizards must have perceived the need to harness the house-elves' enormously powerful brand of magic. It must have been perceived as rather advantageous for them to have such powerful beings at their service—"creatures" with speech and human-level intelligence, who were legally bound to expressing canine-like loyalty to wizards. And so, centuries ago when wizards first targeted the house-elf group for enslavement, they sought to bind these so-called "lesser" creatures into a state of artificial co-dependency; and they obviously succeeded in doing so.

But as we can see from Dobby's example, the slave's "dependency" is merely a "legal status," and not a '*natural*

[31] See the aforementioned document, "The Willie Lynch Letter."

obligation or inclination. And yet, over time, it does become 'second nature' for the slave to think of himself as dependent on the master for everything—including making the most basic choices. As an example, in *Chamber of Secrets*, we learn that the house-elf's dependency status is fully institutional, when Fred Weasley explains to Harry that "house-elves have got powerful magic of their own, but they can't usually use it without their masters' permission" (p. 27). As a result, Harry and the Weasleys believed that Dobby must have been sent by the Malfoys as a ploy to keep him from returning to school. But, as we know, Dobby had come of his own free will to warn and "protect" Harry, whom he had no legal obligation to serve or protect.

And yet, despite all the evidence to the contrary, Dobby persists in believing that he "needs" the Malfoys' permission to seek his freedom. And so, the first sign of the extent to which Dobby embraces his dependency status is when he informs Harry that "a house-elf must be set free," and that he will have to punish himself even though his masters remain unaware that he has come to warn Harry.[32] The very idea that he "needs to be freed" by his masters is a mitigated form of mental bondage: The slave has the ability to leave the master at any time, but the walls inside his mind (mostly fear) hinder him from making such an empowered decision. And so, despite glaring evidence to the contrary, Dobby still accepts that he is *physically* bound by the rules. And so, instead of leaving the Malfoys of his own free will—and for good—he simply returns to the Manor to shut his ears in the oven as punishment for going against his sense of duty.

In addition, Dobby does not even hope for the courage to free himself; instead, one gets the impression that he is waiting for one of the Malfoys to 'slip up' and set him free by mistake:

> 'The family is careful not to pass Dobby even a sock, sir, for then he would be free to leave their house for ever.' (*Chamber of Secrets*, p. 133)

---

[32] *Chamber of Secrets*, p. 16.

It is not without a sense of intense longing that Dobby makes the above observation: Clearly, his mind was already free—in the sense that, unlike other elves, he desired his freedom—long before Harry tricked Lucius Malfoy into throwing him a sock in the second book.[33] And so, Dobby remained psychologically imprisoned by the idea that he "must be set free," until another master class member (Harry) facilitated his freedom.

Nevertheless, as I have noted before, Dobby has made a gigantic leap by simply being *aware* that he is being treated poorly, and acknowledging it. Furthermore, he also realizes that he can live without the Malfoys, and that they can live without him. This is a significant contrast to Winky, who continues to pine for the Crouches long after her master has let her go, insisting how much they "need" her even though she has been dismissed ("My poor Mr. Crouch, what is he doing without Winky?"[34]).

Winky was probably introduced to the story to provide a deliberate—and striking—contrast to Dobby (and perhaps Kreacher as well). After all, it is ironic that she resists her fully bestowed freedom, while Dobby revels in freedom that he was never meant to have.

***

To summarize my arguments thus far and conclude the chapter, I must say that although the house-elf enslavement subplot is one of the most alarming aspects of the *Harry Potter* novels, it is also the series' most hopeful storyline. As I stated before, it is no small feat for Dobby to defy centuries of enchantments and embrace freedom. Nor is it a trivial matter that Ron comes to value elf lives as much as his own: In the final battle in *Deathly Hallows*, he refuses to allow the Hogwarts elves to die for him; and he earns Hermione's long-awaited affections when he suggests evacuating them.[35]

---

[33] Harry gives Malfoy Tom Riddle's ruined diary, wrapped inside his sock. Angry and inattentive, Malfoy throws the sock in Dobby's presence; the elf catches it and is set free. (*Chamber of Secrets*, pp. 248-249)

[34] *Goblet of Fire*, p. 332

[35] See *Deathly Hallows*, p. 502, where Hermione kisses Ron for the first time.

My main argument in this chapter is that the house-elves must have become slaves through extreme physical and psychological violence. But most modern wizards remain ignorant of their history, and so, they carry on with their victimizing traditions, thus prolonging the oppression of the elf race through ignorance and indifference. For example, when Dobby first started looking for a new job and demanded a salary, he was turned away by everyone except Dumbledore: "That's not the point of a house-elf," [36] other wizards had responded. They failed to understand that house-elves did not become slaves because of their '*natures*,' but rather because wizards had initially used force and gruesome acts of violence to manipulate them into perpetual enslavement.

Once the original elf slaves' minds were broken by violence and the threat of violence, they soon came to embrace the aforementioned artificially (and strategically) imposed psychologies as part of their so-called "nature." And ironically, so did the society at large—even those among the master class who were versed in the technique of slave-making, and who had deliberately sought to rid the elves of their humanity. And so, after centuries of elf subordination, what unites both master class and slave class now is what Allport described as "fallacious theories concerning the inherent inferiority and 'animal-like' mentality" of the slave class (1954/1979, p. 11). In other words, the slave is deemed—both by himself and by the society at large—as a lesser human or "sub-human," who "likes" being a slave because he "needs" the master class to rule and control him. However, as demonstrated in previous sections of this chapter, all of these beliefs are part of the victimizing lie of the slave's innate inferiority.

But if the slaves believe it, and if the society at large believes it, and if the slaves teach their children to 'believe in' and 'act out' the ascribed subservient role, and if the descendants of the master class are taught that 'things have always been this way' because 'it is in the slave's "nature" to be subservient,' then, soon enough, everyone will be walking under a cloud of universal misinformation. Basically, such is

---

[36] *Goblet of Fire*, p. 330.

the state of things in J.K. Rowling's wizarding world, where elf slavery is unabashedly accepted as a societal norm.

And so, as far as insurmountable tasks go, even Harry's victory over Voldemort cannot surpass what Dobby has accomplished ... Having murdered Harry's parents, Voldemort is the boy's natural enemy; and so, Harry is merely fulfilling a task for which he had been elected—perhaps even before he was born.[37] Dobby, on the other hand, has to defeat his own mind, the collective mindset of his entire race, *and* contradict centuries worth of misconceptions amongst wizards regarding the house-elves' "humanity." And by simply leaving the Malfoys for a moment to go and warn Harry Potter, and by telling The Boy Who Lived about how poorly he was being treated by his wizard family, Dobby triumphed over centuries of violence and oppression, thus setting a new standard for his race.

The enslavement of the elves is perhaps second only to the genocide of the giants—assuming, of course, that living in slavery and deemed "liking it" is a slightly better option than being exterminated. Thus, Rowling issues crucial advice to her readership through the wise Dumbledore, who sympathizes with Kreacher after Sirius's death. Harry's anger at the Headmaster is justifiable, as Dumbledore seems to lack sympathy for both Sirius and Phineas Nigellus—a distinguished ancestor of the Black family whose portrait sits in the Headmaster's office and is directly linked with another frame in Order Headquarters.

After Kreacher betrays his master, Dumbledore seems to suggest that Sirius was merely reaping the fruits of enmity that he himself had sewn, being the last descendant in a dynasty of pure-blood snobs who had always mistreated elves. Dumbledore explains to an enraged Harry that, "indifference and neglect often do much more damage than outright dislike." And although "Sirius was not a cruel man ... [and] was kind to house-elves in general," he had never tried to overcome his pure-blood attitude towards elves, or to look beyond his prejudice towards Kreacher, who represented

---

[37] That is, if we are to take the Prophecy in *Order of the Phoenix* (p. 741) seriously.

everything that Harry's godfather had hated about his own family and upbringing.[38]

Through no fault of his own, Sirius was born into a family of bigotry-prone extremists. Still, the character had (commendably) overcome many of his ancestors' prejudices: He was accepting and respectful towards Muggle-borns, and he loved his werewolf friend (Remus Lupin). But like most wizards of his generation, Sirius's acceptance threshold did not extend to house-elves. As Dumbledore rightly insists—in spite of Harry's defiance at this stage—Sirius failed to recognize Kreacher as a being with human feelings.[39] And by remaining indifferent to the house-elves' plight, he missed a great opportunity to make a real difference.

However, as I stated earlier in the chapter, the elves are more than complicit in their own demise, which brings to mind the Shakespearean adage: "self love ... is not so vile a sin as self-neglecting."[40] Nevertheless, they are not entirely to blame, and their enslavement effectively demonstrates how prejudice and discrimination can become so intricately woven into the fabric of society that they are no longer recognized as gross injustice. It is also an implicit warning that, in order to prevent prejudicial beliefs and behavior from becoming societal norms, human beings need to continuously re-examine their social consciences, and to exercise constant vigilance where discrimination is concerned.

***

****

*****

As a post-script to the chapter, I would like to add that most of what is deemed acceptable or unacceptable in our own world comes down to what Chomsky and Barsamian described as "orthodoxies."[41] In other words, we believe certain things about ourselves, about social situations and about social Others because we were raised to think in a

---

[38] *Order of the Phoenix*, p. 735.

[39] *Order of the Phoenix*, p. 733.

[40] Henry V. [Act II. Scene IV]

[41] A quote from David Barsamian's interview with Noam Chomsky (May, 2001).

certain way. And most of us simply '*follow the leader*': We act and think the way we do "because our leaders say"[42] it is the appropriate way to act and think.

Here, the term "leaders" may refer to parents, teachers, politicians, religious officials, and so forth. And, of course, the same social rules (in terms of the dominance of orthodoxies and ordinary 'leader + follower' dynamics) are operating in Rowling's wizarding world.

As a result, the enslavement of elves is no longer a '*moral*' issue for wizards—simply because it is the established orthodoxy. Therefore, when Ron grumbles about being overworked "like a house-elf,"[43] or when Draco Malfoy ridicules Lupin, saying "he dresses like our old house-elf,"[44] they are obviously alluding to the dominant orthodoxy of elf slavery and poverty. From the conventional wizarding perspective of these two pure-blood children, a house-elf is the archetype of the downtrodden, overworked and poverty-stricken—or the "dregs of the magical world," in Dobby's words.[45]

To make a pertinent comparison: as recent as thirty-five years ago, in Great Britain, it was still socially acceptable for a person to say that he was "working like a Black." Obviously, Blacks were still recognized as the manual-laboring underclass; and the orthodoxy of Black inferiority and tendency to work in menial jobs was once so powerful that, the Black race might still have to contend with this 'residual perception' for another three decades. Likewise, even if house-elves are granted freedom in the near future, the perception of their group as inferior or enslaved beings will not disappear overnight. Nor will the elves themselves easily relinquish their mindset of subservience.

It is no wonder, then, that elf rights activist Hermione is initially perceived (both by her peers and by the oppressed elf race) as an obsessive, delusional, naïve idealist. Hermione stands alone not only against the establishment (social rules, lawmakers, her superiors, and so forth), but also against a

---

[42] Ibid.

[43] *Order of the Phoenix*, p. 145.

[44] *Prisoner of Azkaban*, p. 107.

[45] *Chamber of Secrets*, p. 133.

long History of the universal acceptance of house-elf oppression. And, at first, Hermione displays great naivety in assuming that her peers care enough about elf rights to pursue activism with her, and that the elves will be compliant and grateful. Thus, she initially fails to grasp the magnitude of the task she has taken upon herself: It is not just about instilling the wizard race with empathy for house-elves, but also the far more challenging task of convincing the elves that they are just as worthy of dignity, respect and social opportunities as any other race. We have seen that even Dobby—who had successfully defied the orthodoxy and embraced his freedom—was still in many ways restricted by its conventions[46] until the day he died.

In short, orthodoxies are not destroyed in a day; nor are they denounced by the voice of the one against the many. Also, as we can see with the orthodoxy of elf slavery, this severe manifestation of prejudice can not be qualified with the 'good-people-versus-evil-people' dichotomy. As Sirius rightly instructs the still-naïve trio in *Order of the Phoenix*, "the world isn't split into good people and Death Eaters." (p. 271) However, ironically, this leads me to raising one of the few criticisms that I have about Rowling's work...

While the author does a great job of endowing her beloved characters[47] with a complex, flawed humanity, the characters on the "dark side" appear to be polarized and irredeemable. Take Dolores Umbridge, for example. From the toad-like features to the high-pitched, sugary sweet fakeness, the character comes across as a kind of cartoonish villain. A consummately evil Ministry official, Umbridge derives great satisfaction from inflicting pain on others and propping up the perverted justice system that she has played such an integral role in creating. In short, there is absolutely nothing redeemable about Dolores Umbridge.

But if we think about our own world, there are a lot of 'decent' or so-called 'good' people who are flawed in exactly the same way as this character. Her chief motivation is simply to remain on the favorable side of the power paradigm. She

---

[46] For example, the slave's intro-punitive or self-punishing impulse.

[47] Included among these are the protagonist (Harry), Ron Weasley, Dumbledore and Sirius Black.

basically shifts the focus of her prejudice "from one minority group to another, based on prevailing social, cultural and political acceptability and expediency."[48]

But whether she is acting as Fudge's over-meddling, devious Undersecretary, or High Inquisitor at Hogwarts, or Chief Prosecutor in the Department of Regulation of Magical Creatures under Voldemort's new regime, Umbridge is merely one digit on the long arm of a corrupt Ministry. And, like many people in the real world, she aligns herself with whoever is at the helm of power, thus joining forces with the establishment in bullying whichever group or individual is being singled out for persecution at that particular moment in History. Whether it is Harry and Dumbledore in *Order of the Phoenix*, or Muggle-borns in *Deathly Hallows*, or werewolves in general, Umbridge is merely a follower of the established orthodoxy. And, unfortunately, followers tend to be serial oppressors...

And to make matters worse, Umbridge is also a fanatical (shall we say "extremely right wing"?) member of the Ministry staff who just happens to be endowed with power and the opportunity to abuse it. And we can safely assume that she is just as indifferent to the house-elves' plight as any other Pure-blood or Half-blood Ministry worker. And so, my only gripe is that Rowling could have created an even more effective metaphor if she had written Umbridge's character as more humane and identifiable with the average orthodoxy-supporting lawmaker or public official.

If we look at our own world, for example, the proto-type orthodoxy-supporter is neither rare nor a polarized, evil villain, as Umbridge clearly is. Many people embrace discriminatory orthodoxies, such as using racial or homophobic epithets, or making antilocutory statements about minority groups or persecuted individuals. And they do so because

i. it is either socially accepted or customary.
ii. they can get away with it.

---

[48] Ouseley, 2001, p. 15

Therefore, one could argue that the world *is* indeed split between those who continuously re-examine established orthodoxies, and those who accept everything without questioning—and in so doing, perpetuate and/or condone gross injustices. But it could hardly be said that the latter are invariably or incorrigibly 'evil' people like Dolores Umbridge. In fact, they are quite the contrary in many cases...

For instance, current orthodoxy dictates that the persecution of Jews and the enslavement of human beings are unacceptable. And so, we look back upon the Holocaust and the Trans-Atlantic Slave Trade with shock and regret. But during the 1930s-40s, many of the people who actually lived under the Nazi regime were either unaware of what was taking place or unconcerned—because it did not directly affect them. And, two hundred years ago, most people in the Western world did not question the legitimacy of African slavery: It was simply the way things were. The average member of the dominant race/class probably accepted that the slaves were inferior beings who should be kept in their place.

During both of these human tragedies, many people who belonged to the dominant classes probably derived a sense of gratification from their privileged position, and continuously articulated their own superiority over the oppressed or enslaved race. And those who abused or exploited Jews or African slaves were rarely compelled to question the morality of their actions.

And so, if nothing else, the house-elf subplot in the *Harry Potter* novels might at least encourage the reader to question and/or re-examine some of the current orthodoxies in our own world. What practices do we condone and accept now that we might look back upon with shock and regret a century from now?

Chapter 4

On Squibs and Werewolves: A Closer Look at the Disability Issue

Despite the choice of title for this chapter, it must be emphasized, once again, that my overall objective is not to make any absolute equations between *Harry Potter* subplots and 'real world' issues, but rather to demonstrate the conditions in which prejudice spawns and thrives. And by doing so, I hope to expose and examine some of the insidious beliefs and discriminatory practices that keep the oppressed firmly rooted in their place—at times without any hope of social (or upward) mobility.

I decided to focus on 'real world' disability-related issues for two reasons: First, as in our world, the magically Disabled are not excluded on racial or "pure-blood" terms, but rather for physically disempowering conditions that they were either born with, or acquired through personal misfortune. And in the case of both Squibs and werewolves, their conditions would not necessarily have been disempowering if society had taken a different view on it. In other words, if wizarding society had allowed them to assume suitable roles for themselves within the magical community—instead of stigmatizing and excluding them for what they are—both their social outlook and social status would be entirely different from what they are now.

And secondly, legislation alone (in favor of Squibs and werewolves) cannot temper wizarding society's negative attitudes or beliefs. Instead, acceptance and equality can only be achieved through deliberate and concerted efforts from the empowered group: Wizards must re-educate themselves about Squibs and werewolves in order to increase general awareness and reduce fear (or in some cases, a mere sense of *awkwardness*).

***

In the previous chapter we discussed how institutional discrimination—in the form of old wizarding laws which instituted elf slavery—helped to foster habits and perceptions that became increasingly difficult to eradicate over time. Hence, as a collective, the elves developed a fixed social identity which led to their embracing slavery indefinitely. And so, on the one hand, we could say that privilege within the magical community is the product of circumstance and history (as in our own world). But on the other hand, rather unlike some of the more liberal societies in our world, there appears to be little chance of social mobility for some out-groups in *Harry Potter*'s world.

Ironically, access to wizarding society is also extremely limited for some humans with direct biological links to the dominant group. Squibs and werewolves are most relevant in this regard; but Muggles could also be included. After all, their inability to do magic makes them inherently *disabled* in a way that wizards are not. And the parents of Muggle-borns are directly linked with the wizarding world. Nevertheless, since my aim is to examine prejudice and discrimination themes in the wizarding world, as they pertain to what Rowling describes as "*magical beings*" or "*magical races*," Muggles will not be a part of the discussion here.

Also, I wish to emphasize the fact that, although some wizards consider werewolves to be "part-human,"[1] for the purpose of the discussion in this chapter, werewolves must be placed firmly in the "human" category. After all, they are fully human in the absence of the full moon.

***

As was mentioned in Chapter 1, wizarding law prohibits Squibs and werewolves from accessing privileges such as formal magical education (at Hogwarts) and employment in the wider magical community. But even in the absence of such discriminatory laws, both groups suffer from the intense social stigma associated with their kind. For example, while there is no mention of anti-Squib legislation in the books, the mere fact that Squibs are not included in the magical registry[2]

---

[1] Umbridge hates werewolves on the grounds that they are "part-humans" or "half-breeds." (See *Order of the Phoenix*, p. 271)

[2] See *Order of the Phoenix*, p. 131.

underlines their 'non-entity' status within the magical community: It is almost as though they had never been born and do not exist.

Also, intense anti-werewolf feelings had been thriving long before the likes of Dolores Umbridge created discriminatory legislation to keep werewolves out of wizarding workplaces.[3] In fact, one could say that an already flourishing prejudice amongst the wizard class made it easy for the Ministry of Magic to legalize anti-werewolf discrimination. Fear, as well as other prevailing negative sentiments within wizarding society, facilitated discriminatory legislation against werewolves in much the same way that contemporary fears about Islamic terrorism have made it easy for some countries to single out Muslims and people of certain stigmatized nationalities in international airports.

And although racial, nationality and religious biases are not usually linked with disability issues, these two very different *Harry Potter* subplots both encapsulate the outsider status of people who are deemed to be '*different*,' due to circumstances that are totally out of their control. The plight of Squibs and werewolves can be interpreted in numerous ways. And also, though the issue of the outsider being perceived as a (violent) physical threat only applies to the werewolves, from a *disability* standpoint, they do share some common ground: The discrimination these two groups experience is primarily influenced by fear and ignorance. And in this respect, their condition is no different from that of any other stigmatized or disadvantaged group within the magical community or in our own world. Both groups have committed the unpardonable crime of being inalterably different...

***

In a recent study to determine social attitudes towards disability and its portrayal on British television, media researcher Jane Sancho cited "the psychology of difference" as the basis for disability-related prejudice:

---

[3] See *Order of the Phoenix*, p. 271.

> When people are confronted by something very different to themselves, often the first response–the so-called fear response–is to reject it. Difference, as a psychological phenomenon, is something of a challenge that some people need to overcome in order to reach acceptance.[4]

Naturally, the degree of difference impacts both physical and psychological responses to the outsider. Thus, by juxtaposing Squibs and werewolves, we are able to contrast two groups at opposite ends of the fear spectrum. Having two extremely contrasting groups helps to further demonstrate that, prejudice and discrimination on any level (from mild to extreme) can be detrimental to the individual and to the society at large.

The crucial issue here is that which relates to social desirability: Both groups are directly (as in biologically) linked to the wizarding world; but one group has a far less desirable presence than the other. Squibs are non-threatening outsiders who are excluded because they are not magical. In other words, they are not 'counted' among wizards; but their presence is tolerated due to the fact that they are usually non-aggressive. But while they do not typify the militancy and anger of werewolves, the resentment they feel towards their families, and towards wizards in general, must have a negative impact on social harmony within the magical community.

Where we see werewolves being isolated and stigmatized because they pose a physical threat (as a result of the damage they can cause when they transform, as well as the incurability of what we could call 'werewolf syndrome'), Squibs are shunned simply because they are an embarrassment to their wizarding families.[5] And it is certainly a mark of the lack of moral progression in wizarding society, that those who are condemned to live with permanent physical shortcomings should be treated so poorly.

Sancho's research suggests that there are different "attitudinal types" when it comes to acceptance of or reactions towards disability-related difference. She identified seven

---

[4] Sancho, Jane. "Disabling Prejudice: Attitudes towards disability and its portrayal on television," 2003, p. 49.

[5] See *Deathly Hallows*, pp. 129-130.

different "defining characteristics" in the subjects of her study: *Children, Followers, In-Stasis, Issue-driven, Transformers, Progressives* and *Traditionalists.* The rest of this chapter will provide examples of each attitudinal type—though not necessarily in the same order—as they relate to the Squib and werewolf subplots in the *Harry Potter* novels.

In-Stasis

The subjects of the study who fall into this category are those who "have become disabled recently" and have not yet come to terms with having a disability. Therefore, they "find it hard to consider disability objectively."[6] In comparison, since Squibs are inflicted with their condition from birth, they are not likely to experience the sudden emotional trauma of "becoming" disabled. In contrast, the recent victims of werewolf bites are understandably traumatized, not only because of the violence they have just experienced, but also because of what they know the future has in store for them: a lifetime of social stigma and exclusion, and possible abandonment by close relations.

In *Order of the Phoenix* we see a recently-bitten werewolf sharing a hospital room with Arthur Weasley, after the latter has been bitten by Voldemort's snake. The werewolf has no visitors at Christmas. And the author seems to purposefully contrast his situation with that of Arthur, who has his family, Harry, as well as members of the Order visiting him (p. 448). In addition, when Arthur attempts to comfort and reassure his traumatized roommate, the man's reaction is typical of trauma sufferers who, as Sancho suggests, "are entirely focused on themselves and unable to communicate objectively about their disability," especially due to the recentness of the traumatic event:[7]

---

[6] Sancho, 2003, p. 31

[7] A subject from Sancho's study said: *"Sorry, I don't want to elaborate on my disability – it all happened recently and I don't like talking about it in detail."* [Female, 35-60, mobile impairment] Another subject said: *"I only lost my sight last year. I don't think of myself as disabled ... I'm finding it very difficult. I lost my job. It's changed my life."* [Male, 30-45, sensory impairment]

> '...But that fellow over there,' [Arthur] said, dropping his voice and nodding towards the bed opposite, in which a man lay looking green and sickly and staring at the ceiling. 'Bitten by a *werewolf*, poor chap. No cure at all.'
>
> 'A werewolf?' whispered Mrs. Weasley, looking alarmed. 'Is he safe in a public ward? Shouldn't he be in a private room?'
>
> 'It's two weeks till full moon,' Mr. Weasley reminded her quietly. They've been talking to him this morning, the Healers, you know, trying to persuade him he'll be able to lead an almost normal life. I said to him—didn't mention names, of course—but I said I knew a werewolf personally, very nice man, who finds the condition quite easy to manage.'
>
> 'What did he say?' asked George.
>
> 'Said he'd give me another bite if I didn't shut up...'
>
> (*Order of the Phoenix*, pp. 431-432)

As we can see here, the recently bitten werewolf victim experiences a more heightened sense of trauma in cases where he or she had held anti-werewolf prejudice prior to being bitten: All of a sudden, they have now become the very thing that they have feared and rejected all their lives. Not surprisingly, they find it very difficult to cope with their new condition, and could therefore be described as "In-Stasis."

Issue-Driven

This group is perhaps the direct opposite of the "*In-Stasis*" group, in that they are by far the most outspoken and militant segment of society when it comes to disability issues. According to Sancho, they are "quite angry with society, which they feel is prejudiced against disabled people."[8]

Both able-bodied and Disabled people constitute this group, as they are the lobbyists and committed political activists who "see disability and the representation of disability within society as a 'cause' that needs to be promoted and supported."[9] They concern themselves with promoting

---

[8] Sancho, 2003, p. 23.

[9] Ibid.

public awareness and inclusion, and "have a greater sense of disabled people being underrepresented.[10]"

The latter is somewhat reminiscent of the anger and militancy which led Hermione to found S.P.E.W. on behalf of the house-elves, whom she insisted were "shockingly under-represented" in the Department for the Regulation and Control of Magical Creatures.[11] And while there are no characters in the novels who engage in political activism on behalf of the magically Disabled (Squibs and werewolves) in the same way Hermione has done for house-elves, we can still detect varying degrees of anger from Squib and werewolf characters throughout the series.

However, neither of the two main Squib characters (Argus Filch, the caretaker at Hogwarts and Mrs. Figg, Harry's cat-loving neighbor in the Muggle world) can be easily categorized as *Issue-driven*. Basically, they are not politically-minded, militant or outspoken enough to be categorized as such. For instance, Filch does not speak up about his Squib status until he feels targeted—shortly after his cat Mrs. Norris is petrified by Slytherin's monster in *Chamber of Secrets*. And besides, when a very inquisitive and puzzled Harry discovers the caretaker's Kwickspell course[12] brochures sticking out of a drawer in his office, Filch seems terrified that a student has finally discovered his Squib status. The following citation reveals the caretaker's unnecessary embarrassment:

> Filch hobbled across to his desk, snatched up the envelope and threw it into a drawer.
>
> 'Have you—did you read—?' he spluttered.
>
> 'No,' Harry lied quickly.
>
> Filch's knobbly hands were twisting together.
>
> 'If I thought that you'd read my private ... not that it's mine ... for a friend ... be that as it may... however ... Very well ... go ... and don't breathe a word ... not that ... however, if you didn't read ... go now...'
>
> (*Chamber of Secrets*, pp. 98-99)

---

[10] Sancho, 2003, p.24.

[11] *Goblet of Fire*, p. 198.

[12] This is a sort of mail order program for learning how to do magic.

Here, we see that Filch's initial reaction is denial, as he claims that his brochures belong to a friend, not him. The character has obviously embraced societal notions about his inferiority as a Squib. And so, "he would willingly rid himself of everything that makes him what he is."[13] Filch therefore lacks the pride and defiance of a true *Issue-driven* subject.

Mrs. Figg displays a similar compliance with wizarding perceptions, as she seems overwhelmed by the occasion when called as a witness at Harry's hearing in *Order of the Phoenix*. Militant activists usually portray a degree of fearlessness in such situations. They relish the opportunity to have a platform from which to air their grievances. Nevertheless, it is not without a sense of deep disgruntlement that she reminds Minister Fudge that Squibs are not included in the wizard registry, and that they can indeed see Dementors, just like witches and wizards can (p. 131). And so, Mrs. Figg is far more *issue-driven* than Argus Filch, in the sense that she recognizes the unfairness of anti-Squib discrimination and vocalizes her frustration whenever the opportunity arises. However, as will be discussed later, her character is more suited for the "*Transformers*" group.

Unfortunately, the examples of *issue-driven* werewolves in the series—people like Fenrir Greyback—are violently militant villains who are endlessly seeking retribution against wizards:

> 'Fenrir Greyback is, perhaps, the most savage werewolf alive today. He regards it as his mission in life to bite and contaminate as many people as possible; he wants to create enough werewolves to overcome the wizards. Voldemort has promised him prey in return for his services. Greyback specializes in children ... bite them young, he says, and raise them away from their parents, raise them to hate normal wizards ... At the full moon, he positions himself close to victims, ensuring that he is near enough to strike. He plans it all. And this is the man Voldemort is using the marshal the werewolves...' [Remus Lupin quote] (*Half-blood Prince*, pp. 313-314)

[13] Allport (1954/1979, p. 151) quotes de Tocqueville's 18th century text *Democracy in America* (p. 334). De Tocqueville was discussing self-esteem issues amongst Blacks.

One could argue that planned werewolf attacks are a sort of reverse-discrimination, whereby the despised seek revenge for the exclusion and persecution that they have experienced at the hands of the dominant and empowered. And so, extreme *Issue-driven* werewolves reclaim empowerment by destroying the lives of as many wizards as possible, whenever they get a chance to do so.

In his discussion on violent militancy, Allport quoted Spinoza, who asserted that "He who conceives himself hated by another, and believes that he has given him no cause for hatred, will hate that other in return."[14] Werewolf attacks are also attention-grabbers: Some werewolves might feel that violence is the only means of getting the Ministry to consider their plight. Once again, the motivations and grievances of Rowling's most militant werewolves are somewhat similar to the causes behind some acts of terrorism in our own world: It is difficult to end the cycle of reprisal attacks because the anger runs deep; and both sides eventually lose the ability (and/or the willingness) to communicate with each other.

Transformers

The *Transformers* in Sancho's study are distinctly different from the *issue-driven* subjects, in that their group is comprised of younger disabled people and children, who tend not to make "advocacy" their priority. Rather, they focus on "creating and taking advantage of opportunities and maximizing their potential." *Transformers* are constantly in the pursuit of self-enhancement. In addition, "they present themselves as agents of change," emphasizing "inclusion, rather than representation." Disabled *Transformers* place emphasis on "being able to prove themselves as people who can compete on the same level as non-disabled people."[15] Hence, though they are aware of the limitations that their

---

[14] Allport, 1954/1979, p. 155.

[15] A subject from Sancho's study said: *"I go to drama classes. I'm the only disabled person there. I go to karate and do what I can. I don't like to feel I can't do the things I want to do."* (Sancho, 2003, p. 24)

disability poses for them, they do not define themselves by these boundaries.

Within their respective groups, both Arabella Figg and Remus Lupin display *transformer* tendencies. As I mentioned in the previous section, Mrs. Figg does not conceal her indignation when Fudge implies that Squibs cannot see Dementors. Through sheer ignorance, the Minister displays the typical 'able-bodied' tendency of assuming that disabled persons are incapacitated in every way; and Mrs. Figg hastens to correct him. She also shows bravery and a strong sense of civic duty by simply showing up to give testimony in a wizard trial, even though people like Fudge do not consider her to be a "convincing" witness.[16]

And finally, she takes up the charge of watching over Harry during the summer holidays, despite her inability to use a wand. And when Harry and his cousin are attacked by Dementors, she proves to be far more reliable than the magically empowered Mundungus Fletcher.[17]

Remus Lupin displays similar *transformer* tendencies, in that he aspires to normal wizarding professions such as teaching and Aurorship—despite the fact that the general wizarding public would prefer not to have werewolves in their midst, especially in the professional arena. Most importantly, whenever Lupin gets the chance, he proves himself to be superbly competent. For instance, students like Harry and Dean Thomas constantly laud Professor Lupin as "the best" Defense Against the Dark Arts teacher they ever had.[18] And in *Order of the Phoenix* we also discover that Remus was a model student and a prefect during his school years (p. 155).

Lupin is also more open-minded and compassionate than the exceedingly militant Greyback. He chooses to integrate with wizarding society instead of glorifying the werewolf's outsider status:

---

[16] See *Order of the Phoenix*, p. 133.

[17] See *Order of the Phoenix*, pp. 23-27.

[18] For example, they both contradict Umbridge in *Order of the Phoenix*, where Dean praises Lupin unreservedly, despite Umbridge's anger (p. 219). And in *Prisoner of Azkaban*, Harry pleads for Lupin to stay at Hogwarts, saying "You're the best Defense Against the Dark Arts teacher we've ever had! Don't go!" (p. 309).

> '...I bear the unmistakable signs of having tried to live among wizards, you see, whereas they have shunned normal society and live on the margins, stealing—and sometimes killing—to eat.'
> (*Half-blood Prince*, p. 313)

Here, the *Transformer* Lupin is contrasted with the *Issue-driven* of his kind. Other werewolves like Greyback probably perceive Lupin as a shameful '*Token*,' whose frustrated attempts at assimilation have merely led to conformity and 'begging' for an ever elusive social acceptance. The last quote also suggests that Lupin sympathizes with both wizards and werewolves, as he is a part of both worlds. However, he recognizes the need for integration and acceptance far more readily than other wizards or werewolves do.

In addition, an important *transformer* characteristic is social and political awareness. Sancho suggested that "*Transformers* recognize shifts in representation and inclusion in general" more than other groups do.[19] Hence, as Lupin is a werewolf trying to find jobs amongst wizards, he remains at all times aware of changes in representation and law-making which can either facilitate his inclusion or further marginalize him.

And finally, as Sancho explained, *Transformers* "understand the power of role models in changing people's mindsets." And so we see a very repentant Lupin in *Prisoner of Azkaban*, when he resigns from his post as Defense Against the Dark Arts teacher: He does so partly out of regret for having placed Harry, Hermione and Ron in harm's way, and partly out of shame for having breached Dumbledore's trust many years before, when he used to roam the school grounds as a werewolf with his friends. It is difficult for the character to forgive himself for such lapses in judgment, because he perceives 'good behavior' and 'setting a good example' as essential for a lone werewolf living among wizards.

---

[19] Sancho, 2003, p. 25.

Children

This category is quite peculiar in that, we could describe children as '*Transformers/Progressives/Issue-driven-in-the-making*'—depending, of course, on the social context in which they are raised. Hence, Greyback's method of "biting them young and raising them to hate wizards," is effective for the simple reason that children develop fundamental values and character traits early and usually stick with them throughout their lifetimes. But Greyback fails to consider the other side of the coin: There are children, like the young Remus Lupin, who are not shunned by their families after being bitten. Instead, they continue to be raised in mainstream wizarding society, hoping for social change and equality rather than being indoctrinated to embrace bitterness and hatred towards non-contaminated wizards.

To make a comparison with disability issues in our own world, Sancho maintained that "current trends in education, support and schooling...encourage disabled children to consider themselves as having special abilities and parity with non-disabled society."[20] Her research findings also proved that disabled *Transformer* children prefer to identify with the able-bodied population, instead of being perceived as disadvantaged or different.

This is an entirely different issue from the "self-hatred" inclinations briefly discussed here (with regards to Filch) and in the previous chapter (with regards to house-elves), where we saw the enslaved and marginalized Kreacher identifying completely with the master class's prejudiced outlook. Instead, rather than denying or ignoring what they are, or blaming or casting aspersions upon social Others, it is imperative that the Disabled acknowledge their disability, but refuse to accept that it is (or should be) a hindrance to their inclusion or social advancement.

We can certainly see the latter exemplified in the wizarding world through the young Remus Lupin. The fact that Remus was competent enough as a student to be made prefect, shows that he was a *Transformer-in-the-making*—eager to prove himself and to excel among his wizard peers, despite the fact that he was severely ill once a month.

---

[20] Sancho, 2003, p. 32.

Also, as demonstrated by Mr. Weasley's hospital roommate, the recently bitten adult werewolf is encouraged as well to perceive himself as a normal member of the community. However, there is a strange irony in such advice, because strategic laws and customs already prohibit the werewolf from making a living amongst wizards ... Perhaps he is required to disclose his werewolf status; and this, in turn, leads to stigma-related exclusion from the vast majority, who are probably uninformed and therefore paranoid and unintentionally cruel. And moreover, in the same way that it is far more difficult for recently disabled adults to adapt to life with a disability in the real world, it is also much easier for young werewolves to learn to integrate socially or to see themselves as 'on par' with their non-contaminated peers.

***

Perhaps the *Children* category should also include non-disabled children who are close friends of the Disabled. As children, Sirius Black and James Potter treated Remus as an equal, despite his condition. Hence, they are '*Child Transformers*' by association because of their friendship and faith in Remus. And furthermore, by regarding him as their equal, they implicitly encouraged him to think of himself as one of the empowered elite; and that, in itself, is a most *progressive* gesture.

Peter Pettigrew, however, is not included here as a *child Transformer* or *Progressive* because there are strong hints in the series that he was never really interested in Remus; nor was he at all knowledgeable about the werewolf's condition:

> 'Did you like question ten, Moony?' asked Sirius as they emerged into the Entrance Hall.
>
> 'Loved it,' said Lupin briskly. '*Give five signs that identify the werewolf.* Excellent question.'
>
> 'D'you think you managed to get all the signs?' said James in tones of mock concern.
>
> 'Think I did,' said Lupin seriously ... 'One: he's sitting on my chair. Two: he's wearing my clothes. Three: his name is Remus Lupin.'
>
> Wormtail was the only one who didn't laugh.

> 'I got the snout shape, the pupils of the eyes and the tufted tail,' he said anxiously, 'but I couldn't think what else—'
> 'How thick are you, Wormtail?' said James impatiently. You run round with a werewolf once a month [!]'
> (*Order of the Phoenix* pp. 566-567)

The young Pettigrew (Wormtail) was a classic *Follower*, as he simply went along with whatever his popular and far more talented peers were doing, without any sincere interest in their cause. Still, *not* all *Followers* are cowardly or disinterested. As we will observe later, both Harry and Ron display some *follower* tendencies where the magically Disabled are concerned. Hermione is the only member of the trio with the level of awareness or the acute social conscience of a 'true' *Progressive*. After the war, all three members of the trio will have become staunch *Progressives*;[21] but during their early teenage years, Harry and Ron follow Hermione's example more than they lead in matters concerning the magically Disabled.

And so, perhaps the young Pettigrew should at least be commended for being part of a group that was much more open-minded and inclusive than either their peers or their parents. The three Marauders found a way to keep Remus' company without exposing themselves to contaminating bites. Therefore, in a sense, they—along with Dumbledore—'facilitated' Lupin's disability. They accomplished something that most wizards during that era would never have even considered for a moment. And of course, Sirius and James grew up to become *Progressives*, remaining accommodating and accepting towards Remus and, presumably, other non-hostile werewolves.

Progressives

In the context of Sancho's research on disability prejudice, the *progressive* group consists of "younger, non-

---

[21] Here, I refer again to a recent interview in which J.K. Rowling revealed that, following the last war against Voldemort, the trio will play a significant role in ridding the Ministry of discrimination. [J.K. Rowling Live Chat, Bloomsbury.com. July 30, 2007 (2.00-3.00pm BST).]

disabled people, and some carers."[22] But in the context of Rowling's wizarding world, it also includes older, more enlightened (and perhaps young-at-heart) wizards like Albus Dumbledore, who are well informed about minority issues in general. Such persons "embrace change in practice and take notice of things they can do to support inclusion and representation."[23]

We discover in *Prisoner of Azkaban* that Dumbledore was the first headmaster to allow a werewolf child to attend Hogwarts "when no other Headmaster would have done so" (pp. 258-260); and when he hired the disenfranchised Lupin to teach, "he had to work very hard to convince certain teachers" that the werewolf was trustworthy (p. 254). Also, we learn that the Whomping Willow—a vicious magical tree that guards the Shrieking Shack, was planted as part of the "precautions" that Dumbledore had taken, before the child Remus arrived at Hogwarts years ago. Rumors had spread that the Shrieking Shack was haunted, and Dumbledore encouraged them, so that other students would not go near the place where Remus had to be quarantined during his full moon transformations (pp. 258-259).

Dumbledore obviously regarded Lupin as just a boy—hence, on equal terms with any other student. But he also appreciated the fact that the young werewolf had certain specific needs; and he was willing to use his power as Headmaster to facilitate that student's special needs. All these actions make him a true *Progressive* where the magically Disabled are concerned. But, based on his inclusion of other marginalized individuals—Hagrid the half-giant, Trelawney the reputedly fraudulent Seer,[24] Filch the Squib, and so forth—Dumbledore is obviously an all-round *Progressive* thinker.

***

---

[22] The term is "Caregivers" in American Standard English.

[23] Sancho, 2003, p. 26.

[24] When she comes under fire from Umbridge in *Order of the Phoenix*, Professor Trelawney tells her class that "Seers have always been feared, always persecuted … it is—alas—our fate" (p. 325).

Harry and Hermione both exhibit *progressive* behavior—although, as I will later explain, Hermione is far more *progressive* than Harry. Basically, they both recognize wizarding prejudice more readily than peers like Ron. But most importantly, they are more suited for the *Child Progressive* category because none of the trio members qualify as *Child Transformers.* And this is simply because they are neither magically disabled nor close friends with a disabled peer. In contrast, James Potter and Sirius Black were Lupin's best friends at school; hence, they were once *Child Transformers.* Still, from their examples, we may surmise that non-disabled *Child Transformers* usually grow to be adult *Progressives.* In *Half-blood Prince* we see Harry, a generation later, echoing his father's sympathy and *progressive* attitude towards Lupin:

> '...I cannot pretend that my particular brand of reasoned argument is making much headway against Greyback's insistence that we werewolves deserve blood, that we ought to revenge ourselves on normal people.'
>
> 'But you are normal,' said Harry fiercely. You've just got a—a problem—'
>
> Lupin burst out laughing.
>
> 'Sometimes you remind me a lot of James. He called it my "fury little problem" in company. Many people were under the impression that I owned a badly behaved rabbit.'
>
> He accepted a glass of eggnog from Mr. Weasley with a word of thanks, looking slightly more cheerful... (*Half-blood Prince*, p. 314)

Here, we see Harry showing strong emotional support for Lupin (a person whom he cares for deeply), and a *progressive* understanding that the werewolf is essentially 'just like everybody else.' However, as I will make clear later, during their early teenage years, both Harry and Ron would be more suited for the "*Followers*" group, as Harry, unlike Hermione, is not 'socially aware' enough to be a true *Child Progressive.*

For instance, Hermione is far more informed about wizarding history, and often comments on the one-sided bias typical of most history textbooks—written, of course, by empowered witches and wizards.[25] In contrast, Harry shows little or no interest in his History of Magic classes; nor does he overly concern himself with the plight of out-groups like house-elves, the way Hermione does.

Social awareness is a key *progressive* trait: It helps the true *Progressive* to recognize prejudicial trends in society, to comment on them and to counteract them through speech and actions whenever they get a chance to do so. Hermione embodies this quality almost to perfection, as we see her keeping Lupin's secret for many months in *Prisoner of Azkaban.*[26] She protects and supports Lupin by choosing not to disclose personal information that would drastically affect how he is treated by others at the school.

And later, in a discussion with her friends in *Goblet of Fire*, we see her highlighting the similarities between anti-werewolf feeling and the next most severe form of wizarding prejudice—that which pertains to giants. Naturally, Ron's insistence (that wizards are right) stems from his own ignorance about what constitutes prejudice, and how it is usually manifested in society:

> '...They can't *all* be horrible ... it's the same sort of prejudice that people have towards werewolves ... it's just bigotry, isn't it?'
>
> Ron looked as though he would have liked to reply scathingly, but perhaps he didn't want another row,[27] because he contented himself with shaking his head disbelievingly while Hermione wasn't looking.
> (*Goblet of Fire*, p. 377)

---

[25] See *Goblet of Fire*, pp. 209-210, where she berates her *Hogwarts: A History* textbook, renaming it "A Highly Biased and *Selective* History of Hogwarts, Which Glosses Over the Nastier Aspects of the School," and *Deathly Hallows*, p. 409, where she reminds Harry and Ron that "wizarding history often skates over what wizards have done to other magical races."

[26] Hermione is the first and only student to accurately deduce that the teacher is a werewolf. But she remains quiet about it, refusing to disclose the information to even her two closest friends for almost the entire school year. (See *Prisoner of Azkaban*, p. 253)

[27] The term "row" is the equivalent of "quarrel" in American Standard English.

Here, we see Hermione providing what Sancho called "word-of-mouth support" for the two out-groups, by citing the wizarding world's socio-political failings. At this stage, Hermione is many steps ahead of Harry (who is still not fully informed about giant and werewolf discrimination) and Ron (who still actively portrays the typical negative pure-blood beliefs and attitudes towards such groups).

Therefore, although Dumbledore and Hermione's outlook and actions are not 'activism' or 'role-modeling' on par with that of *Issue-driven* or *Transformer* subjects, their *progressive* behavior is crucial in fighting prejudice. Both characters are aware that the only way to fight discriminatory orthodoxies is by being a good example. As Chomsky iterates, there is no other "methodology"[28] of fighting ignorance and intolerance.

In addition, this is just one of the ways in which Hermione's social outlook significantly impacts upon the emotional development of the other two main characters: Both Ron and Harry are empowered, either by being pure-blood (Ron) or by having pure-blood connections and a sort of "celebrity"[29] status (Harry). Therefore, both boys are less 'socially aware' than the Muggle-born Hermione. They are not *progressive* thinkers during their early teenage years, simply because they are inexperienced, uninformed, and not affected by wizarding prejudice in the same way as Hermione.

Finally, as was previously mentioned, most *non*-disabled *Child Transformers* are likely to become adult *Progressives*, as we see in the case of Lupin's childhood friends. I have already discussed how James Potter was inclusive and non-discriminatory towards Lupin during their childhood and adulthood years. But it is also worth noting that the adult Sirius exhibits *progressive* behavior towards werewolves in being "alert to changes in representation and inclusion,"[30] applauding it when it favors the magically Disabled, and expressing disapproval when it does not.

In *Order of the Phoenix* we see that Sirius still sympathizes with Lupin's cause, as he expresses dislike for

[28] In an interview with David Barsamian (May, 2001).

[29] Snape ridicules Harry about his "celebrity" status in *Philosopher's Stone* (p. 101).

[30] Sancho, 2003, p. 26.

Dolores Umbridge because of the anti-werewolf laws she has written. Therefore, though Sirius's character may have failed in recognizing house-elves as beings with human feelings, he partially compensates for the flaw by espousing *progressive* attitudes towards werewolves.

Followers

This is a very important group, not only because two of the main characters have been characterized as *Followers* (though **only** as far as the term relates to their attitudes towards the magically Disabled), but also because history shows that humans beings are far more likely to follow the dominant trends in society, as opposed to actively seeking to formulate their own sense of social morals.

During their early teenage years, both Ron and Harry are more suited for the *Followers* group because they "identify primarily with mainstream, non-disabled society." Sancho's research found that there were not many disabled people in this group—just 1% according to the quantitative survey which she completed for the study. Furthermore, she explained that "*Followers* lack a specific interest in disability," and may come in contact with the Disabled through work, social situations or when a family member or close friend becomes disabled. They therefore "learn" to deal with disability, but it does not become "a cause or an issue" because, "as far as they are concerned, it is incidental to their lives."[31]

Admittedly, Harry already has a lot on his plate—with all his parental figures and mentors dying off, and Voldemort on the loose. And so, although the young hero is a *Follower* at first, he is also a *Progressive-in-the-making*, who always does whatever he can for stigmatized *individuals* who are dear to him. (These include Dobby the elf, the giants Hagrid and Grawp and Remus Lupin the werewolf). Beyond that, he shows no inclination towards political activism on behalf of marginalized groups. But, once again in Harry's defense, he rids the wizarding world of Voldemort, thus effectively facilitating a more tolerant environment. And, as we know, he will later play a key role in improving the Ministry.

---

[31] Sancho, 2003, p. 28.

***

While other characters display a more diverse range of traits—Hermione, for example, is very *issue-driven* when it comes to house-elves, but *progressive* towards werewolves and giants—Ron's character is most suited for the *Followers* category, in terms of the way he relates to out-groups in general. Whether it is his light-hearted derision of Filch ("He's bitter.")[32], or his open hostility towards Lupin when he first discovers the teacher's werewolf status ("*Get away from me, werewolf!*")[33], or his undisguised repulsion upon discovering that Hagrid is half-giant ("blimey, no wonder he keeps it quiet")[34], Ron effectively embodies most wizarding prejudices towards out-groups—magically disabled or otherwise.

Ron's character exemplifies the convenience of what Fiske calls "over-generalized categories,"[35] or what is more widely referred to as 'essentialism.' And, as Allport explained, "it takes less effort" to over-generalize; and "effort ... is disagreeable."[36]

Therefore, it is his friendship with the open-minded Harry and the socially-aware Hermione—plus the adventures they encounter through meeting other magical groups—that helps Ron to become a better person. Over the course of the seven novels, we witness Ron's personal development, as he overcomes certain deeply-engrained prejudices which he has held since childhood. Without his friends, the teenage Ron would be a *Traditionalist-in-the-making*, as we see that he has held onto a lot of deep-seated stereotypes for a long time; and it takes him a while to learn to care about marginalized groups in general. For instance, under Hermione's scrutiny, Ron's attitude towards house-elves eventually changes, but it does not happen instantaneously. In fact, it takes several years and a certain amount of trauma.

---

[32] *Chamber of Secrets*, p. 111.

[33] *Prisoner of Azkaban*, p. 253

[34] *Goblet of Fire*, p. 374.

[35] In her essay entitled "Social Condition and the Normality of Prejudgment" in *On the Nature of Prejudice*. (Edited by Dovidio et al., 2005, p. 40)

[36] Allport, 1954/1979, p. 21.

And yet, it is a mark of significant social progression when *Followers* become true *Progressives*, as is certainly the case with Ron towards the end of the series.

Traditionalists

The *Traditionalists* are the last group relevant to both Sancho's research on disability portrayal in the British media and our discussion on disability-related issues in the *Harry Potter* novels. This group is extremely important for the mere fact that it encompasses a very broad cross-section of society. First of all, it includes both non-disabled and disabled people of all ages. And secondly, *Transformers* "differ from *Followers* in that they can be quite resistant to change."[37]

In the *Harry Potter* novels, we see characters on both sides of the 'good-versus-evil' dichotomy expressing *traditionalist* views towards the magically Disabled. For instance, while we expect the likes of Cornelius Fudge and Dolores Umbridge to show open disdain for both werewolf and Squib characters, we surprisingly see beloved personalities like Molly Weasley also being somewhat intolerant towards social Others—for instance, the werewolf who shares her husband's hospital room.[38]

According to Sancho, *Traditionalists* often assume that "people with physical disabilities also have mental disabilities."[39] Likewise, we see Fudge dismissing Mrs. Figg as an unconvincing witness, disregarding everything she has to say, simply because she is a Squib. And as for Umbridge, she categorically "loathes part-humans"[40] for apparently no rational cause. And Molly Weasley is uncomfortable about her husband sharing a hospital room with a werewolf for fear that Arthur might be attacked—even though it is two weeks before the full moon.[41] Here, we see that Molly's incorrect assumption—that the werewolf is not just demented in his wolf state but all the time—signals a resolutely *traditionalist*

---

[37] Sancho, 2003, p. 30.

[38] See *Order of the Phoenix* (pp. 431-432) quote above, cited on page 125 of this volume.

[39] Sancho, 2003, p. 30.

[40] *Order of the Phoenix*, p. 271.

[41] See *Order of the Phoenix*, pp. 431-432.

perspective: Although Molly is kind, accommodating and compassionate towards Remus Lupin, this fails to temper her traditional fears and suspicions about werewolves in general. This is why *Traditionalists* like Molly are usually described as "very set in their ways."[42]

Most importantly, Molly's example proves that a person can have friends, acquaintances, or even family members who belong to a minority group, and still hold deep-seated prejudices against that group in general. And so, it is of no consequence when a person counters accusations of discrimination with arguments such as: "I've got loads of gay/Disabled/Black/Asian/White/Arab/female/poor friends, so I am clearly not prejudiced."

***

Ironically, the Squib character Argus Filch is a consummate *Traditionalist*: First of all, he perceives any acknowledgement of 'Squibhood' as 'victimhood.' And second, it is not without a hint of self-loathing that he finally admits that he is a Squib, whilst fiercely accusing Harry of attacking his cat.[43] It is as though Filch has been 'cornered' into admission of his 'inferior' status: he is far too "set in his ways" to be proud of who/what he is, and to perceive himself as the social equal of wizards—regardless of the physical shortcoming of not having magical powers.

Likewise, although the other Squib character, Mrs. Figg, mostly exemplifies *transformer* leanings, she also displays the *traditionalist* habit of focusing too much on the things she *cannot* do, rather than on the things she *can* do. For example, after revealing her Squib identity to Harry, following the Dementor attack in *Order of the Phoenix*, we see her continuously stressing her ***in***ability to use a wand, to Apparate, or to do any kind of magic—even repeating herself sometimes (pp. 23-27). And so, both Squib characters have moments where they seem to be saying: *'I'm **just** a Squib.'*

***

[42] Sancho, 2003, p. 30.

[43] See *Chamber of Secrets*, pp. 108-109.

Another *Transformer* who finds it difficult to divorce himself from *traditionalist* habits is Remus Lupin. In *Deathly Hallows*, we see him torturing himself over his decision to marry Nymphadora Tonks. And as the following citation shows, his personal insecurities have led him to do something that Harry considers to be unpardonable:

> 'I—I made a grave mistake in marrying Tonks. I did it against my better judgment and I have regretted it very much since.'
>
> 'I see,' said Harry, 'so you're just going to dump her and the kid and run off with us?'
>
> Lupin sprang to his feet: his chair toppled over backwards, and he glared at them so fiercely that Harry saw, for the first time ever, the shadow of the wolf upon his human face.
>
> 'Don't you understand what I've done to my wife and unborn child? I should never have married her, I've made her an outcast!'
>
> Lupin kicked the chair he had overturned.
>
> 'You have only ever seen me amongst the Order, or under Dumbledore's protection at Hogwarts! You don't know how most of the wizarding world sees creatures like me! When they know of my affliction, they can barely talk to me! Don't you see what I've done to her? Even her own family is disgusted by our marriage, what parents want their only daughter to marry a werewolf? And the child—the child—'
>
> Lupin actually seized handfuls of his own hair; he looked quite deranged.
>
> 'My kind don't usually breed! It will be like me, I am convinced of it—how can I forgive myself, when I knowingly risked passing on my own condition to an innocent child? And if, by some miracle, it is not like me, then it will be better off, a hundred times so, without a father of whom it must always be ashamed!' (*Deathly Hallows*, pp. 175-176)

Here, we see Lupin carrying out his own self-inflicted dehumanization with the use of the term "breed," thus emphasizing his animal traits over his human ones. He therefore 'objectifies' his self in the same way society does on a daily basis.

Lupin clearly espouses *traditionalist* opinions (much of which is merely false doctrine) about his ability (or perhaps his *right*) to procreate. And, by assuming that his unborn child *must* be ashamed of him as a father, and that it will *almost certainly* be inflicted with the werewolf condition, he displays all the traits of negative self-categorization: His entire existence has been scripted by someone else—down to his ability to procreate. And, unfortunately, the character seems to have lost the ability to resist the script, despite the *Transformer* tendencies he displayed during his youth.

Lupin's fears are later proved to be unfounded and irrational: first, because the love and acceptance he continues to receive from friends and loved ones should normally disprove the notion that he is *unworthy* of such things. And second, 'werewolf syndrome' is transmitted through the animal's bites at the full moon, and not through sexual reproduction between two humans. Thus, contrary to Remus's fears, Teddy Lupin turns out to be a Metamorphmagus[44]—just like his mother—and not at all inflicted with 'werewolf syndrome.'

The important conclusion to be drawn from all of this is that, anti-werewolf stigma is mostly based on flawed reasoning and misinformation. In our own world, we could compare this situation to the belief that some people have about the reproductive abilities of humans who carry the HIV virus. In addition, some people even still fear that they could catch the virus if an infected person breathes on them or shakes their hand ... By the same token, in *Prisoner of Azkaban* we see Ron recoiling from an untransformed Lupin ("*Get away from me, werewolf!*"[p. 253]), as though the teacher could infect him with a simple touch.

Furthermore, the werewolf group is indeed adversely psychologically affected by the social stigma, if, as Lupin suggests, it has so far restricted their procreation. In being repulsed by the very idea that he could reproduce, and in fearing that his child will be a sort of *beast* or *monster* like

[44] A Metamorphmagus is a witch or wizard who can alter their physical appearance at will.

himself, Lupin effectively demonstrates how much he has internalized wizarding society's hatred and repulsion toward his kind. This 'intropunitive' manifestation of self-hate is somewhat similar to what we see in house-elves, who have fully assimilated the value judgments of the master class. And, we may deduce that many of the violent *issue-driven* werewolves such as Greyback have also internalized this dehumanizing self-image, as if to say: *'Society treats me like a monster anyway, so I might as well act like one.'*

***

From the politically powerful, such as Minister Fudge, to widely disseminated media voices like the *Daily Prophet* journalist Rita Skeeter, the *Traditionalists* in wizarding society are the primary purveyors of negative and unhelpful stereotypes. And this trend has some rather striking parallels in our own world:

> The thing that sets *Traditionalists* apart is that they have embedded, firm beliefs about a whole range of other prejudices, for example, sexism and racism. They are set in their ways and exhibit a lot of prejudice and stereotyping, irrespective of whether they are disabled or not. This prejudice or stereotyping is not necessarily directed at disabled people...
>
> > *We've got black people reading the news now—people like Trevor McDonald*
> > – (Female, 30-60, carer)
>
> [Furthermore] ... they tend to see disabled people as victims, as being disadvantaged and, at worst, as second class citizens.
>
> (Sancho, 2003, p. 30)

Similarly, in *Goblet of Fire*, we see Skeeter inciting widespread public disdain for Dumbledore by simply highlighting the fact that the Headmaster hired a half-giant and a werewolf to teach at Hogwarts.[45] The fact that she manages to demonize Dumbledore by merely associating him with werewolves and giants is not only symbolic of the media's power to influence public opinion; but it also points to mainstream anxieties and prejudice towards these out-groups within the magical community.

Also in the same book, we see Cornelius Fudge voicing reservations about allowing Dumbledore "to hire werewolves or keep Hagrid" (p. 615). This proves that the majority of the wizarding public—including the Minister himself—espouses *traditionalist* feelings about such groups. And besides, Severus Snape's jeering remark in the third novel—about Remus Lupin being a "tame werewolf"[46]—indicates that the very idea of a docile, compassionate werewolf is universally regarded as an oxymoron. Also, Snape's use of the word "tame" further emphasizes the "animal" side of Lupin's character, as opposed to his humanity. And, as we know, attributing a lack of humanity or a sense of 'diminished' humanity to a group is a crucial strategy for justifying institutional discrimination.

Ironically, Minister Fudge displays similar hostility towards Harry in *Goblet of Fire*, on the grounds that the Killing Curse that had backfired on Voldemort when Harry was a baby must have "addled his brains" (p. 612). Through rumors put about by Rita Skeeter in the *Daily Prophet*,[47] most people, including Fudge, now believe Harry to be a piteous, attention-seeking little boy who still cries over his parents' deaths. An illegal Animagus, Skeeter disguises herself as a beetle in order to eavesdrop on the school staff's conversations—as we know, this is how Hagrid's half-giant heritage is discovered and publicized—and she attends Harry's classes in secret. When Harry falls asleep in Divination and wakes up screaming from a vision in which Voldemort is torturing Wormtail, Skeeter capitalizes on the occasion. She publishes an article shortly afterwards entitled "HARRY POTTER 'DISTURBED AND DANGEROUS'", in

---

[45] See *Goblet of Fire*, pp. 380-382 & 531-532.

[46] *Prisoner of Azkaban*, p. 263.

[47] This is the largest daily newspaper in the wizarding world. Other printed media include the *Evening Prophet* and the *Quibbler*.

which she casts aspersions on Harry's sanity and quotes other students saying "he's made friends with werewolves and giants too. We think he'd do anything for a bit of power" (pp. 531-532). This subplot may be read as a metaphor of prejudice against the mentally Disabled in our own world, as it demonstrates how effectively society has constructed the notion of 'insanity' as a pejorative, whereby the supposedly insane are either to be severely stigmatized or shunned and pitied, but never respected or taken seriously.

Furthermore, Fudge sets a poor example in his derision of Harry, particularly on grounds of mental illness: When a leader fails to exemplify acceptance and respect, it becomes common practice within the establishment to discriminate against disadvantaged groups, such as those with (mental or physical) disabilities.

To conclude this section, I must emphasize that the *traditionalist* stances (towards the magically Disabled) that I have so far described in this chapter, appear to be the social 'norm' in J.K. Rowling's wizarding world. But there are other types of *traditionalist* attitudes to disability in our own world that I have not addressed. For example, thus far, I have not examined the 'pity response' to disability at all.

To a certain degree, pity undermines respectability and can be regarded as a mild, non-aggressive form of prejudice. Beth Haller suggests that pity is the typical response to disability in our own world, as narratives on disability usually portray the Disabled as "coping with adversity." And so, instead of promoting acceptance, "they sometimes promote pity."[48] This is an issue that I would have liked to address in far greater detail; but I lacked the opportunity to do so, simply because 'pity' does not feature much in the *Harry Potter* series where Squibs and werewolves are concerned.

Then again, this is probably because the Squib and werewolf personalities in the series are only minor characters. Harry and the rest of Rita Skeeter's audience certainly feel pity for Dumbledore's fabled Squib sister in *Deathly Hallows*; and there is certainly a hint of pity in Ron's assertion that

---

[48] News article entitled: "Confusing Disability with Tragedy," *The Sun*. Baltimore, Maryland. April 29, 2001.

Filch is "bitter."[49] Still, although it does not disguise Ron's contempt for the caretaker, it would probably be unfair to accuse Ron of prejudice towards Squibs in general.

Neither does Aunt Muriel's narrative (about how Squibs used to be purposefully suppressed due to shame) give us any indication that the 'pity response' towards Squibs was a dominant feature in wizarding society. And, once again, this lack of perspective is due to the fact that Squib characters are restricted to very minor roles; and they are usually 'spoken about' rather than given a voice.

Where werewolves are concerned, the 'fear response' is obviously far greater than the 'pity response.' We are also restricted to Greyback's blood-curdling threats and Lupin reminiscing about how James Potter used to stand up for him. Perhaps it would have been useful to hear mention of autobiographies written by Squib or werewolf characters—specific information about how well they sold or how such books were received by the general wizarding public might have been useful.

***

To conclude the chapter, I join ranks with the *Transformers* in Sancho's study, in the belief that it is crucial for the Disabled in our own world to perceive themselves as equally "worthy" and just as "empowered" as able-bodied people. The same principle applies to the magically Disabled (Squibs and werewolves) in J.K. Rowling's wizarding world.

But the need for acceptance is frustrated by *traditionalist* attitudes and beliefs about disability in both worlds. Moreover, we have seen how, over time, persecuted groups and individuals may come to adopt the negative societal attitudes and views projected upon them throughout their lifetimes. The discussion in Chapter 3 of this volume, where I examined the mindset of Rowling's house-elves, explained some of the ramifications of negative self-categorization: It is one of the more dangerous consequences of prejudice and institutional discrimination, because the social outcast may gradually come to embrace a sense of inferiority. And this can

[49] *Chamber of Secrets*, p. 111.

have various destructive consequences for the individual, as well as the society at large.

Also, as discussed in this chapter, the more insidious forms of prejudice, which sometimes affect disabled groups, can have the following negative effects:

i. As we see in the Squibs' case, disabled outsiders may become unhealthily obsessed with the perceived advantage or power of the able-bodied 'elite'. Filch, for example, is literally 'living a lie' until forced to accept the truth about himself. His lack of self-esteem and failed self-acceptance exemplify Allport's notion of the outsider's acquired "self-hatred," after so readily assimilating the outlook and prejudice of the dominant group. And, once again, as we may deduce from Ron's unsympathetic observation that Filch is just "bitter", self-hatred among the oppressed is far too casually accepted and dismissed by the dominant, empowered elite.

ii. As we see in the werewolf's case, the shunned outsider may respond to being scorned by seeking retribution, projecting his own anger and self-loathing at society through extremist violence.

In the most extreme cases, it can have devastating consequences for the collective. After all, the sort of criminality typified by Fenrir Greyback's band of mercenary werewolves is, effectively, a mitigated form of terrorism. And so, once again, we see that *ignorance* of the social Other not only increases unjustified fear—thus fuelling prejudice and discrimination—but can also have significant psychological effects on marginalized individuals and groups, and can be extremely detrimental to the wider society in the long run.

Chapter 5

What's Wrong with Hermione Calling Herself a "Mudblood"? : Examining the Politics of Naming and Self-Naming in the Harry Potter *Novels*

Recently, a distinguished actor was fired from a popular U.S. television drama series for allegedly referring to another cast member as a 'faggot.' And whilst denying the allegations on national television, the actor used the forbidden word again ("*No, I did not call So & So a faggot*"), causing widespread shock and disgruntlement amongst the audience and his colleagues. Obviously the use of the word—in any circumstance—is '*tabooed*,' as most epithets are. And yet, many homosexuals have embraced the term and use it casually amongst themselves. Similarly, Whites are forbidden from using 'the "n" word'[1] to refer to Blacks, although it is commonly thrown about in rap songs and in the African-American film industry.

Likewise, in Rowling's series finale (*Deathly Hallows*), we see a major character using a renowned wizarding world 'hate speech' term to refer to her self. In the meantime, her peers can only observe her sudden liberation but not participate in it—because it still remains a *taboo* for them.

And so, in this chapter, I will examine the politics of "naming" (or more specifically, "name-calling") and "self-naming," and discuss their social significance in Rowling's magical community, as well as in the real world.

***

In the last two chapters, I touched upon the importance of marginalized groups and individuals having healthy self-images, particularly in order to counteract the self-loathing-related consequences of systematic discrimination. In this chapter, I will discuss how *naming* (or name-calling) and *self-*

[1] Variations of the "*nigger*" epithet include "nigga," which is pluralized as "niggaz" in African-American Ebonics.

naming reflect upon the self-image of some of the characters in the *Harry Potter* novels.

Allport maintained that "intense hostility is reflected in the antilocution of name-calling," and epithets ("like 'kike,' 'nigger,' 'wop'") generally issue from deep and long-standing hostility" (1954/1979, p. 50). Likewise, the abusive, degrading nature of J.K. Rowling's "Mudblood" pejorative is apparent even before the author explains the social, historical and political contexts of the term to her readers. We easily deduce that "Mudblood" is fraught with biological significance; and the coining of the term was obviously based on the notion that Muggles—and by extension Muggle-borns—are '*unclean*.'

In *Chamber of Secrets*, Ron informs Hermione and Harry that the pejorative literally denotes "dirty blood" (p. 89). And in *Deathly Hallows* we see the Death Eaters using the same rhetoric to indoctrinate Hogwarts students in their "Muggle Studies" classes, where the young minds are filled with lies about Muggles being "like animals, stupid and dirty" (p. 462). It is also noteworthy that, in a wizarding world ruled by Voldemort, Muggle Studies is no longer optional, but mandatory for all Hogwarts students: Wizard children must therefore be subjected to a compulsory mis-education. Clearly, Voldemort aims to use doctrine to engender hostility towards Muggles and Muggle-borns. Perhaps he believes that he will gain more support from the wider wizarding population by creating an "us-versus-them" dynamic where Muggles are concerned.

Of course, there are violent consequences for all who resist the indoctrination or oppose the new social order. For instance, in *Deathly Hallows*, we see some of Harry's classmates—all members of the Defense group (Dumbledore's Army) that he had founded in *Order of the Phoenix*—nursing horrific injuries as a result of opposing the new curriculum or speaking out against the latest anti-Muggle/Muggle-born movement.[2] These students, as well as the general wizarding public, had always denounced the use of the "Mudblood" epithet. And so, it might have set off a few figurative alarm bells amongst the *Harry Potter* readership when Hermione

---

[2] *Deathly Hallows*, pp. 459-463.

Granger finally declared herself to be "Mudblood, and proud of it" (p. 395).

Considering the notions of 'stupidity,' 'dirtiness' and downgraded humanity traditionally associated with being a "Mudblood", does Hermione have the right to use the term to refer to anyone—including her self? Does it trivialize the Muggle-born's historical struggle for social equality within the wizarding world? And finally, if it becomes socially acceptable for Muggle-borns to refer to themselves as "Mudbloods," what are the social ramifications for Half-bloods and Pure-bloods like Harry and Ron?

***

In his volume on *Naming and Identity* (1988), Richard Alford attributes identity-creation to the act of naming, and consequently bestows irrevocable empowerment upon the namer or self-namer—particularly in the Foucauldian sense of power being an act upon another act.[3] For example, Judaic traditions dictate that a person's fate is linked to his or her given name, and so, renaming a sick or otherwise condemned person can give them hope and protection. Likewise, names and the act of naming are also frequently linked with 'power' in fantasy and children's literature. For example, in Tolkien's *Lord of the Rings*, the murderous Gollum shows uncharacteristic humanity and compassion when Frodo addresses him by his birth name, Smeagol.[4] Also, in Tolkien's work, naming often denotes the character of the namer(s), as we learn that each race in "Middle Earth" has a different name for the wizard Gandalf.[5] The name itself not only reflects how the wizard is perceived by each civilization; it also encapsulates aspects of that culture's identity.

---

[3] See Michel Foucault's essay, 'The subject and power', Afterword to H.L. Dreyfus and P. Rabinow, *Michel Foucault: Beyond Structuralism and Hermeneutics* (1982, p. 220).

[4] See "The Taming of Smeagol" in Tolkien's *The Lord of the Rings: The Two Towers* ([Collectors Edition-Complete Works Volume] 1991, pp. 627-644).

[5] *"Many are my names in many countries, [Gandalf] said. Mithrandir among the Elves, Tharkûn to the Dwarves; Olórin I was in my youth in the West that is forgotten, in the South Incánus, in the North Gandalf; to the East I go not."* (Tolkien, 1991, p. 697)

Other 'acquired' names in Tolkien's work include "Wormtongue," "Láthspell"[6] and "Barad-dur,"[7] which are all used to denote degeneracy or loss of good character. Here, we see that the discontinued use of a person's birth name or the original name of a place coincides with a loss of morality or reputation. In this sense, names are equated with identity and character...

But to return to the 'naming=power' principle, other fantasy writers have written various works in which this rule applies. For example, in Jonathan Stroud's *Bartimaeus* series, so-called "demons" gain power over wizards by learning their birth names. And naming is synonymous with reciting magical incantations in Ursula Le Guin's *A Wizard of Earthsea*—a work in which Le Guin also utilizes the institutional structure of a magic school. But where Rowling uses Latin-based "incantations" that her young witches and wizards must learn in order to master magic, Le Guin's younglings endure a challenging year in the "Isolate Tower" studying with the "Master Namer." Le Guin's entire magical education system is based on the principle that a wizard must learn the original or 'true' name of a thing (in "Old Speech") in order to have power over it.[8]

J.K. Rowling attributes similar power to names and the act of naming in *Harry Potter*'s world, but not always in the same way. She often uses names in a sort of 'self-evident' way to symbolize a character's physical or emotional qualities or defects: For example, we have the lupine Remus Lupin, a werewolf; the *severe*, embittered Severus Snape, a sniping and vindictive mentor; and the cowardly Wormtail who worms his way into the favor of popular peers and powerful superiors. Rowling often uses names in a sort of comical, all-encompassing manner: for example, a well-published author of Transfiguration books is called "Emeric Switch," a Potions

---

[6] "Láthspell" means "ill news." In *The Two Towers* (1991, p. 535), the corrupt Wormtongue invents this name for Gandalf, in an effort to defame the wizard in front of the people of Rohan.

[7] Barad-dur is the tower where Tolkien's Dark Lord Sauron resides and keeps a sinister eye on "MiddleEarth." We are told that it used to be a wholesome place, but now no one dares enter it because of Sauron's evil influence.

[8] See Le Guin's *A Wizard of Earthsea*, p. 16.

Master named "Arsenius Jigger," and the author of a book entitled *Curses and Counter-Curses (Bewitch your Friends and Befuddle your Enemies with the Latest Revenges...)* is called "Vindictus Viridian".[9]

Such names border on caricature; but these characters are merely authors of magical text-books, and are not instrumental to the story's plot. However, their names are almost 'too appropriate' or '*too coincidental*.' And so, one could postulate the theory that these magical text-book authors have different birth names: They simply took on memorable, fitting monikers (or pseudonyms) in order to stress their authority and expertise in their chosen fields.

After all, the idea that self-naming has a vital '*purpose*' is a crucial theme in the novels. The theme first surfaces in *Chamber of Secrets*, where we discovered the reason behind Voldemort shedding his birth name (Tom Riddle). Here, we can see that Riddle's self-naming act also had a purpose that was inextricably linked to his professional reputation:

> He pulled Harry's wand from his pocket and began to trace it through the air, writing three shimmering words:
>
> TOM MARVOLO RIDDLE
>
> Then he waved the wand once, and the letters of his name rearranged themselves:
>
> I AM LORD VOLDEMORT
>
> 'You see?' he whispered. 'It was a name I was already using at Hogwarts, to my most intimate friends only, of course. You think I was going to use my filthy Muggle father's name forever? I, in whose veins runs the blood of Salazar Slytherin himself, through my mother's side? I, keep the name of a foul, common Muggle, who abandoned me even before I was born, just because he found out his wife was a witch? No, Harry. I fashioned myself a new name, a name I knew wizards everywhere would one day fear to speak, when I had become the greatest sorcerer in the world?'
>
> (*Chamber of Secrets*, p. 231)

---

[9] *Philosopher's Stone*, p. 52 & p. 62.

The above citation also betrays the fact that Riddle renamed himself initially out of shame for his Muggle heritage—a connection he had come to associate with the weakness and cruelty of his father's abandonment. One also perceives the character's overwhelming sense of self-loathing—at least for the Muggle part of his self. The teenage Riddle evidently believed that he could create his own identity—at least one that he could be proud of—through the act of self-naming. Coincidentally, Alford also maintained that "name changes actually help to effect identity change" (1988, p. 85).

And moreover, having been sorted into Slytherin House when he first came to Hogwarts, it was not long before the eleven-year-old Tom Riddle assimilated the value systems dictated by the wizarding world's social and 'racial' elite. With "close friends" like Bellatrix and other future Death Eaters, he soon discovered the privileges associated with being a Pure-blood, as well as the wizarding world's degrading perception of Muggles and Muggle-borns. His lust for power, along with a resolute belief in his own superiority, caused him to regard his Muggle attachment as a smear on his character and detrimental to his reputation of academic brilliance and distinguished wizard blood ties. Naturally, Riddle's Muggle parentage was a part of his self that had to be severed, rather like a gangrened limb is compulsorily amputated. And later in the series we see him encouraging his followers to do the same with their own families:

> 'Many of the oldest family trees become a little diseased over time,' he said, as Bellatrix gazed at him, breathless and imploring.
>
> 'You must prune yours, must you not, to keep it healthy? Cut away those parts that threaten the health of the rest.'
>
> (*Deathly Hallows*, pp. 16-17)

Since Voldemort had murdered his own Muggle father and grandparents[10] to "cut away" what he regarded as degeneracy

[10] In *Goblet of Fire*, p. 560, he boasts to Harry about how he murdered his Muggle relatives.

and weakness, here, he refers to Bellatrix recently acquiring a highly stigmatized relative, [11] who presumably infected the family tree and had to be pruned away.

Also worth noting is the fact that, although the stigma associated with Muggles and Muggle-borns is not quite as severe as werewolf stigma, people like Hermione are still highly persecuted in the relatively peaceful wizarding world—prior to Voldemort's first rise to power and after his fall in the early 1980s. Hence, the term "Mudblood" encapsulates both subverted and overt dichotomies of empowerment—which is why Hermione finally embracing the pejorative in *Deathly Hallows* constitutes a significant turning point in the series.

Hermione's momentary outburst could easily be mistaken for rash self-deprecation, as we see an alarmed Ron imploring her not to take on the epithet (p. 395). However, I believe Hermione embraces the term precisely because she has a far better insight into the aforementioned dichotomies of empowerment than Ron does: "I've got no higher position under this new order than you have," she says empathetically to a persecuted goblin. "I'm quite as hunted as any goblin or elf, Griphook! I'm a Mudblood!" (p. 395).

The last statement is crucial both for Hermione and for Rowling's readership, because although her vulnerability has been made clear since *Chamber of Secrets*, this is the first self-status-evaluating declaration from the character in the entire series. And, understandably, it takes her friends by surprise, because Ron and Harry have always perceived her as their social equal—and certainly as their superior in terms of academic achievement. Neither of them understands the insidious nature of wizarding world prejudice and politics the way Hermione does: She alone can see that the Muggle-born now stands on common ground with elves and goblins under Voldemort's new regime.

In addition, notice how the voicing of the "Mudblood" pejorative has so far been restricted to pure-blood and half-blood characters (Voldemort, Snape, the Malfoys, the Blacks—including their lifelong servant, Kreacher—and the Death Eaters). This trend signals the Pure-blood's empowerment as the *namer* (the one with the power to define and/or determine

[11] Her niece (Nymphadora Tonks) had just married the werewolf Remus Lupin.

the role and *place* of the social Other), and the Muggle-born's objectified, inferior status as the *named*. Therefore, embracing the term is, in essence, Hermione's way of turning the hierarchy on its head and reclaiming empowerment for herself. But before we examine the social consequences of this act, we must first understand the context and the extent of antilocution towards Muggle-borns in the wizarding world...

***

A seething undercurrent of hostility towards Muggle-borns becomes apparent quite early in the series, particularly through the Malfoys' attitude towards Hermione Granger in *Chamber of Secrets*. Here, Arthur Weasley has a public altercation with Lucius Malfoy, after the latter comments derisively on Arthur's poor choice of "company" (the Grangers): "I thought your family could sink no lower" (pp. 51-52). And later, after several Muggle-borns have been attacked by Slytherin's monster, Draco tells Ron and Harry (who have drunk Polyjuice Potion and are now posing as Draco's friends Crabbe and Goyle) to "go up to the hospital wing and give all those Mudbloods a good kick from me" (p. 166). He also informs them that a Muggle-born student (whom we later discover to be a school ghost nicknamed Moaning Myrtle) had died fifty years before, when the legendary chamber was opened for the first time (p. 167).

At this stage, Draco also expresses his own resentment towards Harry Potter, not only because the famous "Boy Who Lived" had rejected his friendship the previous year, but rather for the same reason that Draco and his family have always despised the Weasleys—a lack of "proper wizarding feeling" (p. 166). "Proper [wizarding] pride," according to Draco, would morally restrain Harry from being friends with "that jumped up Mudblood Granger" (p. 166)—perhaps in the same way that the young Tom Riddle's "pride" had impelled him to destroy everything that linked him to the Muggle world. Here, Draco's use of the term "jumped up" implies that Hermione does not '*know her place*.' In other words, she is trespassing on wizard territory by daring to aspire to academic excellence, when she should rather resign herself to '*knowing*' that she is an inferior specimen, and '*act*' out that inferior role.

Therefore, it is no surprise that when Voldemort's return culminates in open warfare in the seventh book, Muggle-borns are stripped of their wands, dismissed from their Ministry jobs and reduced to a class of beggars. Those who protest are violently silenced. And in their new status as "the Wandless," they are forced to sustain harmful propaganda that they "stole" their magic powers. Some wizards even go as far as to completely deny their humanity; for instance, in the series finale, we see the Death Eater Travers referring to a downgraded, down-trodden Muggle-born wizard as "it."[12]

Ironically, the house-elf Kreacher had expressed similar disdain for Hermione in previous books, long before we reached this pivotal point in the series. In Book 6, we see that although house-elves are supposed to be lower in the social hierarchy than humans, Kreacher voices his own 'superior feelings' and is overtly disrespectful toward Hermione:

> "The Mudblood is speaking to Kreacher, Kreacher will pretend he cannot hear"
> (*Half-blood Prince*, p. 425).

And in *Order of the Phoenix*, the elf disparages Hermione for simply "standing there bold as brass" in the Blacks' ancient house (p. 101). Kreacher is a slave (albeit of a pure-blood family), and yet he genuinely believes that he is entitled to a more privileged position than Hermione. But, as I stated in Chapter 3, Kreacher is merely reflecting his own self-loathing: He has completely assimilated the persecutory habits, beliefs and value system of his pure-blood masters.

As a member of the wizarding world's most downtrodden class, the elf has no business being a racist; and yet, somewhat comically, he embraces ideas about racial purity even more readily than most wizards. But what is most important here is that Kreacher's openly-acknowledged prejudice is further proof that antilocution towards Muggle-borns had never really gone out of fashion, even in a war-free wizarding world.

---

[12] *Deathly Hallows*, p. 425.

It is also worth noting that many wizards who claim to have no animosity or prejudice towards Muggle-borns still dismissively relegate them to inferior roles. As was briefly mentioned in Chapter 2, Professor Slughorn expresses total surprise when Muggle-born students prove to be more talented than their pure-blood peers:

> 'Your mother was Muggle-born, of course. Couldn't believe it when I found out. Thought she must have been pure-blood, she was so good.'
>
> 'One of my best friends is Muggle-born,' said Harry, 'and she's the best in our year.'
>
> 'Funny how that sometimes happens, isn't it?' said Slughorn.
>
> 'Not really,' said Harry coldly.
>
> Slughorn looked down on him in surprise.
>
> 'You mustn't think I am prejudiced!' he said. 'No, no, no. Haven't I just said your mother was one of my favorite students?' And there was Dirk Creswell in the year after her, too—now Head of the Goblin Liaison Office, of course—another Muggle-born, a very gifted student, and still gives me excellent inside information on the goings-on at Gringotts!'
>
> ...Harry wasn't sure whether he liked Slughorn or not. He supposed he had been pleasant in his way, but he had also seemed vain and, whatever he said to the contrary, much too surprised that a Muggle-born should make a good witch.
>
> (*Half-blood Prince*, pp. 71-72 & 75)

Unfortunately, Slughorn appeals to the same school of thought as the former Minister for Magic, Cornelius Fudge, whom Dumbledore once chastised for placing "too much importance ... on the so-called purity of blood," and failing to realize that "it matters not what someone is born, but what they grow to be."[13] Herein lies the Muggle-born's dilemma: He or she is permanently straight-jacketed in wizarding society as a 'second-rate' wizard or witch, despite their ability and desire to achieve the same success as Pure-bloods.

[13] *Goblet of Fire*, pp. 614-615.

But note how Slughorn denies his prejudice and justifies his deep-seated, racist beliefs by emphasizing his connections with a few accomplished Muggle-borns. And besides, the few Muggle-borns whom he respects are highly distinguished; and still, by his own reasoning, Muggle-borns do not have what it takes to be in the same league as Pure-bloods. Slughorn is carrying out an action which Spencer and Horowitz[14] defined as the "systematic destruction of racial pride and individual self esteem" amongst persons from racial minority groups (p. 246). And he does so whilst ignoring the glowing examples of the few revered '*Tokens*' like Lily Potter and Dirk Creswell. This suggests that the Professor only (and somewhat grudgingly) attributes 'giftedness' or academic brilliance to a select few Muggle-borns—who are freaks of nature, by his own reasoning—, but not to the group as a whole.

Slughorn's case is an important example of the futility of tokenism as a means of establishing social or racial equality, even in our own world. The select few who are called upon to 'represent' outsider or minority groups in the mainstream—for instance, one Disabled person, a few brown faces here and there, and perhaps an apparently 'flaming' homosexual, just to show how open-minded and accepting the establishment has become—cannot bear the burden of representation for long. Tokenism is detrimental to the minority group, as a whole, because some Tokens tend to assimilate mainstream values to the point where they are no longer identified or identifiable with the minority groups they are supposed to be representing.

And furthermore, tokenism serves the dual purpose of glossing over glaring social inequalities and assuaging collective guilt: Tokens are *necessarily* vastly outnumbered by the mainstream. Hence, they are virtually powerless when it comes to *transforming* the prevailing perceptions (or stereotypes) about the minority groups to which they belong. And so, Slughorn's rationalization of his prejudice is reminiscent of familiar responses to accusations of racism in

---

[14] "Effects of Systematic Social and Token Reinforcement on the Modification of Racial and Color Concept Attitudes in Black and in White Preschool Children." *Journal of Developmental Psychology, Vol.9 No.2*, University of Kansas Press, 1973, pp. 246-254.

the real world: "*I know I'm not an anti-Semitist because I have a Jewish professor I really like*" or "*I'm not racist: I've got loads of Black/Arab/Asian friends*," and so forth, which are all expressions of racial tokenism.

In essence, Slughorn, Kreacher and the Malfoys are all expressing the same fundamental belief: that Muggle-borns are innately inferior to Pure-bloods and Half-bloods, and should not, *under normal circumstances*, be entitled to the same treatment or be capable of similar achievements. In other words, the Muggle-born is an inferior being who is *not supposed to* be confident, outspoken, ambitious or brilliant.

Also, each of these prejudiced characters has different intentions and varying levels of awareness of what actually constitutes prejudice. For instance, whereas Draco is perfectly aware of his own antipathy towards Muggle-borns and revels in it, Slughorn appears to be completely unaware that his beliefs are prejudicial; and, admittedly, he has no real intent to harm. And then there is Kreacher, who is physically and psychologically duty-bound to embracing the value systems of his pure-blood masters.

But Slughorn embodies the most insidious, unnoticeable and arguably the most dangerous form of prejudice, because it is happily disguised as '*popular opinion*.' Kreacher and the Malfoys openly embrace their extremist values, as the Malfoys feel that superiority is their birthright. But Slughorn hides his true feelings under a feeble façade of political correctness. His casually-expressed views, concerning Muggle-borns' innate inferior ability, have made it clear that he believes in the Pure-blood's right to superiority as much as the Malfoys do. The only difference is that Slughorn does not perceive Muggle-borns to be a social threat because there are not that many of them occupying positions of power. And so, the character is temporarily assured in his status as part of the mainstream or dominant (Half-blood + Pure-blood) majority.

Slughorn's beliefs are deeply rooted in tradition and intricately woven into the fabric of his own social consciousness and that of many others like him. And so, despite the offensive nature of his convictions, he is not recognizable—neither to himself nor to others who share his views—as someone who is prejudiced against Muggle-borns. Moreover, his remarks would not bother most Half-bloods, who, unlike Harry, may not have brilliant Muggle-born friends or a Muggle-born mother. And so, Slughorn's muted and easily disguised prejudice is probably the greatest hindrance to the Muggle-borns' quest for social equality in the wizarding world...

***

As I stated in the previous section, distinguished Muggle-borns like Hermione, Lily Potter and Dirk Creswell (the Tokens) are regarded as mere exceptions to the norm—["Funny how that sometimes happens, isn't it?"[15]]. But why is this so? Is this dominant view of Muggle-borns grounded in any sort of historical fact?

One may speculate that Muggle-borns have historically lacked the opportunity to develop their talents. Evidence from the novels suggests that Muggle-borns—like werewolves—were not always allowed to attend Hogwarts.[16] And even when they were allowed to attend, unnoticeably prejudiced and perfectly likeable teachers like Slughorn may have directly or indirectly influenced their perceptions of themselves: We see Slughorn portraying his unwholesome beliefs as facts of '*nature*' as well as the social norm. And, over time, after continuous exposure to such doctrine, Muggle-born students would easily internalize these notions (of their own 'inferior ability') and perform poorly as a result.

Here, we could draw some pertinent comparisons with our own world: For example, in a recent speech, British Member of Parliament John Hutton cited poverty as the "breeding ground for low aspiration and low achievement,"[17] as various sociological research findings suggest that children and women from certain ethnic minority and poorer class backgrounds rarely aspire to high-paying professions or admission to elite universities like Oxford or Cambridge—

---

[15] From the famous Slughorn quote in *Half-blood Prince* (p. 71).

[16] For example, Lucius Malfoy's desire to see the wizarding world return to the "old ways" in *Chamber of Secrets*, and his insistence that someone "of no wizard family" (like Hermione) should not be academically superior to his son (pp. 43-44).

[17] "Ethnic Minority Employment in Britain-Recognizing Women's Potential"—Women's Enterprise Project-Bethnal Green. See Works Consulted page for the URL reference for Minister Hutton's speech, given on February 28, 2007.

simply because they do not believe themselves to be capable of such achievements. Also, they have so far lacked the opportunities to develop their talents and prove themselves. Likewise, since wizarding society does not expect much from Muggle-borns, we may deduce that, as a group, they have traditionally failed to aspire to the highest offices, or even above-average academic achievement.

Naturally, the average Muggle-born student will feel somewhat "out of place"[18] at Hogwarts, at least initially. Even the famous Harry Potter—who had two magical parents—initially feels apprehensive about his own wizarding merits when he comes to Hogwarts. At first, Harry worry's whether the fact that he was raised by Muggles will put him at a disadvantage academically, but Ron assures him that many students come from Muggle families, and they still do well.[19]

We may also infer that Muggle-borns who do not realize that they have magical powers until much later in life, are quite frightened of integrating with the wizarding world, which must seem awfully frightening to them. As a result, the Muggle-born group might simply be plagued by a sort of collective lack of self-esteem with regards to their abilities, or simply their '*right*' to be a part of wizarding society. But the suppression and de-humanizing violence inflicted upon their group in the series finale must remind the reader of the house-elves' plight: The slave-making processes discussed earlier[20] have much in common with the way we see the Death Eaters treating Muggle-borns in *Deathly Hallows.* Therefore, Ron is right to be alarmed when Hermione refers to herself as a "Mudblood."

Even Ron is aware of the victimizing power of pejoratives in general, and how they can affect a person's self-perception, or what Charles Taylor referred to as the "recognition" and "self-*recognition*" of the social Other.[21] In this case, it affects Hermione, who is someone very dear to Ron. He obviously

---

[18] Edward Saïd expresses his own sentiments of perpetual outsiderhood in his memoir, *Out of Place* (1999).

[19] *Philosopher's Stone*, pp. 75-76.

[20] See Chapter 3 of this volume, where I examined the mindset of the house-elves and theorized how they may have come to be an enslaved class.

[21] In his essay entitled "The Politics of Recognition" in *Multiculturalism: Examining the Politics of Recognition* (1994), edited by Amy Gutmann.

does not '*recognize*' her in the same way that other Pure-bloods do, but he is perfectly aware that "Mudblood" entails degeneracy and inferiority.

And so, we see that even Ron—who is far less socially aware than Hermione—equates notions of *personal identity* with the external construct that is *recognition*. Taylor explained that recognition from an external source, especially where dissimilar power dynamics are involved, eventually becomes self-recognition. He elaborated on this concept using the example of Blacks during both the *pre* and *post* colonial era, explaining that "their own self-depreciation...becomes one of the most potent instruments of their own oppression," and therefore, "their first task ought to be to purge themselves of this imposed and destructive identity."[22]

Evidently, recognition is a political act which can reflect both empowerment and disenfranchisement. Taylor's main argument is that personal identity is "partly shaped by recognition or its absence, often by the *mis*recognition of others, and so a person or group of people can suffer real damage, real distortion, if the people or society around them mirror back to them a confining or demeaning or contemptible picture of themselves" (1994, p. 25). And this is precisely what troubles Ron: He does not wish to see his friend assimilating the sort of degraded self-image that Pure-bloods like the Malfoys would inflict upon her.

However, Hermione's reasons for saying "I'm a Mudblood" are clearly advantageous rather than self-depreciatory. One certain advantage is that it stokes the fires of empathy and solidarity in Griphook's heart, thus convincing the goblin to give them the assistance which they needed. But more important, it transforms the social identity of the Muggle-born from an externally inflicted one to one that is more of a personal choice. In other words, embracing the pejorative not only robs it of its power to wound and belittle her, it also takes the powers of *naming* and *defining* out of the Pure-blood's hand and bestows it upon her instead. Thus, Hermione now has the power to define what being a Muggle-born entails—on her own terms. It is she who *chooses*

---

[22] From "The Politics of Recognition" in *Multiculturalism* (Edited by Amy Gutmann, 1994, p. 26).

to use the epithet, rather than having it inflicted upon her. And she only uses it in the full knowledge that she herself does not and will never conform to the Pure-blood's contemptible image of so-called "Mudbloods". And so, in the end, Hermione decides that although she cannot change the historical significance of the pejorative, she can at least *choose* to alter her response to it.

Nevertheless, her self-inflicted use of the term is still quite problematic because it creates a sort of 'semantic barrier' which shuts out Ron and Harry, who dare not speak it, even when she herself uses it freely. Note how Ron says "Don't call yourself *that*,"[23] but he dares not repeat the epithet...

I will return to this matter later in the chapter, but before we discuss the significance of Hermione partaking in the privilege of naming—albeit by *self-naming* with a forbidden epithet—, we must first consider the general implications of the acts of naming and self-naming in the series. And to do so, we must first deconstruct the self-naming act of a far more socially empowered character: Lord Voldemort.

***

Earlier in the chapter, I mentioned some of the curiously appropriate names of Rowling's magical textbook authors. And I used their example to show that self-naming can be a means of projecting a desired image of the self, or creating the required mode of recognition for professional reasons. But the act of self-naming can also be a means of contesting the Taylorian notion of *mis*recognition, because a self-chosen name often reflects the character's self-perception or fundamental life principle. For instance, if we look at the Dark Lord's self-chosen name (*Vol-de-mort*), it literally translates as "flight from death," which is an apt pseudonym for a character intent on attaining immortality.

The name "Voldemort" also alludes to the fear of death that most mortals feel. Thus, it serves the dual purpose of (semantically) embodying fear and causing fear responses

---

[23] *Deathly Hallows*, p. 395. Emphasis added.

(physical and otherwise) in others. And besides, the self-chosen moniker has clearly achieved its projection purposes, in the sense that most beings in the wizarding world have now accepted it as the Dark Lord's *only* name: Many wizards are either unaware of his birth name or have forgotten it. For instance, in *Chamber of Secrets*, we see Dumbledore informing Arthur and Molly Weasley that "very few people know that Lord Voldemort was once called Tom Riddle" (p. 242). Moreover, beings of all magical races fear to speak the Dark Lord's chosen name. And so, having conquered the very thing which most mortals fear, Voldemort is now perceived as even more powerful and more fearsome than death itself.

Harry gets a sense of this when he meets the wandmaker Ollivander for the first time in Book 1:

> '...I think we must expect great things from you, Mr. Potter ... After all, He Who Must Not Be Named did great things—terrible, yes, but great.'
>
> Harry shivered. He wasn't sure he liked Mr. Ollivander too much.
>
> (*Philosopher's Stone*, p. 65).

Here, Harry detects a hint of admiration for the Dark Lord in the wandmaker's choice of words. Ollivander's unwavering veneration for Voldemort is later confirmed in the series finale, where he informs the trio about Voldemort's obsession with the Elder Wand. In the following citation, we can see that the wandmaker remains in awe of the antagonist:

> 'The owner of the Elder Wand must always fear attack,' said Ollivander, 'but the idea of the Dark Lord in possession of the Deathstick is, I must admit ... formidable.'
>
> Harry was suddenly reminded of how he had been unsure, when they first met, of how much he liked Ollivander. Even now, having been tortured and imprisoned by Voldemort, the idea of the Dark wizard in possession of this wand seemed to enthrall him as much as it repulsed him.
>
> (*Deathly Hallows*, pp. 401-402)

Ollivander's persistent admiration, despite the tremendous sufferings inflicted upon him by Voldemort, is reminiscent of the reverence shown to an impious deity—or the "holy dread" which Freud partially equates with the "taboo."[24] Here, Rowling highlights the curious connection between admiration and fear, and, most notably, the notion of fear as reverence for the sacred—best elucidated, of course, through Freud's discussion of the *taboo* concept.

In addition, Voldemort's nicknames, "You-Know-Who" and "He Who Must Not Be Named," may remind the reader of another Dark Lord: Tolkien's Sauron in *The Lord of the Rings*. The people of Gondor also referred to Sauron as the "Shadow of the Unnamed" or simply "the Unnamed."[25] And, as in Rowling's work, the act of *naming* the dark force is synonymous with breaking a social or cultural taboo.

However, in certain cultures in our own world, it is simply forbidden to speak a person's real name because the name itself is sacred. For example, as Freud explained, the names of revered public officials in Polynesia become "taboo"—as in '*unspeakable*'—when they die. As a result, a new word must be invented if the deceased person's name is the same as an everyday concept or commonly-used object. And so, the Polynesian origins of the word "taboo" have evolved to translate as "sacred," "consecrated" or "forbidden." But there are also other layers to the term, which include "uncanny," "unclean" and "dangerous."[26]

The converse of "taboo" in Polynesian is "noa" which denotes "common" or "generally accessible."[27] And so, Voldemort uses his own transgression of social and moral taboos—such as killing and delving into the Dark Arts—to continuously emphasize his 'uncommonness' or 'above-ness' in relation to other humans. For example, in *Chamber of Secrets*, we see the teenage Tom Riddle referring to his father as a "common Muggle" (p. 231); and in *Half-blood Prince*, when Harry and Dumbledore explore Riddle's past, we

[24] As examined in *Totem und Taboo* (1913).

[25] *The Lord of the Rings* (Harper Collins Complete Works Edition, 1991, p. 702).

[26] Freudian references here are taken from the latest edition of Strachey's translation of *Totem and Taboo* (2001, pp. 21-25).

[27] Ibid.

discover that his given name was a nuisance to him, primarily because of its ordinariness and widespread use:

> '...I hope you noticed Riddle's reaction when I mentioned that another shared his first name, "Tom"?' [Dumbledore said] ... 'There he showed his contempt for anything that tied him to other people, anything that made him ordinary. Even then, he wished to be different, separate, notorious. He shed his name, as you know, within a few short years of that conversation and created the mask of "Lord Voldemort" behind which he has hidden for so long.'
> *(Half-blood Prince*, p. 259*)*.

Dumbledore also perceives the '*forbidden*' nature of the "*mask*" of the pseudonym. It transforms Voldemort's true identity into a veiled countenance that looks upon a world that cannot access it in return. And it is this "mask" that facilitates the taboo. And moreover, the real man—the real Tom Riddle—is hidden behind a pseudonym which ultimately proves to be a falsehood.

Also, in *Goblet of Fire*, we see that even though the fact that Voldemort had split his soul was supposed to be a closely-guarded secret, he makes several suggestive remarks (boasts, really) to his Death Eaters about exploring the Horcrux method of survival:

> "I, who have gone further than anybody along the path that leads to immortality. You know my goal—to conquer death."
> (*Goblet of Fire*, p. 566)

Here, once again, he emphasizes the fact that he has "gone further" than anyone else. In other words, he has excessively used the taboo-breaking act in order to transform himself into the ultimate taboo: "sacred" in the sense that he is worshipped by his followers and "untouchable" and "dangerous" in the sense that no one else has dared to commit similar atrocities.

We also see an unabashed teenage Tom Riddle discussing Horcruxes with Professor Slughorn in *Half-blood Prince*, where we learn that even creating one Horcrux is a monumental taboo (pp. 464-466). Later in the same book, we discover that Voldemort created no less than six Horcruxes (p. 470). And in *Deathly Hallows*, he finally protects his deified status by instituting a literal taboo, with severe consequences for those who dare to speak his self-bestowed name.

Through this particular subplot, Rowling establishes a sort of intertextual link with George Orwell's "Big Brother" concept in the novel *1984,* similarly metaphorizing oppression as an unnamable (forbidden), omnipresent and untouchable force that dominates the lives of the populace. We also learn that this so-called "taboo" on Voldemort's name was a feature of the first war, sixteen years earlier. Members of the Order of the Phoenix could easily be traced, due to the fact that they were the only ones who dared to speak the name.

And so, whereas some taboos are upheld by the fear of breaking with sacred tradition, the fear of becoming a social outcast or the fear of becoming unclean, Voldemort's taboo serves the purpose of self-deification, and is sustained by the fear of pain and death. One may also surmise that the universal fear of a spoken name signals further empowerment of the feared entity: In a world ruled by Lord Voldemort, only he has the power to speak his self-bestowed name without retribution.

Even the Death Eaters dare not say it; and we see an outraged Bellatrix slating Harry for "besmirching" the name with his "unworthy ... half-blood's tongue."[28] Naturally, as Harry's mentor, Dumbledore has always encouraged him—from the beginning of the series—to say "Voldemort," because "fear of a name increases fear of the thing itself."[29] And, once again, we see the act of 'naming a dark force' being equated with 'gaining power' over it. The same theme appears in many other examples of fantasy literature and children's books. Most notably, in Annie Dalton's *Naming the Dark*, the act of naming also constitutes a semantic and social taboo.

It is also highly symbolic that, in *Deathly Hallows*, the reader learns about the recently instituted physical taboo (on speaking Voldemort's name) through Ron's character: Ron is

[28] *Order of the Phoenix*, p. 691.

[29] *Philosopher's Stone*, p. 216.

the only pure-blood member of the trio, and the only one who has never overcome the fear of saying "Voldemort" out loud.

Finally, one could argue that Riddle's act of renaming himself *Vol-de-mort*, coupled with his emphatic insistence on his own uniqueness, effectively projects his desired self-image upon the wizarding world: superior, infallible, fearsome and most of all, immortal. Consequently, the juxtaposition of 'repulsion' and 'enthrallment', as exemplified by Ollivander's ambiguous feelings, is precisely the sort of admiration that the Dark Lord has always craved. And Harry's suspicions about Ollivander have been quite accurate from the start: On the one hand, Voldemort is repulsive to the old man in the "unclean," "dangerous" sense, because he has done things that no decent wizard would do; but on the other hand, the extent of the Dark Lord's power and audacity is also enthrallingly admirable to over-awed wizards like Ollivander.

I will therefore summarize this section by stating that self-naming in the *Harry Potter* novels has three main functions. First, it helps the namer to project a desired self-image: This has been demonstrated not only through Voldemort but also the almost *'too-aptly'* named magical textbook authors mentioned earlier in the chapter. Second, Voldemort's example demonstrates that self-naming can create new notions of the sacred and generate powerful taboos, which, like all taboos, may either be revered or defied (as in 'broken'). And finally, self-naming can be an act of self-affirmation. The latter has mostly positive connotations; but it may also serve the purpose of deceit—whether self-deception or deceiving others—, particularly where there are tremendous insecurities in the self-namer...

***

And now, for a moment I would like to return to the discussion of Hermione's self-directed use of the tabooed "Mudblood" pejorative, which certainly carries out some—though not all—of the aforementioned functions of self-naming. In our own world, the appropriation of names that identify some minority groups (such as gay, Black, Muslim, Jewish and so forth) is also a political act. Similar to social trends in Rowling's wizarding world, epithets used to qualify out-groups in the real world also create considerable social anxieties. For instance, the example provided in the introduction to the chapter proves that the gay epithet ("faggot") is a powerful social taboo. So is the word "nigger."

But since the 1980s there has been a systematic de-politicization of "nigger" amongst Black Americans, as the term is rather casually disseminated in rap songs and in the African-American film industry. In addition, Aitken once maintained that "a new movement is brewing to embrace former pejoratives such as 'queer' and even 'faggot', the way black Americans have reclaimed 'nigga'."[30] Here, Aitken argues that the use of these words is political, and claims that "they have more power when the minority group fears their usage: Hence *Queer as Folk.*"[31]

Likewise, we see that the intensity of public reaction to the "Mudblood" epithet in Rowling's wizarding world is matched only by the universal fear of the spoken name, "Voldemort." Moreover, even the act of addressing someone has similar associations with 'exercising power' in the magical context of the *Harry Potter* series, as we learn that Dumbledore is the only one Voldemort ever feared.[32] And coincidentally, Dumbledore has always insisted on calling Voldemort "Tom Riddle"—of course, to the Dark Lord's annoyance.[33] Harry therefore follows his mentor's example in the final battle, where Voldemort repeatedly responds to the loss of his self-naming empowerment with the same expression of outraged incredulity:

> '*You dare—!*' said Voldemort.
> 'Yes, I dare,' said Harry.
> (*Deathly Hallows*, pp. 591-593)

[30] Aitken, Paul. "The Appropriation of 'Gay'." [News Article – April 23, 2007].

[31] A popular, turn-of-the-century TV drama which focused on gay relationships.

[32] This is first mentioned in *Philosopher's Stone*, where Professor McGonagall tells Dumbledore that "everyone knows you're the only one ... Voldemort was frightened of" (p.14). The idea recurs throughout the series, most notably in *Order of the Phoenix* where Dumbledore duels with the newly restored Dark Lord (pp. 712-722).

[33] See *Half-blood Prince*, p. 414 & *Order of the Phoenix*, p. 717-719.

When Harry calls Voldemort "Tom," it is not merely an insult, but rather an unpardonable transgression—a callous violation of the wizarding world's most powerful taboo. For the Dark Lord, being called "Tom Riddle" is synonymous with being called a "Mudblood," because his birth name associates him with Muggles—hence inferiority, fallibility and mortality. And all of these things contradict the projection motives of his self-naming act.

Notably, Hermione's projection motives (for embracing the "Mudblood" pejorative) are completely different from Tom Riddle's reasons for renaming himself. For example, unlike Riddle, Hermione wants to establish solidarity with other persecuted magical creatures like goblins and elves—as is evident in her conversation with Griphook. Here, she justifiably contradicts the goblin's assertion that no one "amongst the wand-carriers protests" against the new social order, in which goblins and elves are even more exploited and abused than before. "We do! We protest!" Hermione insists, as she reminds Griphook that Muggle-borns are in the same predicament as the so-called "lesser" magical creatures.[34]

And so, where Voldemort desperately needs to project a self-image of superiority, Hermione wants to project that of one who seeks solidarity with social Others. In addition, the Dark Lord had rejected his birth name largely due to the anger he felt, after learning that his father had abandoned his mother when he found out that she was a witch. As a result, the young Riddle came to associate being a Muggle with being "weak." He therefore changed his name as an emphatic affirmation of his allegiance to what he perceived as the "might" of wizardkind; and we see the new social order in *Deathly Hallows* being propped up by the political slogan—"MAGIC IS MIGHT" (p. 198).

In contrast, Hermione has loving Muggle parents; she is proud of her Muggle heritage and values it just as much as she cherishes her affiliation with the wizarding world. And so, where Voldemort professes a lack of pride in what he regards as an inferior, defective lineage, Hermione celebrates her Muggle parentage.

---

[34] *Deathly Hallows*, p. 395.

Also, I mentioned earlier that Hermione claims a sense of empowerment from being able to embrace the pejorative on her own terms—with defiance and pride—, which strips it of its power to victimize and offend her. Being proud of her Muggle heritage is an assertion that Muggles are equal to wizards in terms of humanity[35] and personal worth, even though they lack magical ability. And furthermore, by accepting who she is and being "proud" of it, she affirms her own right to occupy wizarding space: In other words, she is neither '*trespassing*' nor '*usurping*'; she has the right to be there as much as any Half-blood or Pure-blood. And instead of being ashamed that she has no biological wizarding world connections, she is proud of the fact that having no wizard blood has never prevented her from being a good witch.

Therefore, Hermione defiantly proclaims her inalienable right to a level of humanity on par with Pure-bloods, by assuming the pre-designated Pure-blood role of 'defining' social Others. (However, she restricts the definition to her self). And if we compare Hermione's attitude to that of the Squib character Argus Filch, we see a marked difference. In the previous chapter, I characterized Filch as a *Traditionalist* because, instead of accepting the Squib part of his identity and being proud of it, he hides (and therefore denies) his Squib status. Also, by taking "Kwikspell" courses, perhaps Filch is trying to become something that he can never be.

Also, we see the character nearly reduced to tears when word gets out about his Squib status. And here, Filch demonstrates his own acceptance of the notion that Squibs are 'lesser beings' than wizards. And, once again, Rowling sends a clear message to her readership that it is not ability that defines a person but choices, and also that self-acceptance is a much better option than denial.

***

Before moving on to the next stage of the discussion, I would like to make a few pertinent comparisons between the

---

[35] See the introduction to Chapter 1 of this volume (pp. 36-38) for the two definitions of the term "humanity," in the context of Rowling's wizarding world.

perception of Muggle-borns in *Harry Potter*'s world, and that which relates to minority groups in our own world.

Take Hermione, for example. Perhaps she is indeed innately brilliant, but she is also an extremely hard worker who takes pride in her work and is constantly in the pursuit of knowledge. But Pure-bloods do not give her credit for her hard work and diligence. Consequently, the character has always been discursively aware that the "Mudblood" epithet is meant to induce performance in the Butlerian sense, where individuals play out the identity traits that they are "purported" to have.[36] Hence, when Kreacher criticizes her for being "bold as brass"—for simply entering a pure-blood house and "standing"[37] there—he is merely voicing the age-old pure-blood belief that Muggle-borns are innately inferior and irremediably unworthy. People like Hermione are therefore expected to act out an inferior role by refraining from aspirations to higher (pure-blood) circles and being ashamed of having no wizard blood. As a result, we see the Death Eaters suppressing Muggle-borns in the series finale by forbidding them to think of themselves as worthy of holding magic powers, and treating them, essentially, like animals.[38]

Images from the latest novel (of the disenfranchised, wandless Muggle-borns in Diagon Alley) are reminiscent of Nazi persecution of Jewish people during the Second World War. Many historians have documented how the Jews were de-humanized and stripped of their wealth during Hitler's regime.[39] Thus, a wizard's wand may symbolize empowerment in the same way that financial security empowers people in the real world. In addition, the new social order in *Deathly Hallows* dictates that magical ability can only be legitimately transferred from parent to child. As a result, individuals of double lineage—Half-bloods—are allowed, to a certain extent, to occupy the privileged position of the racially superior (Pure-bloods). Thus, if it were not for their direct biological

---

[36] See Judith Butler's *Gender Trouble* (1990, p. 25).

[37] *Order of the Phoenix*, p. 101.

[38] See *Deathly Hallows*, Chapter 13, (pp. 203-220), where Muggle-borns are put on trial for "stealing" magical powers, and p. 425, where the Death Eater Travers refers to a Muggle-born as "it."

[39] See, for example, *The Plunder of Jewish Wealth During the Holocaust: Confronting European History* (2001), edited by Avi Beker.

link to a pure-blood family, Half-bloods would normally be excluded, just like Muggle-borns.

The '*half-blood versus no-blood*' dichotomy may be compared with the disparity between the social privileges enjoyed by lighter-skinned Blacks during the colonial and postcolonial eras. Even as recent as the mid-to-late twentieth century, lighter-skinned individuals of African descent were more socially accepted in higher social spheres, and far more represented in the visual media[40] than their darker-skinned counterparts. Even today, in many postcolonial cultures such as Pakistan, India and the West Indies, lighter skin is still considered to be what Yusuf calls «le symbôle suprême de la beauté» ("the supreme symbol of beauty").[41] As Yusuf explains, this obsession with pale skin was inherited from colonial domination and the self-loathing corollaries of the natives (Blacks, Indians, Pakistanis and so forth) learning to privilege European standards of beauty over their own—a practice which remains "profoundly embedded" in the postcolonial identity even to this day.

The privileging of lighter skin in India's caste system is beautifully dealt with in Arundhati Roy's masterpiece, *The God of Small Things* (1998). And in many other cultures of the developing world, women and men are still required to meet European standards of beauty—for example, having softer-textured hair or a straighter nose—in order to have access to opportunities for social advancement, including ordinary jobs and more lucrative media and modeling careers. Also, the British and European modeling industries have continuously encountered criticism for racial profiling in their choice of models.[42]

Also, if we observe the example of South Africa, we can see that the language of the European master class is a persisting colonial/postcolonial marker of privilege. As Harvey wrote in his thesis on *The Fall of Apartheid* (2001) in

---

[40] Visual media includes television, cinema, billboards, magazines, music videos, brochures, and so forth.

[41] In her article «*Culte de la blancheur au Pakistan et en Inde: Vive les visages pales!*» ("A Thriving Bleaching Culture in Pakistan and India: Hurray to Pale Faces!"). *Courier International*, 2-8 September, 2004, pp. 42-43.

[42] See, for example, Emily Dugan's article in *The Independent*: "Modelling Agencies Blamed for Racist Culture" (October, 2007).

South Africa, the mere fact that the Dutch-rooted Afrikaans—"the language of the oppressor" (p. 71)—was used to educate black children in schools, signaled the continued de-valorization of Blacks and the linguistic/naming power of Whites. And, of course, many among the so-called "Colored" race/group (in the South African context) were perhaps less perturbed by the plight of Blacks because they shared in some of the privileges of the dominant race/group: For instance, perhaps they had better opportunities to learn Afrikaans as a result of being biologically linked to the dominant race. In much the same way, in Rowling's wizarding world, Half-bloods are allowed to partake in Pure-blood privileges at a time when Muggle-borns are completely marginalized and oppressed. And, presumably, just as the Coloreds in South Africa were distinguishable from the Blacks, likewise, the Muggle-born's outsider status in the wizarding world is also grounded in certain aspects of physical appearance...

Although this concept is not fully developed in the novels, Rowling drops a few hints that Pure-bloods have ways of identifying Muggle-borns,[43] which suggests that there is some sort of physical trait which helps to distinguish Muggle-borns from Half-bloods and Pure-bloods. Hence, the Muggle-born group is disenfranchised on both outward appearance and blood status terms. And with no wizard relatives to vouch for them, they are trapped in a static social status, irremediably disempowered under Voldemort's new regime.

As a result, Ron gallantly proposes that they tell people that Hermione is his cousin,[44] but by then it is too late because the entire magical community already knows that she is a Muggle-born and also one of Harry Potter's best friends. And so, due to her disenfranchised social status, Hermione is consummately aware of the "Mudblood" epithet's oppressive role in Voldemort's regime—a role effectively played out because of the power of pejoratives, in general, to coerce and induce performance through verbal violence.

---

[43] For example, Draco warns Hermione to "keep that bushy head down" because Voldemort's supporters know exactly how to "spot a Mudblood" (*Goblet of Fire*, pp. 110-111). And in *Half-blood Prince*, Marvolo Gaunt identifies Muggles and Muggle-borns by the shapes of their noses (pp. 192-194).

[44] See *Deathly Hallows*, p. 173.

Allport ascribed a similar power to the "nigger" epithet, which he believed induced many Blacks during the twentieth century to live according to a designated script of inferiority:

> Ask yourself what would happen to your own personality if you heard it said over and over again that you were lazy, a simple child of nature, expected to steal, and had inferior blood. Suppose this opinion were forced upon you by the majority of your fellow citizens. And suppose nothing you could do would change this opinion—because you happen to have black skin.
> (Allport, 1954/1979, p. 142)

As Jones surmises, "Allport assumed that the constancy of denigration and discrimination took a psychological toll on Black children and Black people generally."[45] Likewise, as I pointed out in Chapter 3 of this volume, the house-elves' minds were broken into submission centuries ago through the use of a similar rhetoric and, of course, physical violence. Similarly, in their attempt to suppress Muggle-borns during the second war, the Death Eaters use physical violence, the threat of violence and the language of violence and denigration to induce a performance of inferiority. And eventually, the Muggle-borns' disenfranchised status becomes instituted: As we see in *Deathly Hallows*, the vast majority of them are now either on the run from the Ministry or begging in the streets.[46]

Still, the defiant resistance displayed by some of the persecuted Muggle-borns in the series finale brings to mind a rather jarring image from Alex Haley's *Roots*, where the African Kunta Kinte is excessively beaten for refusing to accept his European name (Toby). Eventually, Kunta is beaten into submission,[47] but throughout his lifetime he continues to resist the slave's scripted existence and aspire to freedom for himself and his descendants.

---

[45] In his essay "Mechanisms for Coping with Victimization..." in *On the Nature of Prejudice*. (Edited by Dovidio et al., 2005, p. 156)

[46] See, for example, *Deathly Hallows*, p. 425, where a Death Eater refers to Muggle-borns as "the Wandless."

[47] Haley, 1976, p. 214.

Likewise, it is clear that Hermione knows how much her personal pride (in being a Muggle-born) is frustrating to Pure-bloods who would wish to project an image of inferiority upon her. And she refuses to give in. Her self-directed use of the epithet is therefore an act of rebellion against what Taylor and Appiah described as *mis*recognition.[48] For her, embracing the epithet is an act of defiance and resistance which clearly states:

- *I am not ashamed of being a Muggle-born; nor should I be expected to feel that way.*
- *I do not have "dirty blood."*
- *I was born with magical ability and I am deserving of my talents.*
- *I have worked very hard and am deserving of all my achievements.*
- *I am just as worthy and capable as any Pure-blood or Half-blood.*
- *I am entitled to having and displaying confidence and ambition.*
- *You can call me a "Mudblood" but I do not have to perform that ascribed role ... The word has no power over me.*

Hence, the character single-handedly tackles what Adam and Moodley[49] once termed "the psychology of oppression" by engaging in the violence of a broken taboo—the spoken epithet. Hermione's reaction to the new social order in *Deathly Hallows* is obviously one of *non*-compliance: She refuses to admit inferiority, or to sever or deny her connections with the Muggle world. In fact, we even see her subconsciously maintaining the link...

In order to protect Harry and keep their Horcrux quest secret, the trio must temporarily assume fake identities after they are captured by a group of Snatchers. On this occasion, Harry uses an inverted form of his Muggle cousin's name (Vernon Dudley); Ron immediately thinks of Stan Shunpike;

---

[48] See Anthony Appiah and Charles Taylor's essays in *Multiculturalism: Examining the Politics of Recognition*. (1994, pp. 25-73 & 149-163).

[49] In the volume entitled *The Opening of the Apartheid Mind* (1993, p. 110).

but the first name that comes to Hermione's mind is "Penelope Clearwater"[50]—a peripheral Muggle-born character briefly mentioned in *Chamber of Secrets*. And so, even the character's instinctive, non-deliberate actions are emblematic of a refusal to deny her heritage and identity.

***

Now that I have explained why Hermione's acceptance and self-directed use of the "Mudblood" epithet is self-affirmative rather than self-depreciatory, I will now discuss the consequences of this political act for wizarding society as a whole—not all of which prove to be favorable.

Thus far, I have discussed the political significance of the acts of naming and self-naming, as well as highlighted some of the functions served by the self-naming process—such as projecting a desired self-image and expressing a sort of 'self-affirmation.' I have also interpreted Voldemort's self-naming act as one that has generated powerful social taboos and created new notions of the 'sacred.' And so, finally, I will discuss the extent to which Hermione's employment of the "Mudblood" epithet transgresses social boundaries and other notions of the sacred taboo.

In *Chamber of Secrets*, where Draco calls Hermione a "filthy little Mudblood" (p. 86) for the first time, the severity of the insult is reflected in the furious response it provokes from Ron and the entire Gryffindor Quidditch team—except Harry, who, like Hermione, was raised in a Muggle home and therefore had no idea what the word meant:

> Harry knew at once that Malfoy had said something really bad because there was an instant uproar at his words. Flint had to dive in front of Malfoy to stop Fred and George from jumping on him, Alicia shrieked *'How dare you!'* and Ron plunged his hand into his robes, pulled out his wand, yelling, 'You'll pay for that one, Malfoy!' and pointed it furiously under Flint's arm at Malfoy's face.
> (*Chamber of Secrets*, p. 87)

---

[50] *Deathly Hallows*, p. 363.

Based on these characters' reactions, it is clear that vocalizing the "Mudblood" epithet is as powerful a social taboo in the wizarding world as the "nigger," "kike" or "faggot" epithets are in the real world. And, as previously mentioned, the word itself suggests that Muggle-borns are '*unclean.*' But the act of *saying* the epithet also makes the speaker unclean. In other words, Draco projects an unclean (as in 'foul-mouthed') image of himself by transgressing this social taboo.

Likewise, when Hermione uses the "Mudblood" pejorative for self-reference, it is also an act of transgression which projects a dually '*unclean*' image of her self: First, breaking the social taboo of using foul language commits her to the realm of the '*unclean*' (or foul-mouthed), as with Draco. Second, unlike real-world pejoratives such as "queer" or even "nigger," due to its semantic content, "Mudblood" can never really be taken out of its historical context. In other words, because of its unavoidable association with 'mud,' or 'dirt,' Mudblood will never denote anything other than "dirty blood." Therefore, in a sense, Hermione is literally admitting that she is "dirty"—although, as we have already surmised, this is not her intention. And so, although the taboo-breaking act is a significantly revolutionary step for Hermione, and although her motivations for using the word are primarily positive, it also has some drastically negative consequences, which she has clearly not considered.

Most notably, she has created yet another social taboo: Even in our own world, many a political career has ended over rancor caused by the use of the scorching epithet, "faggot"—although, as I already mentioned, many homosexuals use the term jokingly to refer to each other. And it is still forbidden for a white person to refer to a black person as a "nigger," although the term is casually used amongst Blacks. And so, one could argue that, when an out-group embraces injurious epithets, it might send the wrong messages to the society at large: i.e., either that the historical context of the term is no longer central to the group's contemporary social issues, or that it is suddenly permissible for everyone to transgress the social taboo and use the forbidden term freely. But, as we know, neither of these statements is true. And so, the use of tabooed epithets could have inauspicious social consequences for both out-groups and the mainstream.

In the same way that the socio-moral imperatives of '*political correctness*' now forbid the dominant heterosexual group from referring to homosexuals as "faggots," or Whites from calling Blacks as "niggers" without retribution, likewise, it will never be socially acceptable for Ron and Harry to call Hermione a "Mudblood"—not even in jest. And so, while being able to use the word without fear empowers her, it effectively distances her from her best friends.

And besides, if we compare Hermione's transgressive act to that of Harry saying "Voldemort" throughout the series—whilst most of his peers and elders avoid using the name—we can see that Harry's taboo-breaking is, ironically, more socially acceptable and 'inclusive' than Hermione's. For example, in *Philosopher's Stone*, we see Harry—new to the wizarding world— finding it much easier to break the taboo of saying "Voldemort" than using the more socially acceptable "You-Know-Who" or "He Who Must Not Be Named." And he was commended for this, because back then it was perceived as an act of bravery to break the taboo. In fact, Dumbledore encouraged the boy to speak the forbidden word, insisting that one must "always use the proper name for things" (p. 216). And by saying the name out loud, Harry stripped it of its fear-inducing power; and, like Hermione, his daring put him on another level, separate from those who refused to break the taboo of speaking the forbidden name.

However, what distinguishes Harry's taboo-breaking (at age 11) from that of Hermione in the series finale, is that, if people wanted to overcome the fear of saying "Voldemort,"[51] social conventions 'allowed' them to imitate Harry. And, we see that, throughout the series, Harry rightly encourages his peers—often ignoring Ron's apprehensive whimpers—to defy the taboo just as Dumbledore had taught him. However, in contrast, Hermione will never be able to say '*it's OK to call me a "Mudblood"*.'

After all, as Freud once explained, one of the objectives of the traditional Polynesian taboo was to protect and safeguard

[51] In *Order of the Phoenix*, Hermione says the Dark Lord's name for the first time (p. 293), while Ron remains afraid to do so.

certain individuals (famous people or vulnerable persons such as targeted minority groups or the aged) from harm.[52] Hence, the social, political and cultural taboo that is placed on the "Mudblood" pejorative serves the purpose of protecting Muggle-borns from verbal violence. And, as we see in *Deathly Hallows*, where Harry has to face the harsh consequence of seeing his friends captured when he says Voldemort's name, the breaker of any taboo becomes, himself, tabooed: i.e., cut off from others and punished.[53]

Therefore, by violating the prohibition on saying "Mudblood," Hermione has created a sort of Freudian quarantine around herself, which all social Others—especially 'racial'[54] elites like Ron and Harry—are forbidden to access. Similar to the discriminatory politics that aim to maintain social distance[55] between the dominant Pure-blood/Half-blood group and all social Others—by keeping people like Hermione or Remus Lupin out of pure-blood spaces (including Hogwarts, the Ministry of Magic and the Top Box at the Quidditch World Cup)—, Hermione has created a new space that further distinguishes her from Ron and Harry. Thus, boldly going where her friends cannot follow is a sort of micro-reversal of empowerment for her, but it remains uncertain whether her taboo-breaking act has any other meaningful or useful outcome.

***

In conclusion, even after a rather lengthy discussion in this chapter, we are still left to ponder the socio-political conundrum of minority groups embracing abusive epithets. As demonstrated through Hermione's intentional, self-targeted use of the "Mudblood" pejorative, embracing an epithet can be a means of reclaiming the power of naming from the dominant group or racial elite. However, we must

---

[52] See Strachey's translation of *Totem and Taboo*, 2001, p. 23

[53] Ibid, p. 38.

[54] I continue to use this word with apprehension, obviously for want of a better word.

[55] See Katz's work for a closer examination of the theories related to social distance.

ask ourselves whether it ought to be socially acceptable for minority groups to casually use hate speech terms, while everyone else (or any other group) must necessarily be chastised for using the same words. Is this a kind of social hypocrisy? And besides, since Dumbledore emphasizes the importance of referring to things by their real names, and since we know that Hermione is not, in any sense of the word, a "Mudblood", should she be referring to herself as such?

In coining the term *"Vol de mort"* for himself, the Dark Lord believed he could literally escape death and attain immortality. Likewise, Hermione embraces the "Mudblood" epithet, partly out of a belief that she can deny or overcome the derogatory denotations of its historical and semantic contexts. In a sense, both characters are mistaken: As we know, Voldemort's immortality is conditional upon no one ever finding out about his Horcruxes. And the fact that Hermione embraces the pejorative does not necessarily mean that she will be henceforth impenetrable to its offensiveness—particularly when the term is employed by malicious pure-blood elitists.

And so, defying the taboo empowers her only as far as the transgression allows her to redefine the pejorative *for herself*, thus reducing the fear and intense sensitivity associated with it, and ridding it *momentarily* and *conditionally* (depending on who uses it) of its power to offend or belittle. But the fact that she can utter the epithet unreservedly does not rid it of its historical significance. Nor does it nullify or erase the term's biological denotations of degeneracy and "dirtiness" because, as previously surmised, the association with 'dirt' and 'mud' makes traditional denotations of "Mudblood" virtually inalterable. And, most importantly, Hermione's use of the pejorative creates a towering semantic wall between her self and her half-blood and pure-blood peers.

Finally, our own world history is littered with words that were once coercively imposed to diminish the outsider's humanity; and while some social commentators maintain that it is a self-dehumanizing act to embrace a historically abusive epithet, others insist that the out-group's use of the forbidden word strips it of its power to victimize them. Conversely, one could also argue that embracing a pejorative does not necessarily rid it of its power to offend, but instead creates a strange sort of inverted dichotomy of empowerment, whereby further barriers are erected—this time to keep 'insiders' from meddling in 'outsider' territory. As a result, instead of more cohesiveness and unity between socially dominant groups and minority groups, we have further separations (or inversions) of privilege and power.

Chapter 6

Parenting and Prejudice

There are examples of various kinds of parenting in the *Harry Potter* novels. From Harry's Muggle relatives (the Dursleys) to wizard parents such as the Weasleys and the Malfoys, and even minor characters like Remus Lupin and the Gaunts (Voldemort's wizard relatives), Rowling uses her parental figures to demonstrate how prejudice becomes what Allison[1] calls "a chronic or major life event" from early childhood onwards. Naturally, some prejudices acquired during childhood become "normative" over a person's lifetime, through what Allport described as "sheer conformity."[2] And so, in this chapter I will examine the roles that child upbringing or parenting play in forming the social outlook and personalities of some of the characters in the *Harry Potter* series.

***

At this stage in our discussion, the one truth that should be clear by now is that prejudice is not unique to malevolent or 'evil' people, in the same way that sadness is not monopolized by the clinically depressed. I have stated in previous chapters that prejudice is sometimes difficult to recognize, particularly when it has become a social 'norm.' And so, acquiring prejudice is mostly—though not uniquely—a matter of upbringing, because it results from what Devine and Sinclair et al. describe as "non-conscious, non-volitional (i.e. implicit) attitudes" towards social Others. These attitudes "develop via exposure to socializing agents (e.g., parents, peers and the media)."[3]

In other words, we learn to think and feel a certain way about certain things or certain kinds of people because of

---

[1] In his article entitled "Stress and Oppressed Social Category Membership," from *Prejudice: The Target's Perspective*. (Edited by Swim and Stangor, 1998, p. 150).

[2] Allport, 1954/1979, pp. 285-296.

[3] See abstract to essay entitled "The Relationship Between Parental Racial Attitudes and Children's Implicit Prejudice." (Sinclair et al., 2005, p. 283).

images and opinions projected upon us throughout our lives, since childhood. And, as a result, we come to have certain expectations of ourselves as well as social Others; and these thoughts and/or opinions are based upon what can best be described as our 'sense of *entitlement*.'

We could argue that the least malevolent forms of prejudice do not '*purposefully*' dictate or encroach upon the entitlement of social Others. In contrast, the more overt kinds of prejudice occur when people genuinely believe that they are entitled to certain things—privileges normally denied to other individuals or groups—because they are innately superior. And, as J.K. Rowling skillfully demonstrates in the *Harry Potter* novels, both kinds of prejudiced thinking and behavior have their roots in child upbringing, or parenting.

Although Allport explained that there are "certain conditions of child training that are likely to prevail in prejudiced homes,"[4] he also cautioned against over-generalizing the parental role in prejudice acquisition in children. But while children do not become "mirror images" of their parents, they will assimilate many of their parents' value judgments, or what Allport described as "idiosyncrasies":

> Although conformity with the home atmosphere is undoubtedly the most important single source of prejudice, it must not be thought that the child grows up to be a mirror image of his parent's attitudes. Nor is it true that the parents' attitudes are always in conformity with the prejudices prevailing in their community.
>
> What the father and mother transmit to their offspring is their own personal version of cultural traditions. They may be skeptical concerning the stereotypes current in their community, and pass their skepticism on to their children. They may have a few pet prejudices of their own that are not represented in their cultural group. Unless the child picks up outside the home the standard attitudes of the community, his pattern of prejudice will reflect whatever idiosyncrasies the parents have imposed.
>
> (Allport, 1954/1979, p. 294)

---

[4] Allport, 1954/1979, p. 398.

Allport later added that children may sometimes come to question their parents' value-attitudes and prejudices. And later in this chapter I will highlight some examples from the *Harry Potter* novels, where similar developments take place. But for now, I wish to focus on the "idiosyncrasies" mentioned above, many of which are merely '*gut feelings*' or traditional views about social Others, which are not necessarily hostile but still covertly prejudiced.

***

One example of a covert, less intentional expression of prejudice occurs in *Deathly Hallows*, where Harry, Hermione and Ron are on the run and scrounging for food. An injured, moody and hungry Ron complains about Hermione's cooking, saying that his own mother "can make food appear out of thin air" (p. 240). Hermione later complains that the boys expect her to be the one to prepare food because she is a *girl* (p. 241), which implies that—at least from Hermione's point of view—gender roles in the wizarding world are still submitted to occupational segregation,[5] or what Siltanen and Murgatroyd called "the sex-typing of jobs."[6]

But Ron denies the implied accusation of sexism, insisting that Hermione is only expected to cook because she is better at magic than him or Harry (p. 241). Perhaps Hermione is indeed a bit sensitive about being the only girl in the trio; nevertheless, the unfair and somewhat spiteful comparison with his mother incriminates Ron, who, at this stage, is still extremely immature and takes his mother's attentions and care for granted.

Ron displays an unconscious bias regarding gender roles, partly because he has yet to realize how privileged he is to have a stay-at-home mother who looks after him and caters to his every need. His situation is obviously very different from the orphaned Harry, who has been treated poorly by the Dursleys nearly all his life. Ron's twin brothers, Fred and

---

[5] Beechey, 1979 & 1983.

[6] In Siltanen's essay entitled "Domestic Responsibilities and the Structuring of Employment," from *Gender Stratification*, 1986, p. 99.

George, show due appreciation to Molly in the sixth book, after moving away from home to start their business:

> "Well, we find we appreciate you more and more, Mum, now we're washing our own socks."
> (*Half-blood Prince*, p. 318)

But most importantly, Ron's remark demonstrates what Rudman describes as "the ordinariness of gender prejudice"[7]—a topic which does not feature at all in *The Nature of Prejudice*, because Allport's definition of prejudice was somewhat limited to the notion of "antipathy" towards out-groups. Ron's feelings towards Hermione are clearly not "antipathetic"; nor does he "reject" or perceive her as a member of an out-group. His sexist attitudes merely comply with societal norms, which are primarily based on the overriding ideology of patriarchy.

I mentioned in Chapter 3 of this volume that some of the *Harry Potter* readers whom I had interviewed for this project perceived the house-elf slavery subplot as symbolic of motherhood—the daily grind of providing and caring for children being so often a thankless job, plus the fact that most mothers adore and serve their children unconditionally. Similarly, the comparison Ron makes between Hermione and his mother (as cooks)—and Hermione's reaction to it—brings to mind Gustave Flaubert's assertion that male-dominated culture and religion are enslavement mechanisms for women. The protagonist (Emma) in *Madame Bovary* also rejects the sexual politics of her time, but unlike Hermione, her choices, as well as her ability to voice her discontentment, are extremely limited.

Also, although Ron is not intentionally 'sexist,' he does have certain expectations which are perhaps best qualified by using Rudman's concept of *implicit prejudice stereotypes*,[8] which are maintained not only by males like Ron but also by

---

[7] From the Introduction to *On the Nature of Prejudice*. (Edited by Dovidio et al., 2005, p. 11)

[8] In her essay entitled "Rejection of Women? Beyond Prejudice as Antipathy" in *On the Nature of Prejudice*. (Edited by Dovidio et al., 2005, pp. 110-111)

women who embrace their designated societal roles as simply 'the way things ought to be.' Ron's attitude certainly betrays a sense of entitlement to care and comfort provided by a female; and, of course, the ever politically conscious Hermione tries to bring this to his attention.

But Ron's gender prejudice has not necessarily been directly transmitted from parent to child: According to Rupert Brown, sociologists have struggled to establish empirical evidence to support the claim that parents directly influence their children's gender attitudes (1995, p. 152).[9] Still, Ron's attitudes were certainly acquired on a societal level which is grounded in home life. After all, children inevitably assimilate or acquire normative beliefs through observing others in their social environment. These include parents, peers, siblings, television programs, and so forth. And the idea that the roles of 'homemaker' and 'nurturer' are more suited for girls and women than for boys and men is one example of dominant ideologies which can be easily assimilated without any overt expression from an external source.

In addition, throughout the series Ron's character is constantly portrayed as someone who does not easily rethink his assumptions about social Others. And in Chapter 3 of this volume, I discussed how, rather unlike Hermione and Harry, Ron usually accepts wizarding society's stereotypes about out-groups without scrutinizing the information for himself. On numerous occasions, we see him expressing deep-seated antipathetic feelings about out-groups such as goblins,[10] werewolves[11] and giants.[12] Consequently, we may deduce from Molly Weasley's aversion to the idea of a werewolf sharing her husband's hospital room—two weeks before the full moon[13]—that much of Ron's social outlook was acquired at home.

---

[9] See also Maccoby and Jacklin (1987) and Zuckerman et al. (1980).

[10] See *Deathly Hallows*, pp. 409-410, where Ron questions Griphook's integrity and slates goblins in general, blaming them for the acrimonious relationship between their group and the wizard race.

[11] See *Prisoner of Azkaban*, p. 253, where Ron expresses disgust and shrinks away from Lupin's touch, after discovering the Professor's werewolf status.

[12] See *Goblet of Fire*, pp. 373-377, where Ron reacts aversely to the discovery that Hagrid is half-giant.

[13] As I mentioned in Chapter 4, Molly is categorized as a '*Traditionalist*' because of her general attitude towards out-groups. See also *Order of the Phoenix*, pp. 431-432.

Even his tolerance towards Muggles and his open acceptance of Muggle-borns are tempered by an air of superiority which, ironically, he might have learned from an extremely kind-hearted father. Gupta rightly observes that, in his obsession with all things concerning Muggles, Arthur Weasley has "an air of an entomologist studying insects ... and could be thought of as rather patronizing towards Muggles."[14] Hermione identifies similar attitudes in Ron, who, like his father, is very much interested in hearing about Muggle activities. But Ron's interest in Muggles mostly gives him reason to amuse himself by commenting on their strangeness.

For example, in *Order of the Phoenix*, we see him making fun of Hermione's family, questioning why anyone would want to slide down a mountain on a pair of sticks (or go skiing). Most of Ron's jibes are harmless banter, but it is clear that Hermione sometimes takes offence to it. For instance, she later asks Harry not to tell Ron how much she herself dislikes skiing: "I told him skiing's really good because he kept laughing so much" (p. 440). Ron's patronizing view of Muggles is obviously not meant to be taken as seriously as his antipathy towards the aforementioned magical out-groups. But it still stems from an intrinsic belief in wizard superiority and Muggle inferiority—as opposed to simply acknowledging that Muggles are *different* from wizards.

However, the aforementioned Weasley examples are only 'mild' expressions of prejudice. And besides, one would expect a highly maternal figure such as Molly to worry about harm coming to her family from werewolves—an out-group that has a justified reputation for violence towards wizards. Likewise, it is natural that a magically empowered, benevolent wizard like Arthur should be inclined to regard Muggles with an endearing and slightly condescending eye. And moreover, the fact that Hermione ends up marrying Ron[15] will give Arthur a chance to rethink his assumptions about Muggles, and to learn to view them as equals rather than patronizing them.

And so, although Molly and Arthur are to a certain extent responsible for their son's varying degrees and manifestations

---

[14] Gupta, 2003, p. 106.

[15] The series finale's Epilogue ("Nineteen Years Later") confirms that Harry and Ginny have started a family together; so have Hermione and Ron.

of prejudice towards out-groups, it must be said that their own beliefs and attitudes are as influenced by societal norms as Ron's.

In addition, J.K. Rowling constantly alludes to the role that environment plays in shaping not only social outlook but also personal sensitivity to social issues. For example, by contrasting Hermione and Harry with Ron in *Chamber of Secrets* (in terms of how differently they react when Draco calls Hermione a "Mudblood"), she shows how society dictates and influences people's feelings about everything—including pejoratives. At this stage in the series, Ron is the only member of the trio who knows what "Mudblood" means, or how offensive it is in the social context of the wizarding world. Hence, Hermione and Harry must learn to recognize the term as an epithet and be offended by its use.

Conversely, Ron and his siblings are initially unable to recognize the house-elves' plight as extreme cruelty and overt prejudice because they (and their parents) have been socially conditioned to believe that slavery is the house-elves' '*natural*' role. However, as we see in *Deathly Hallows*, Ron finally '*un*learns' the flawed knowledge he has held all his life about the inferior humanity of house-elves in relation to that of wizards.[16] And so, the character's sense of loyalty to his friends and his general responsiveness to good role models are commendable traits: Ron responds to the "Mudblood" insult because he sees it as his duty to protect Hermione as a friend and loved one; and, gradually, he comes to attribute similar humanity to the house-elves. And these are, essentially, the qualities and *choices* that distinguish him from elitist Pure-bloods like Draco Malfoy.

We see that both Ron and Draco have been raised by their own wizard parents; but where one is open, accepting and even protective towards some social Others, the other is close-minded, elitist and aggressively '*racist*'[17] towards all out-groups. And so, the fact that Molly and Ron eventually embrace Lupin—a known member of the stigmatized

[16] See *Deathly Hallows*, p. 502, where Ron suggests evacuating the house-elves along with the students, prior to the Battle of Hogwarts.

[17] Once again, I use this adjective only for want of a better word.

werewolf group—and treat him with dignity, shows that they are naturally open-minded, good-hearted people.

And so, despite the fact that they are occasional purveyors of societal stereotypes and mild prejudices towards out-groups, Molly and Arthur at least try to set a good example for their children. Generally, they recognize the humanity of social Others and treat them respectfully.[18] And, as a result, Ron is far more disposed to overcoming his traditionalist views about out-groups than Draco Malfoy will ever be. It is rather admirable that, as a member of the privileged Pure-blood class, Ron so willingly supports his friends as they cross the artificial boundaries of social difference—notwithstanding his initial refusal to join S.P.E.W.

***

In sharp contrast to the main characters (including Ron), Dudley Dursley and Draco Malfoy are the two most conspicuous examples of overtly prejudiced children in the *Harry Potter* novels. And throughout most of the series, these two boys show a total lack of empathy for social Others within their respective environments—Dudley obviously belonging to the Muggle world and Draco to the magical community. Also, Draco and Dudley's expressions of prejudice are far more serious and purposefully malicious than Ron's sexist outburst about Hermione's cooking, or even his initial fear and antipathy towards werewolves, which he soon overcomes.

In both Dudley and Draco's cases, the manner in which the boys acquired their prejudice has less to do with general every-day socialization in the outside world and far more to do with parental behavior and indoctrination at home. And so, in either case, it is difficult to point the finger of blame at anyone but the parents. The two boys have been bombarded (at home) with both subtle suggestion and demonstrations of blatant material disparities between privileged insiders and despised outsiders. And, as a result, both boys have been implicitly and explicitly encouraged by their parents to regard

[18] For instance, in *Goblet of Fire* (pp. 12-124), Arthur Weasley is the only one among the Ministry officials who refers to the house-elf Winky by her name—as opposed to simply addressing her as "elf!"—the way Amos Diggory does repeatedly.

social Others as '*lesser*' beings—less worthy, less capable, less loveable, less human.

Dudley and Draco are, quite literally, worlds apart; and they also differ greatly in terms of physical appearance.[19] But both boys have been spoilt by their mothers and have a tendency to bully other children. They also tend to manipulate their parents into getting what they want. But what incriminates the parents (the Dursleys and the Malfoys) is the flawed sense of entitlement which they have purposefully instilled in these two boys.

For instance, in *Chamber of Secrets* we see Draco criticizing Harry and Arthur Weasley for their lack of "pride" or "proper wizard feeling" (p. 166) because of their sympathy towards Muggles and Muggle-borns. Draco, like his parents, does not believe that Muggle-borns are entitled to being treated the same as other wizards. But a twelve-year-old boy cannot be solely blamed for taking on such a highly prejudiced view: Clearly, his parents have led him to think this way. Similarly, throughout the series, Dudley's parents send a clear message to him that he is entitled to better (as in far more humane) treatment than Harry, simply because he is their son and Harry is not. They also encourage Dudley to perceive Harry as 'less human' or "*abnormal*" because he is a wizard.

Ironically, Dudley is the first child whom Rowling introduces to her readership. The first pages of *Philosopher's Stone* paint the perfect portrait of privilege and parental pampering for the Dursleys' only child, before taking us to the spider-infested cupboard under the stairs to meet the persecuted protagonist, Harry. And so, even the author's ordering of events here symbolizes Harry's status in the Dursley household: second-best and down-trodden. Dudley's introduction is therefore undercut with tremendous sarcasm:

> The Dursleys had a small son called Dudley and in their opinion there was no finer boy anywhere.
> (*Philosopher's Stone*, p. 7)

---

[19] In *Philosopher's Stone* Dudley is described as "four times bigger" than Harry (p. 20), so he obviously has a serious weight problem. In contrast, when we meet Draco for the first time he is described as "pale" and "pointed-faced" (p. 59).

Later we are told that beating up on Harry was Dudley's favorite pastime (p. 24)—a habit which he no doubt picked up from a father who physically threatens ["'*You'll get the stuffing knocked out of you*'"[20]] and verbally abuses his cousin in front of him, and who also encourages him to physically abuse Harry ["'Poke him with your Smeltings stick, Dudley'"[21]].

Harry's aunt, Petunia, also goes out of her way to impress upon Dudley that he is entitled to better treatment than Harry.[22] Not only is he lavished with dozens of expensive presents on his birthdays—in sharp contrast to Harry, who usually gets a pair of old, moldy socks or some other cheap, unwanted object—but also, Petunia has no pictures of her nephew anywhere in the house.[23] And she normally excludes Harry from family outings. Also, the Dursleys often lock Harry away in his room whenever they are entertaining guests,[24] thus making it clear to both boys that Harry is not counted as part of the family.

Therefore, Dudley merely imitates his parents in being hateful and abusive towards his cousin, and these habits, which are incurred and encouraged in the home, are transferred to other social settings such as school and the wider community. For example, we discover in *Goblet of Fire* that teachers have accused Dudley, in their school reports, of bullying his peers (p. 29). And, in *Order of the Phoenix*, we see Dudley joking with his gang about beating up a boy less than half his size: "'...squealed like a pig, didn't he?' Malcolm was saying, to guffaws from the others." (p. 16)

---

[20] *Prisoner of Azkaban*, p. 21.

[21] *Philosopher's Stone*, p. 30.

[22] See, for example, *Goblet of Fire*, p. 30, where Petunia forces her entire family to go on a strict diet because of Dudley's weight problem. At breakfast, Harry gets a much smaller quarter of grapefruit because "Aunt Petunia seemed to feel that the best way to keep up Dudley's morale was to make sure that he did, at least, get more to eat than Harry."

[23] See *Philosopher's Stone*, p. 19, where we see the Dursleys' living room ten years after the death of Harry's parents: "The room held no sign at all that another boy lived in the house, too."

[24] See, for example, the first two chapters of *Chamber of Secrets*, where the Dursleys host the Masons, whom they inform that Harry must be kept locked away because he is "very disturbed" (p. 20).

Of course, Dudley is a parenting disaster; and the only people who fail to recognize this are his own parents. The Dursleys, who never hesitate to speak of Harry's so-called *delinquency*,[25] refuse to acknowledge Dudley's flaws:

> They ... skated over the accusations of bullying in [Dudley's] report—'He's a boisterous little boy, but he wouldn't hurt a fly!' said Aunt Petunia tearfully.
> (*Goblet of Fire*, p. 29)

And so, Petunia and Vernon Dursley purposefully transmit a flawed sense of entitlement to Dudley: first, by very obviously differentiating him from Harry in terms of material comforts, and second, by meting out less than humane treatment to Harry whilst Dudley is being pampered. No doubt, such persistent persecution gives Dudley the impression that Harry *deserves* to be despised.

Allport would have identified the Dursleys' behavior as an example of when "parental words and gestures, along with their concomitant beliefs and antagonisms, are transferred to the child."[26] Through their actions (for example, the extreme preferential treatment they shower on Dudley), Vernon and Petunia Dursley make it clear that Harry is just an unwanted, orphaned nephew (and a 'freakish' outsider), thus projecting the message to both boys that '*Harry is not like us and does not really belong here.*' And this is no different from the mantra of extremists who target social Others with violence because of racial or religious differences.

Petunia's abuse is also an act of vengeance: She always felt that her parents had favored her sister Lily, Harry's mother:

> '...I was the only one who saw her for what she was—a freak! But for my mother and father, oh no, it was Lily

[25] See *Prisoner of Azkaban* (pp. 20-21), where Vernon Dursley forces Harry to tell other people that he goes to "St. Brutus's Secure Centre for Incurably Criminal Boys," and *Order of the Phoenix*, (pp. 15-16), where we are told that the neighbors often comment on Harry's "delinquent appearance."

[26] Allport, 1954/1979, p. 297.

> this and Lily that, they were proud of having a witch in the family!'
> (*Philosopher's Stone*, p. 44)

Petunia was obviously jealous of Lily, because having magical powers entailed a sense of empowerment that she herself had always craved but could not have. Towards the end of the series, we discover that the teenage Petunia had written to Dumbledore, asking him to allow her to attend Hogwarts, despite the fact that she was a Muggle. And so, when she finally realized that Lily's power and achievements were beyond her reach, she turned against her sister and proceeded to despise everything associated with the magical world. Rather than admitting her own jealousy and dealing with it in a more humane, respectable manner, Petunia chose, instead, to curse and persecute Lily (and by extension, Harry), describing them both as "abnormal" and "freaks."[27]

It is also remarkable—and rather amusing—that Vernon and Petunia Dursley would rather have their relatives and neighbors believe that they are harboring an "incurably criminal"[28] boy rather than a wizard. Petunia's animosity toward wizardkind is fuelled, on the one hand, by a desperate need to be, like Lily, accomplished and extraordinary in some way. Hence, the Dursleys glorify the idea of being "normal,"[29] because this is what they are good at; and so, anything or anyone remarkable or exceptional must be regarded with fear and suspicion.

And still, on the other hand, there is also a sense of intense maternal protectiveness for Dudley—as though they are desperately trying to shelter him from something far more insidious ... We may deduce from information provided in the books that Petunia had suffered severely as a child because of what she perceived as her parents' preferential treatment towards the witch Lily. And now, she wants to shelter her son

---

[27] See *Philosopher's Stone*, p. 44 and *Deathly Hallows*, p. 537.

[28] *Prisoner of Azkaban*, p. 20.

[29] The very first sentence of *Philosopher's Stone* tells of how much the Dursleys were "proud to say that they were perfectly normal, thank you very much" (p. 7). And in *Prisoner of Azkaban*, Vernon Dursley warns Harry not to let Aunt Marge discover his "*abnormality*" (p. 20).

from whatever she experienced: Perhaps it was the feeling that she was useless, or that, no matter how hard she tried, she was never going to be as talented or as admired as her sister. And so, Petunia goes to the extreme, treating Harry harshly not only because he belongs to an outsider group that she has come to stigmatize, but also in order to protect her son from feelings of being '*second best*' or '*not good enough*.' Clearly, the idea that Harry is "abnormal" or "freakish" undermines his and Lily's humanity. But from Petunia's point of view, this is a small price to pay for giving Dudley what she believes to be a healthy sense of self-esteem—perhaps his own sense of entitlement to the '*superior feeling*,' or simply the pride or reassurance that comes from being the '*favorite*.'

Unfortunately though, as Dumbledore points out to her in *Half-blood Prince*, in trying to build Dudley's self-esteem at the expense of Harry's humanity, Petunia has done her son more harm than good:

> '...I left [Harry] upon your doorstep fifteen years ago, with a letter explaining about his parents' murder and expressing the hope that you would care for him as though he were your own ... You did not do as I asked. You have never treated Harry as a son. He has known nothing but neglect and often cruelty at your hands. The best that can be said is that he has at least escaped the appalling damage you have inflicted upon the unfortunate boy sitting between you.'
>
> Both Aunt Petunia and Uncle Vernon looked around instinctively, as though expecting to see someone other than Dudley squeezed between them.
>
> ...Dudley was frowning slightly, as though he was ... trying to work out when he had ever been mistreated. (*Half-blood Prince*, pp. 57-58)

And so, Dudley has been raised to be greedy, selfish, abusive and completely lacking in compassion for others—particularly for Harry—and it is mostly Petunia's fault. Petunia's acrimony towards her sister recalls the discussion in Chapter 1, where I briefly cited *envy* as one factor that fuels prejudice.

In this case, we see that, more than a decade after her sister's death, Petunia is still haunted by childhood jealousy: She perceives Dudley's non-magical status as 'ordinariness' in comparison to Harry's 'extraordinary' magical abilities; and she is secretly awed and resentful of Harry's association with wizardkind. It reminds her of feeling ordinary and overlooked alongside her witch sister. Still, while the Evans (Lily and Petunia's parents) may or may not have favored their witch daughter, even if they had, it still would not justify Petunia's hateful words and attitude, or the maltreatment and neglect she would later mete out on an innocent boy.

Nevertheless, Petunia's instinctive (and rather typical) reaction is to deny her own prejudice. She has simply concluded that Lily and Harry '*deserve*' to be treated with resentment and persecution because they are "abnormal." This is an example of an Allportian concept that I briefly mentioned in Chapter 2: "prejudice without compunction."[30] In this case, the bearer of prejudice (Petunia) evades guilt by justifying the conditions or the causes of her hatred for the social Other (her witch sister and/or her wizard nephew). It is clear that Petunia transfers responsibility for her own intolerant feelings from herself to Lily and Harry, thus demonizing them and the out-group to which they belong (magical beings).

And, as Rowling herself has stated in a recent interview, many "years of pretending" have "hardened" Petunia to the point where she is utterly incapable of openly showing compassion to her nephew. [31] For instance, in *Deathly Hallows*, we finally see Dudley reaching out to Harry with expressions of kindness and gratitude because he knows that there is a war going on and that Harry might die (pp. 37-39). But although Petunia has far greater knowledge of the wizarding world than her son, and although she knows that she might never see her nephew again, she remains emotionally stunted, evidently incapacitated by a lifetime of jealousy and bitterness. And so, unlike other characters who have at least shown a willingness to overcome feelings of

[30] Allport, 1954/1979, p. 380.
[31] Interview in October 2007 at Carnegie Hall, Manhattan, NewYork.

antipathy or indifference towards out-groups, Petunia has never learned to overcome her prejudice towards magical beings like Harry and Lily.

***

Ironically, the wizard parents whom Petunia and Vernon Dursley most resemble are some of the most prejudiced (as in 'anti-Muggle') Pure-bloods: Narcissa and Lucius Malfoy. And despite the fact that they inhabit different social spheres, Lucius Malfoy and Vernon Dursley have many things in common: Both are resolutely closed-minded towards social Others; neither one hesitates to resort to physical violence; and both characters believe that the corresponding outsider group is the source of all the world's problems.

For example, when speaking to Harry about wizardkind, Vernon constantly refers to them as "your lot,"[32] and he does so in a manner which suggests that nothing good can be expected from such people. He even expresses surprise that there is a Ministry of Magic:

> 'People like you in *government*? Oh, this explains everything, no wonder the country is going to the dogs.' (*Order of the Phoenix*, p. 32)

Similarly, Lucius Malfoy's annoyance with Dumbledore and Arthur Weasley is mostly because of their sympathetic attitudes towards Muggles and open acceptance of Muggle-borns.[33] It is therefore no surprise that both the Malfoys and the Dursleys have encouraged bullying and purposefully poisoned their children's minds against the social Other (magical people in Dudley's case, and Muggle-borns in Draco's case).

A rather amusing parallel is drawn between Dudley Dursley and Draco Malfoy quite early in the series, as Harry

---

[32] See, for example, *Philosopher's Stone* (p. 11), where he refers to Lily's friends as "*her lot*" and *Order of the Phoenix* (p. 11), where he forbids Harry from watching television on the grounds that "*Your lot* don't get on *our* news."

[33] See, for example, *Chamber of Secrets* (p. 43), where Lucius describes Arthur as a "Muggle-loving fool."

develops a deep dislike for Draco even before learning his name or discovering his family's ties to Slytherin House.

> 'Hullo,' said the boy, 'Hogwarts too?'
>
> 'Yes,' said Harry.
>
> 'My father's next door buying my books and my mother's up the street looking at wands,' said the boy. He had a bored, drawling voice. 'Then I'm going to drag them off to look at racing brooms. I don't see why first-years can't have their own. I think I'll bully father into getting me one and I'll smuggle it in somehow.'
>
> Harry was strongly reminded of Dudley...
>
> '...Why is [Hagrid] with you? Where are your parents?'
>
> 'They're dead,' said Harry shortly. He didn't feel much like going into the matter with this boy.
>
> 'Oh, sorry,' said the other, not sounding sorry at all. 'But they were *our* kind, weren't they?'
>
> 'They were a witch and wizard, if that's what you mean.'
>
> 'I really don't think they should let the other sort in, do you? They're just not the same, they've never been brought up to know our ways.'
>
> (*Philosopher's Stone*, pp. 60-61)

Here, we see a young Draco attempting to establish solidarity with a new acquaintance by expressing "antilocution"[34] towards Muggle-borns—a group he knows absolutely nothing about. Because Harry has two wizard parents, Draco automatically assumes that he agrees with him, and that he shares the same prejudices. Draco's limited world view tells him that, all persons who meet the crucial criterion of having wizard blood must necessarily believe that Muggle-borns are inferior and irreconcilably different. And, as I mentioned earlier, the boy's presumptions are clearly a result of his parents indoctrinating him with ideas about the Muggle-born's innate inferiority—as though it were a universally acknowledged truth. This is somewhat similar to the way the

---

[34] See the 'Definition of Key Terms' section at the beginning of this volume (p. 8), and Allport, 1954/1979, p. 14.

Dursleys demonstrate to their son, on a daily basis, that Harry is *different*—and therefore entitled to *different* (lesser) things and *different* (less humane) treatment. And furthermore, Draco's insistence that they should not "let the other sort" into Hogwarts suggests that he has been exposed to some sort of 'segregation' rhetoric.

Segregationists in post-slavery North America used similar arguments (that Blacks should be kept separate from Whites because they were intrinsically and fundamentally different) to justify Black-White segregation in schools, churches, on buses and so forth. But even as far back as the late 19th Century, social commentators were arguing against racial segregation in schools, emphasizing the fact that prejudice not only had negative effects on Blacks but also on white children. As Litwack explained, many abolitionists believed that segregated schools had a "damaging effect on white youths."

> "We deem it morally injurious to the white children, inasmuch as it tends to create in most, and foster in all, feelings of repugnance and contempt for the colored race as degraded inferiors, whom they may, or must, treat as such. This is the standard of morals and humanity which these schools teach our children, who are thus led to attach to color alone, sentiments and emotions, which should arise, if at all, only in view of character." [35]

Even from the early stages, pro-abolition activists perceived that social outlooks and attitudes acquired during childhood are normally—though not always—maintained over a lifetime, and that neither the parents nor the children stood to gain anything from segregation. And furthermore, raising children to be bigots was not only detrimental to the out-group children in question, but also to the society as a whole.

Similarly, unlike previous Headmasters, Dumbledore had always encouraged diversity at Hogwarts because he perceived it to be beneficial to wizarding society as a whole. And in the end, it proves to be so. We need look no further

---

[35] Litwack, 1961, p. 146.

than the Weasleys to see how wizards' uninformed ideas about out-groups like giants, goblins and werewolves have fuelled prejudice—and in some cases, outright hate. Hence, Dumbledore's insistence on inclusion at Hogwarts helped to establish what could best be likened to multicultural spaces in the real world where social (ethnic, religious, age, gender, sexuality, ability, and so forth) diversity is encouraged.

But it seems that the Headmaster's adaptation of a sort of 'real-world' multicultural model is regarded as a major revolutionary step in the conservative, somewhat archaic social context of J.K. Rowling's wizarding world. And so, although Dumbledore took in Remus Lupin when no other Headmaster would have allowed a werewolf child to attend Hogwarts, and although he had encouraged Armando Dippet (the principal before him) to keep Hagrid on the school grounds as Gamekeeper,[36] he still has to keep these students' (werewolf and part-giant) identities a closely-guarded secret.

And so, in a way, although his actions are quite honorable, he remains perfectly aware that he is contradicting the social order—obviously for the sake of "*the greater good*." Of course, Dumbledore realized that segregation—or keeping so-called '*normal*' wizard children separate from other magical beings—legitimized flawed beliefs (or stereotypes) about other magical races. Allport described such beliefs as "justificatory devices" for severe prejudice.[37] And so, allowing Muggle-borns, werewolves, giants, and so forth to come to Hogwarts, to share the same space with the offspring of the 'racial' elite and also to be submitted to the same rigorous training and evaluation of their magical ability, gives everyone a chance to broaden their knowledge and become more informed about racial/social Others.

Simply put, having Muggle-born companions like Hermione is the perfect opportunity for Pure-bloods like Ron and Draco to learn more about Muggles. A diverse, non-prejudiced environment should normally help pure-blood

---

[36] See *Goblet of Fire* (pp. 394-395), where Hagrid explains to the trio how Dumbledore looked after him after his father's death and helped him to get a job at Hogwarts, after he had been wrongfully accused and expelled for causing a student's death.

[37] Allport, 1954/1979, p. 192.

children to rethink their acquired prejudices, or at least to re-evaluate the (mis)information transmitted to them by their parents. But, as we see in Draco's case, there are other factors which have contributed to his intense antipathetic feelings towards Muggle-borns like Hermione...

Basically, Draco is jealous of Hermione's academic success; and this is what fuels his animosity towards her throughout most of the series. In *Chamber of Secrets*, Lucius Malfoy berates his son for allowing Hermione, "a girl of no wizard family," to beat him in every test (p. 44). Here, Lucius incites Draco to feel not only an inappropriate sense of envy towards another person—as though Hermione has somehow cheated or robbed him personally by getting top marks—but also the Pure-blood's sense of *entitlement* to '*more ability*' and '*better performance*' than Muggle-borns. Draco has therefore been made to understand, from a very young age, that he *ought to be* more successful at school than his Muggle-born peers—simply because he is a Pure-blood.

Of course, this is a viciously inaccurate estimation of the Muggle-borns' ability in comparison with that of Pure-bloods. We all know that it is hard work and commitment that cause Hermione to succeed at school. And to out-perform her, Draco must rely on similar skills and effort—not his wizard blood. And after a year of attending classes with Hermione, Draco should have recognized this. But it is not easy to undo the years of indoctrination his parents have inflicted upon him. Nor is it easy to overcome his own jealousy toward Hermione whilst desperately seeking his father's praise.

And so, most of Draco's disgruntlement with Hermione lies in the fact that she occupies a place which he genuinely believes should be reserved for someone with far more distinguished blood ties—someone like himself. Furthermore, a lot of his anger is actually targeted toward Harry—or as he calls him, "Saint Potter, the Mudblood's friend"[38]—who has allowed a mere Muggle-born to usurp the coveted position of being best friends with the famous Harry Potter. Draco feels doubly cheated: Not only does Hermione get top marks, but she also profits from an association that he has coveted ever

[38] *Chamber of Secrets*, p. 166.

since introducing himself to Harry during their first trip aboard the Hogwarts Express ... In typical Jessica Mitford fashion of "out-snobbing the snobs"[39] Harry had immediately rejected Draco and his cronies: He refused to shake their hands and told Draco that he did not wish to be associated with the "wrong sort."[40] And so, a part of Draco—the irrational part—thinks that Hermione benefits academically from her association with Harry because...

> 'everyone thinks he's so *smart*, wonderful *Potter* with his *scar* and his *broomstick—*.'
> (*Chamber of Secrets*, p. 43)

From Draco's point of view, Hermione shares in the preferential treatment that "Saint Potter" gets from the teachers. Hence, when his father criticizes his academic performance, Draco insists that "it's not my fault," and that Hermione only gets top marks because she is, like Harry, a teacher's favorite.[41]

But of course, as we know, Hermione has earned her results through hard work: We always see her earning points for Gryffindor or getting the rare smile of approval from Professor McGonagall.[42] And so, it is a mark of the Pure-bloods' intense antipathy towards Muggle-borns that, no matter how hard Hermione works or how well she performs, she will always be classed as Draco's inferior.

And there is a similar sense of futility with Harry and the Dursleys—as though no matter how well he behaves or what he does for them, they will always have terrible things to say about him and treat him poorly. Vernon Dursley's attitude toward his nephew never really improves after Harry saves Dudley from the Dementors in *Order of the Phoenix* (pp. 20-42). Similarly, even though Harry saves Draco's life twice in *Deathly Hallows*, it is difficult to imagine Lucius Malfoy ever

---

[39] From her famous novel *Hons and Rebels*, p. 161, about a young girl from a large English family (Unity) who marries a Hitler supporter (Sir Oswald Mosley).

[40] See *Philosopher's Stone*, pp. 81-82, where Harry stands up for Ron and rejects Draco and his gang.

[41] *Chamber of Secrets*, p. 44.

[42] See, for example, *Philosopher's Stone*, p. 100, where Hermione's talent shines in her first Transfiguration lesson.

being civil to him or his friends. And so, both sets of parents (the Dursleys and the Malfoys) have been hardened by a lifetime of hateful beliefs and attitudes. Their children must therefore learn to liberate themselves from these traditions for their own sakes...

Consequently, towards the end of the series, both Draco and Dudley have demonstrated a capacity for change that remains beyond their fathers. Dumbledore's criticisms (cited above), about how Harry had been mistreated by the Dursleys, certainly seem to have resonated with Dudley—even though his parents continue to appear to be indifferent. And so, a year later, we see him thanking Harry for saving his life—something that neither Petunia nor Vernon had ever done. Likewise, Dumbledore's softly spoken assurance that Draco is not a killer—plus perhaps the realization that his parents were extremely hypocritical and on the wrong/losing side—has tempered Draco's inclination to hate Muggle-borns...

In *Deathly Hallows*, when the trio are captured and taken to Malfoy manor, it is clear that Draco recognizes his schoolmates, but in an effort to protect them from Voldemort and his own Death Eater relatives, the boy refuses to identify the trio (pp. 371-372). And so, to a certain extent, both Draco and Dudley eventually embrace a different social outlook from that of their parents. In their own way, both characters symbolize humanity's hope, as societies evolve and younger generations become more open-minded and inclusive towards social Others.

***

Before finishing off this chapter, I feel compelled to return to the 'self-hate' or 'self-loathing' issue which was discussed in previous chapters, because it is extremely relevant to the matter of parenting. So far, I have alluded to notions of social '*entitlement*' as they relate to two privileged boys: Dudley Dursley and Draco Malfoy. One must concede that these two children have been given a positive *personal* sense of entitlement by their parents—regardless of their prejudices and negative attitudes towards social Others. In other words, based on how their parents have taught them to valorize themselves, they '*know*' and '*feel*' that they *deserve* the best things, can accomplish the highest achievements and are entitled to the best treatment within their own social contexts. And, although some of the reasoning behind their feelings of entitlement is flawed and prejudicial towards social Others, their self-belief and elevated sense of entitlement are still positive traits, simply because they are self-affirming rather than self-depreciatory. In other words, Draco Malfoy and Dudley Dursley are empowered in their respective worlds because of their parental background, the care they have received during their upbringing, and the resulting belief in their own worth. And all of these are good things: All things considered, empowered parents tend to raise empowered children—whether it is the kind of empowerment that comes from material wealth, strength of character or self-belief.

But what about situations where parents, or in some cases the society at large, transmit a negative sense of entitlement to the young?

A good example of a character with a negative sense of social entitlement, and who risks transmitting this to his offspring, is the werewolf Remus Lupin. As I mentioned in Chapter 4, being a member of a persecuted group for so long has severely affected Lupin's self-esteem. And, as a result, he assumes that he does not have the capacity to be a good father, and that his unborn child *must* be ashamed of him. A horrified Harry severely chastises Lupin for the choice he makes (namely abandoning his wife and child) because he (Harry) knows the value of having positive, caring parental figures—especially after having lost so many of them:

> Broken images were racing each other through his mind: Sirius falling through the Veil; Dumbledore suspended, broken, in mid-air; a flash of green light and his mother's voice, begging for mercy ...
>
> 'Parents,' [he said], 'shouldn't leave their kids unless—unless they've got to.'
>
> (*Deathly Hallows*, p. 177)

Harry recognizes that his own positive sense of self—despite all that he has been through, particularly the appalling ten years spent under the stairs in the Dursleys' home—comes from having had parental figures who

1. looked after him when they were alive and provided for him.
2. loved him so much that they were willing to sacrifice their own lives to keep him safe and protected.

Also, Harry gradually discovers, throughout the series, just how well his parents (James and Lily Potter) had been loved by their own parents. For example, in *Deathly Hallows*, Harry perceives the remarkable difference between his father and Snape, who apparently came from an abusive home (which partly explains but does not justify Snape's bitterness and cruelty towards the boy)...

When Harry sees his father in Snape's memory, James Potter is described as having "an indefinable air of having been well cared for, even adored, that Snape so conspicuously lacked" (p. 538). Also, Petunia's never-ending rancor about Lily being the favorite must have at least had some basis in actual fact: The Evans obviously loved both girls, but Lily's power inspired great jealousy in Petunia, probably due to the attention that the witch Lily attracted from a pair of awed Muggle parents. Lily was also the younger of the two girls—a fact which may or may not have won her even more attention. Naturally, like James, she had very high self-esteem when she went to Hogwarts because her parents believed in her and supported her. (And we may also assume that Hermione's parents show similar support and belief in their daughter).

And so, from as early as *Philosopher's Stone*, Dumbledore has impressed upon Harry the importance of him being "marked" by his mother's love (p. 216), a powerful emotion that Voldemort does not understand because he has never known real love—neither parental affection nor genuine camaraderie in his friendships. Dumbledore later explains to Harry in the sixth book that, the only kind of love Voldemort understands is the subservient adulation shown by Death Eaters like Bellatrix Lestrange, who only serve and adore him because he is powerful:

> [Voldemort's friends at school] were a motley collection; a mixture of the weak seeking protection, the ambitious seeking some shared glory, and the thuggish, gravitating towards a leader who could show them more refined forms of cruelty. In other words, they were the forerunners of the Death Eaters, and indeed some of them became the first Death Eaters after leaving Hogwarts.
>
> ....
>
> You will hear many of his Death Eaters claiming that they are in his confidence, that they alone are close to him, even understand him. They are deluded. Lord Voldemort has never had a friend, nor do I believe that he has ever wanted one.
>
> (*Deathly Hallows*, pp. 338-339 & p. 260)

Voldemort does not know the kind of unconditional love a parent has for a child: a love that gives and cares without expecting any favors or service in return. Similarly, in *Deathly Hallows*, we learn that Lily Evans and Severus Snape were friends during their childhood, but Snape did not understand why Lily should be so hurt by Petunia's anger and rejection.

> Snape slid open the compartment door and sat down opposite Lily. She glanced at him and then looked back out of the window. She had been crying.
>
> 'I don't want to talk to you,' she said in a constricted voice.
>
> 'Why not?'
>
> 'Tuney h—hates. Because we saw that letter from Dumbledore.'
>
> 'So what?'
>
> She threw him a look of deep dislike.
>
> 'So she's my sister!'
>
> 'She's only a—' He caught himself quickly; Lily, too busy trying to wipe her eyes without being noticed, did not hear him.
>
> (*Deathly Hallows*, p. 538)

Here, we see that part of Snape's sense of entitlement as a wizard is the belief that his feelings and opinions matter far more than those of Muggles. Hence, he does not understand why Lily cares so much what her sister thinks and feels. Regardless of Petunia's lack of power, she is obviously still of worth to Lily as a loved one. And so, Lily is predictably affected by her sister's anger, simply because she cares and wants to be on good terms with her. But as far as the young Severus is concerned, Petunia does not matter because she is "just a Muggle"—as he clearly intended to say. Why would anyone care so much how a 'lesser' human (or any less empowered entity) felt?

Perhaps, because he had been abused during his childhood and always felt a sense of powerlessness, the young Severus quickly learned to value others based on power and privilege, rather than on genuine feelings of solidarity and love. Snape has been, in many ways, as victimized by his past and lack of a positive, caring father figure as Voldemort was. But, rather unlike Voldemort, he at least grew up with a mother who cared for him. And so, in a sense, Snape has fewer reasons (than Voldemort) to be as compassionless as he sometimes seems...

In *Half-blood Prince*, we see that Harry experiences a measure of sympathy for Voldemort, when he discovers the circumstances in which the boy Tom Riddle entered the world. Riddle's mother died in childbirth after Tom Riddle Senior had abandoned her; but Harry fails to understand the reasons for her despair:

> 'But she could do magic!' said Harry impatiently. 'She could have got food and everything for herself by magic, couldn't she?'
>
> 'Ah,' said Dumbledore, 'perhaps she could. But it is my belief...that when her husband abandoned her, Merope stopped using magic. I do not think she wanted to be a witch any longer. Of course, it is also possible that her unrequited love and the attendant despair sapped her of her powers; that can happen. In any case, ...Merope refused to raise her wand even to save her own life.'
>
> 'She wouldn't even stay alive for her son?'
>
> Dumbledore raised his eyebrows.

> 'Could you possibly be feeling sorry for Lord Voldemort?'
>
> 'No,' said Harry quickly, 'but she had a choice, didn't she, not like my mother—'
>
> 'Your mother had a choice, too,' said Dumbledore gently. Yes, Merope Riddle chose death in spite of a son who needed her, but do not judge her too harshly, Harry. She was greatly weakened by long suffering and she never had your mother's courage...'
>
> (*Half-blood Prince*, pp. 245-246)

Harry certainly feels a degree of sympathy for Voldemort, even though he denies it. Furthermore, as other characters have commented on his impulse to save others,[43] it is clear that he inherited his mother's bravery, as he disparages Voldemort's mother for giving up, when she had a son for whom she ought to have wanted to live. Like most human beings, Harry assumes that other people are exactly like him—or that they ought to be...

It is no surprise, therefore, when he rejects Lupin's offer to accompany him on the Horcrux quest. Harry can not in all good conscience allow Lupin to abandon his wife and unborn child—especially based on Lupin's erroneous, self-deprecating view that the child will be "better off"[44] without his father. Regardless of what Lupin thinks the child will turn out to be, or how he thinks it will respond to having a werewolf as a father, he must have the courage to face the responsibilities of parenting, which are not just social and financial, but most importantly, emotional.

One could argue that it is the example of Voldemort's failed upbringing that teaches the protagonist the value of good, compassionate parenting, and which gives him an understanding that rejection and abandonment from parents are devastating acts of emotional violence (which, in turn, breed anger and further violence in the children themselves). In a sense, wizards have created their own worst enemies by rejecting and abandoning werewolf relatives, who respond to

---

[43] See, for example, *Order of the Phoenix* (p. 646), where Hermione tells Harry (to his great annoyance) that he has "a *saving-people thing*."

[44] *Deathly Hallows*, pp. 175-176.

their family and wizarding society's neglect and indifference with physical violence. Of course, this is by no means a justification for werewolf criminality, but rather an explanation of a possible cause for it...

And so, Lupin has a crucial opportunity here to be a true *Transformer*,[45] and to show the wizarding world that, not only can werewolves "breed"[46] but that they also make exceptional parents. We may safely assume that, if it were not for Harry's stern words with Remus, the young Teddy Lupin might have grown up to hate the father who had abandoned a pregnant wife. And he may have come to vilify the werewolf group as a whole—just as Voldemort's anger at his own Muggle father was eventually transferred to Muggles in general.

Also, as I stated in Chapter 3, it sometimes takes the descendants of oppressed peoples several generations to liberate themselves mentally, because the psychologies of oppression and inferiority become so deeply entrenched in their culture and traditions. And so, we may safely deduce that, following the last war against Voldemort, it will take many decades before werewolves become truly integrated into wizarding society. In fact, most wizards will continue to feel apprehensive about them for a long time. Therefore, as a werewolf, it is crucial for Lupin to be a positive role-model for his son.

Similarly, the role model principle applies to all parents belonging to oppressed groups, as they have the power to change the course of the future for their children. In Chapter 3, where I examined the house-elves' mindset, I suggested that enslaved parents usually transmit inferiority or subservience-related attitudes to their offspring, who in turn continue to perpetuate the transmission of negative self-esteem to future generations. Still, as is suggested in the first Allport citation of this chapter, it is not always the case that children adopt their parents' mindsets. Nonetheless, it is the most predictable outcome of parenting.

---

[45] See the definition given in Chapter 4 of this volume, where I discussed the various societal attitudes to disability – both in the wizarding world and in the real world.

[46] See *Deathly Hallows*, p. 176, where Lupin says "my kind don't usually breed."

Likewise, notions of Muggle-born inferiority may or may not be related to parenting. And the average Pure-blood's assumption that Muggle-borns are not as gifted as wizard children, or that they are usually lacking in high-achieving ambitions, might have "no ascertainable basis in fact"—in much the same way that Allport's Armenian example demonstrates that stereotypes often prove to be quite untrue.[47]

Nevertheless, it could also be the case that Muggle-borns have indeed been traditionally out-performed by wizard children—not because of inferior innate ability but rather due to the lack of social opportunity and self-belief. After all, there are still people like Slughorn in the wizarding world who constantly impress upon them that they are not expected to demonstrate equal ability and self-esteem as their peers who have come directly from wizard homes.

In addition, we may safely assume that Muggles are in awe of the wizarding world because of its sheer power and secrecy; and so, as I mentioned in the previous chapter, it would not be surprising if many Muggle-borns felt somewhat *out-of-place* in this new world. After all, their parents and everything they knew before coming to Hogwarts are totally foreign to the magical community. And so, there is certainly a subverted sense of rupture, heartbreak, distance and perhaps irretrievable loss where the parents of Muggle-borns are concerned—because they can never really be a part of the world to which their children now belong.

For instance, very often I have wondered how people like Hermione's parents cope with the fact that their children are absent from their lives for so long and so often. Hermione, for example, on top of spending the entire school year at Hogwarts, sometimes spends Christmas there as well, and some summer holidays with the Weasleys.[48] And so, it would

---

[47] I cited this in Chapter 1 of this volume (p. 63). See also Allport, 1954/1979, pp. 189-190.

[48] Hermione and Ron remain at Hogwarts for Christmas during their second and third years so that Harry would not be alone while Slytherin's monster and the notorious Sirius Black were on the loose. She also stays during the fourth year for the Triwizard Yule Ball. And in *Order of the Phoenix* she cancels a skiing trip with her parents to return to Harry and Ron's side after Arthur Weasley's near-death incident. Also, during her fourth year, before the Triwizard tournament, she

not be surprising if some Muggle parents tried to hold on to their children (as in '*keeping them in their rightful place*') by impressing upon them that they belong to a different world than other wizard children. And so, if it is indeed true that Muggle-borns have been traditionally out-performed by Pure-bloods and Half-bloods, then perhaps it is partly due to constant reminders from their own families that they are '*different*' from other magical children (as in belonging to a different world) and, therefore, should have different expectations of themselves. And this is just one example of how self-perception among parents can affect self-esteem in children—whether in the wizarding world or in our own.

***

To conclude the chapter, I wish to draw a few important comparisons with our own world, particularly where parenting issues and self-esteem or prejudices are concerned. As I have proved throughout this chapter, it is a truth universally acknowledged that parents are largely responsible for the level of self-esteem their children display. And disparities in both self-esteem and a sense of social entitlement are sometimes reflected in the racial divide.

For example, many would argue that (in many Western societies), Caucasian children have far greater access and are far more at ease in certain social contexts, simply because they are more accustomed to moving in these (higher) social circles. In other words, the general perception is that they '*belong*' there, more so than their ethnic peers. And, they have had this sense of entitlement to 'access' and 'ownership' (implicitly or explicitly) transmitted to them by their parents and the wider community since early childhood.

This is partly why, for example, in the UK's top universities, the ratio of ethnic minority (undergraduate) students to white students is still extremely small. The truth is that, even though a relatively small number of students of

---

spends almost the entire summer holidays at the Burrow with Ron's family. And during the fifth year, prior to the Dementor attack on Harry and Dudley, she is at Order Headquarters for the entire summer.

African or Asian descent end up in the Oxbridge[49] system, the vast majority of Blacks and Asians living in Britain might not even think about Oxford or Cambridge as an attainable aspiration. Some pupils do not even bother to apply for a place, even if they have achieved the required A-Level[50] grades. And this is partly because they do not think they would '*fit in*' in a social setting that has been traditionally regarded as 'upper-class' or exclusively for the wealthy or racial elite.

Of course, the many-centuries-old reputation for both excellence and elitism which surrounds the Oxbridge system plays a large role in maintaining these perceptions. But parental guidance should also be perceived as playing a vital role: What messages are parents from working class or ethnic minority backgrounds sending to their children about their potential for academic excellence? Some parents are able to overcome their own underprivileged backgrounds or lack of self-esteem to encourage their children to aspire to heights that they themselves would never have envisioned. But many others—perhaps the majority—do not have the ability to defeat these intangible (but resistant) mental and social barriers. How do you give your child something that you never had in the first place—something that you do not even know how to procure? It is certainly *not* impossible, but the likelihood is not great.

The task therefore falls to the society at large to help such children to rethink their own evaluations of their personal worth and ability, by treating them with equal respect and having the same high expectations of them as the privileged (socio-economic, racial or otherwise) elite. As with Muggle-borns in the wizarding world, teachers and peer groups in the real world must constantly impress upon the non-privileged that they are just as capable of achieving anything, and just as worthy of excellence as their more privileged peers.

Unfortunately though, reality paints a much different picture. Far too often, teachers tend to straight-jacket poorer class or ethnic minority children into less rewarding and/or

[49] Oxford and Cambridge Universities.

[50] Advanced Level subjects to be taken before secondary level students can gain entrance to University in the United Kingdom.

less challenging—and sometimes demeaning—career paths. And they do so by either telling the children explicitly or through role playing, that they are only '*good enough for*' certain kinds of vocations, instead of letting them prove for themselves what they can do.

Similarly, in *Harry Potter*'s world, we see that Slughorn's insistent surprise that a Muggle-born like Lily Potter should be extremely bright and popular sends an implicit message—both to Muggle-born and Pure-blood/Half-blood students—that Muggle-borns are not entitled to academic excellence and popularity. Slughorn's convictions not only display the general view of Muggle-borns amongst wizards, but they also signal the Muggle-born's place in wizarding society as an intrusive outsider—one with no connections or ancestry to justify the privilege of having magic powers. It is a very pervasive, seemingly harmless type of prejudice, which is easily justified because of the view that '*everybody feels/thinks the same way*' ... Lucius Malfoy expresses similar sentiments when he chastises Draco for being outperformed by someone like Hermione. And, of course, a similar sense of lack of social entitlement holds the house-elves firmly rooted in slavery, as we see the newly-freed Dobby being turned away when he starts demanding payment for his work:

> '"That's not the point of a house-elf," they says, and they slammed the door in Dobby's face!'
> (*Goblet of Fire*, p. 330)

Here, we see that Dobby is not encouraged to embrace his humanity or his potential to improve his social status: It is far too deeply engrained inside wizard minds and in wizarding culture that certain kinds of magical creatures are only good for certain kinds of things. In the same way, in our world, we wrongfully associate certain types of people with certain types of jobs, lifestyles, morality and so forth.

Finally, I would like to summarize the arguments put forth in this chapter by saying that, in the same way that parents contribute to prejudiced beliefs and attitudes in their children (as demonstrated in the flawed sense of entitlement typified by Draco Malfoy and Dudley Dursley), they can also encourage a lack of self-esteem, which causes prejudice to have devastating social and psychological consequences. A child may implicitly—and sometimes explicitly—learn from his parents that he is not the social equal of his superiors, therefore he is not entitled to the same rights, the same education, the same amount of love or care or attention, or the same opportunities in life. This is tantamount to a life-sentence of inferiority and self-deprecation, even when the child makes valiant attempts to *transform* society's negative perceptions—as we clearly see in Remus Lupin's case.

And so, in sum, prejudiced children are likely to assume that they alone and others like them are entitled to the aforementioned privileges, whereas the more open-minded, accepting, socially-aware (and therefore non-prejudiced) children recognize that social Others are entitled to the same rights, comforts and opportunities for social advancement as themselves. Hence, the kind of parenting which encourages empathy and respect towards the social Other is the most vital tool in ridding society of prejudice and creating a more tolerant world.

Chapter 7

Harry Potter: The Should-Be Delinquent

Simply put, Harry Potter is a rule-breaker. He lies, steals and disobeys his superiors in order to achieve his aims. And yet, it is unimaginable that a readership that celebrates the Weasley twins' dedication to anarchy would be critical of the protagonist for his instances of rule-breaking. But since rules are important for maintaining social stability, rule-breakers are usually perceived as menaces to society because they work against the social order. Therefore, it is no surprise that the protagonist Harry is frequently compared with his adversary, Tom Riddle (or the self-titled "Voldemort").

The young Riddle certainly showed all the signs of juvenile delinquency before transforming into the monstrosity of the Dark Lord. And although Harry's aims are entirely different from those of his adversary, is this distinction enough to justify the hero's rule-breaking tendencies while we condemn Riddle/Voldemort? When we look at the boy Riddle and the child Harry, why should we be so inclined to regard one as a social delinquent and the other not so? These are some of the questions which I will seek to answer in the final chapter of this volume.

In addition, I will highlight some examples from the series, where Harry is continuously burdened with the stigmas associated with either delinquency or some form of insanity. Intriguingly, the persons who label the boy as "delinquent" or "mad" only know about his parents or some parts of his well-publicized traumatic history; but they are often quite ignorant about the individual, Harry. And so, I will show how the protagonist's situation can be likened to an insidious, somewhat unnoticeable prejudice in our own world, where individuals who have experienced severely traumatic events in their lives are doubly-victimized by the stigma attached to victimhood...

Some common traits shared by many people deemed to be 'hopeless' or irrevocably 'messed up' include coming from a broken home, having been raped or otherwise violently attacked, or simply lacking positive parental figures. And so,

Harry's severe trauma as an infant and his subsequent trials with the Dursleys not only recall the plight of orphans and abandoned children in our own world, but also those who have had parents or guardians who abused them (whether emotionally or physically), or those who grew up in loveless homes. In many cases, such individuals are just as mentally sound and socially conscious as anyone else. Some overcome poverty, severe trauma and even depression to lead fulfilling, successful and happy lives. And many never show any signs of socio-pathology, vengeful bitterness or mental illness throughout their lifetimes. Nevertheless, they are sometimes (pre)judged harshly by relatives or a society that generally expects *'less'* from those who come from abusive, disadvantaged or underprivileged backgrounds.

Also, unfortunately, society still looks unfavorably upon people who are unable to live up to the idealized, flawless images of self-hood portrayed in the mainstream media: For instance, we might automatically *pity*[1] or label people as 'damaged' or 'not well brought up' when their home lives do not conform to the standards of the iconic 'cookie cutter' nuclear family.[2] And so, in this chapter I will also discuss how some of the subplots in the *Harry Potter* novels allude to this form of prejudice.

***

The earliest studies on adolescent delinquency described the condition as "maladaptive behavior."[3] In general terms, delinquency relates to the failure to abide by rules and laws. Therefore, we could argue that children either learn to become delinquent or fail to learn to be law-abiding. Many of the initial delinquency studies linked delinquent behavior with a lack of intellectual aptitude in some areas. For example, Gluek's study found that delinquents showed "less aptitude" in language-based tests, but performed equally to non-

[1] There is an element of scorn in some expressions of pity; and in such cases, pity must be regarded as another way of "acting out" prejudice.

[2] Included among the non-traditional family situations are single-parent settings and same-sex partnerships where children are involved.

[3] See Conger's Preface to *Personality, Social Class and Delinquency* (1966, p. *vii*).

delinquents in examinations that required mathematical or reasoning abilities.[4]

Gluek and other twentieth century sociologists such as Merton (1938) and Cohen (1955) also questioned whether the condition was related to social class and parental love, as most of the major theoretical perspectives[5] on delinquency during the 1950s and 60s suggested that love in the home and socio-economic and family backgrounds played a significant role in determining child delinquency. Later, during the 1970s, researchers such as Johnson still maintained that "parental attachment [occupied] a central place as a determinant," and that the extent of a child's attachment to school and susceptibility to influence from peers was largely affected by the amount of love that child received from his parents.[6]

Although the aforementioned studies on delinquency are quite dated, they were (and still are) legitimate–in the sense that they were based on factual research of social trends which persist in more modern times.

Nevertheless, there can be no '*absolute determinant*' for the social condition of juvenile delinquency. At the end of the day, children still have the free will and the ability to choose how to behave, regardless of the social factors deemed to "determine" their behavior. And moreover, many children nowadays exhibit delinquent behavior despite the fact that they come from relatively prosperous socio-economic backgrounds and nurturing family settings, where they receive copious amounts of love and have a deep sense of attachment to their parents.

These realities are nicely alluded to in the *Harry Potter* novels. For example, in the previous chapter I contrasted Dudley Dursley and Draco Malfoy with the protagonist, Harry. Both Dudley and Draco were raised by loving, caring, attentive mothers and doting fathers. But although these two

---

[4] Gluek's study found that delinquents were outperformed on Vocabulary, Information, and Comprehension tests, but resembled non-delinquents in Arithmetical Reasoning, Memory Span for Digits and Similarities tests (Gluek, 1952, p. 120).

[5] Cohen, 1955; Merton, 1938; Mckay, 1942; Cloward and Ohlin, 1960; Hirschi, 1969; Johnson, 1972 & 1979.

[6] Johnson, 1979, pp. 100-109.

privileged boys have access to money and plenty of parental attention and care, they both tend to bully their peers, or to target social Others with physical violence. In particular, Dudley seems to suffer from an emotional disorder which causes him to express himself mainly through violence (stomping, punching, shouting, and so forth), and to pick on children who are much smaller or weaker than himself.[7] In addition, both Dudley and Draco are out-performed academically by other children in their respective school settings.

Intriguingly, according to the theories cited above, the downtrodden, unloved Harry has far more reasons than either of these boys to perform poorly in school or to be violent towards social Others. And yet, with the exception of History of Magic and Divination,[8] his academic performance is not significantly different from that of his peers. In fact, Harry is the top student in his year in Defense Against the Dark Arts, outperforming even the brilliant, bookish Hermione in this difficult subject.[9] And where power dynamics with social Others are concerned, note that it is Harry who is "kicked around like a football"[10] by Dudley, and who has always taken a stance against Draco's pure-blood snobbery and verbal violence towards Muggle-borns and other magical beings.

Ironically, however, Harry is the one presumed to be the bully, simply because of his abilities and the tragic events of his life. For instance, as I mentioned in an earlier chapter, his peers accuse him of attacking Muggle-borns after a rumor is spread that he hates Muggles—the Dursleys in particular.[11] The students suggest that Harry is a Dark wizard, simply because he can speak Parseltongue; and they partly base their

---

[7] Harry, for example, is much smaller than Dudley and had always been his main target; but that was before Dudley found out about Harry's magical abilities. Another example also appears in *Order of the Phoenix* (p. 17), where we learn that the 17-year-old Dudley and his friends are still beating up 10-year-olds (like little Mark Evans).

[8] These have always been his worst subjects, and they are the only OWL (Ordinary Wizarding Levels) exams in which he gets an outright fail. See *Half-blood Prince*, p. 100.

[9] Ibid. Here, Harry learns that he is the only student to receive top marks ('O' for "Outstanding") in the Defense Against the Dark Arts OWL exam.

[10] *Philosopher's Stone*, p. 47.

[11] See *Chamber of Secrets*, p. 150.

theories on the flawed principle that a wizard must have or use Dark powers in order to overcome a menace like Voldemort (Hence, Harry had to have Dark powers in order to bring about Voldemort's end when he was just a baby.[12]) Notably, the main principle behind these assumptions is that Harry was either 'born' with Dark powers, or that he must have developed them during infancy. Such beliefs would also imply that there is a high degree of '*innateness*' (therefore irredeemableness) in being a Dark wizard.

And so, in *Goblet of Fire*, the slandering journalist Rita Skeeter publishes an article in which she informs the wizarding world that Harry "would do anything for a bit of power" (p. 532). But prior to this, Skeeter had published other misleading stories, painting Harry as a pitiful boy who still cried himself to sleep over his parents' deaths (p. 276) ... Eager to appeal to dominant stereotypes about traumatized children, Skeeter happily promotes the idea that Harry is "damaged," or weakened by the trauma of his infancy.

As a result, Cornelius Fudge later insinuates that Harry's brains were "addled" by Voldemort's curse; and he also accuses the boy of seeking attention just to get more fame (pp. 611-616). And so, it is no surprise when we see an angered, tortured protagonist dealing with similar attitudes and insinuations from his peers and the repressive Dolores Umbridge in *Order of the Phoenix.* Here, we also see Harry being attacked by the Dursleys, who accuse him of breaking wizard law by using magic against Dudley, even though he has just saved his cousin's life (pp. 28-42).

The immense injustice of Harry's situation is evident only to the close friends who truly know him. Only his best friends and the Weasleys seem to know that Harry would never seek power or use his abilities to dominate, oppress or to bully others. And so, a part of the intense sense of frustration surrounding Rowling's protagonist, particularly in later works (such as *Order of the Phoenix* and *Deathly Hallows*) lies in how highly misunderstood he is—not only by wizarding society, but most of all by his own family...

---

[12] *Chamber of Secrets*, p. 148.

The Dursleys fail to see Harry for who he really is; they are blinded by fear, jealousy and resentment. And this is why, although most of Harry's rule-breaking takes place at Hogwarts, the issue of his "delinquency" is mostly raised in the Muggle world: Here, he is stigmatized by his relatives simply because he is a wizard; because being a wizard is an innate ability which Harry alone possesses, and which they cannot control. Hence, Vernon Dursely's view of Harry is that he is "incurably criminal," and one of society's "hopeless cases."[13] Of course, the reader knows that Harry is neither of these things ... A large part of the Dursleys' annoyance with the boy lies in the fact that he cannot be anything other than a wizard—not even in pretence. Nor can he change the horrific events of his life that have led to his relatives having to put up with him in their home. And, of course, Vernon and Petunia's feelings about Harry are based on their own prejudices against wizardkind, and particularly towards Harry's parents.

***

In much the same way, Severus Snape's opinion of Harry is hugely affected by his animosity towards James Potter and Sirius Black—Harry's father and godfather. Snape is unable to see Harry for who he truly is because his vision is clouded by the shadow of a hated rival, with whom the boy shares an uncanny physical resemblance:

> '—mediocre, arrogant as his father, a determined rule-breaker, delighted to find himself famous, attention-seeking and impertinent—'
>
> 'You see what you expect to see, Severus,' said Dumbledore ... 'Other teachers report that the boy is modest, likeable and reasonably talented. Personally, I find him an engaging child.'
>
> (*Deathly Hallows*, p. 545)

Here, we can see that Dumbledore has a far more wholesome (and realistic) view of Harry than the embittered, grudge-

[13] See *Prisoner of Azkaban* (p. 23), where Vernon tells his sister Marge that Harry goes to St. Brutus's, "a first-rate institution for hopeless cases."

ridden Snape, who has never been able to see beyond Harry's outward appearance. Hence, the idea that '*the apple doesn't fall far from the tree*' is a stereotype which has caused Harry an enormous amount of suffering under the Potions Master's tyranny. And yet, from the way that Harry reacts to the discovery of his father's crimes against Snape, we know that his social outlook and his capacity for compassion are completely different from those of either James or Snape:

> What was making Harry feel so horrified and unhappy was not being shouted at or having jars thrown at him; it was that he knew how it felt to be humiliated in the middle of a circle of onlookers, knew exactly how Snape had felt as his father had taunted him, and that judging from what he had just seen, his father had been every bit as arrogant as Snape had always told him.
> (*Order of the Phoenix*, p. 573)

Harry's sympathy for Snape, in the above, says a lot about his overall character. At this stage in the series, Snape is next only to Voldemort, Draco Malfoy and Dolores Umbridge as Harry's antagonists. But where many people would rejoice or at least feel vindicated by the humiliation of a hated foe, Harry, instead, feels understanding and compassion.

Due to the fact that Harry knows exactly what it is like to suffer and to be socially rejected and humiliated, he does not wish this fate upon anyone—not even his worst enemy. And so, while the protagonist is not perfect, he is essentially decent in a way that Snape could never fathom. And, evidently, his decency stems from the way he *chooses* to respond to his disadvantaged upbringing. Harry accepts that no one else, not even Voldemort or Snape, is responsible for his (Harry's) choices, or his capacity to be a decent, humane person. And so, regardless of what happened to him in the past, Harry's hardships have not crippled him emotionally or intellectually. In other words, the protagonist's endless trials have not exhausted his capacity for feeling sympathy for others. In fact, they seem to have had the opposite effect.

And moreover, whereas Harry's perceived delinquency is mostly due to circumstances beyond his control, we can see that James Potter used to purposefully '*perform*' the role of a teenage delinquent: James was constantly roughing up his hair, hexing people in hallways and breaking school rules just for the fun of it.[14] In comparison, Harry is perceived as a delinquent in the Muggle world simply because he has inherited both his father's unruly hair and Dudley's baggy old clothes.[15] And most of his rule-breaking at Hogwarts occurs in situations where he feels he has no choice but to break the rules, because someone's life is in danger. For example, in *Chamber of Secrets* Harry, Ron and Hermione break at least a hundred school rules (according to Professor McGonnagal [p. 241]), in order to unravel the secrets of the legendary Chamber and ultimately save Ginny's life.

In addition, unlike James, Harry is not a braggart. Nor are his actions motivated by any quest for fame, popularity amongst his peers or universal notoriety, as the prejudiced Snape seems to believe. Of course, Harry already has these things in abundance; and so, perhaps the fact that he is not motivated by the need for them is simply an example of how the circumstances of his life have determined his personality and his ambitions: For instance, we could easily speculate that, if James Potter had arrived at Hogwarts as the most famous person of his age group, and then got immediately selected as the youngest Seeker in a century,[16] he might not have been so desperate for praise or admiration from 'cooler,' more affluent peers like Sirius Black. Nevertheless, the 11-year-old Harry must at least be commended for managing to keep a level head, especially after discovering that he was the most famous person in the wizarding world.

There is a remarkable difference between how he and the young James perceive themselves, and also how they interact with adulating, reverent peers or inferiors. For example, if we look at how Harry reacts to the adoring Colin Creevey in *Chamber of Secrets*, we see a 12-year-old protagonist who is far more self-assured than his father was at age 15. In a way,

---

[14] *Order of the Phoenix*, pp. 590-592.

[15] Harry would often hear "disapproving mutters" from people in the Dursleys' neighborhood, as they discussed his "'delinquent' appearance." (*Order of the Phoenix*, p. 16).

[16] *Philosopher's Stone*, p. 113.

Colin is to Harry what Peter Pettigrew (Wormtail) was to James at Hogwarts. Like Wormtail, Creevey is also a Gryffindor; therefore he has far greater access to Harry than students from other houses. Colin is also small in stature, a bit insignificant-looking and only too eager to stroke Harry's ego. But even before learning about the teenage Wormtail's adoration for James, or his subsequent treachery as an adult, Harry is somewhat frightened of Colin and tries to distance himself from this obsessed admirer.[17] The protagonist is obviously far more comfortable socializing with others who are his equals, and also with academically superior peers like Hermione. He simply does not need to hear how good and great he is all the time.

Also, unlike James, who tormented Snape just to entertain a wealthy, upper-class pure-blood friend,[18] Harry does not feel the need to perform to please or entertain his peers. We could say that he is not only more mature than James, but also more socially empowered than his father was as a teenager. We could also argue that his non-privileged (even abusive) upbringing has made him far more compassionate than James was at his age. But Harry still has the *choice* to abuse his fame or to become hard and hateful towards others as a result of the hardships that he has had to live through. Even Dumbledore is amazed at the person the boy has become, as well as his modesty:

> 'But I haven't got uncommon skill and power,' said Harry, before he could stop himself.
>
> 'Yes, you have,' said Dumbledore firmly. 'You have a power that Voldemort has never had. You can...'
>
> 'I know!' said Harry impatiently. 'I can love!' It was only with great difficulty that he stopped himself adding, 'Big deal!'
>
> 'Yes, Harry, you can love,' said Dumbledore, who looked as though he knew perfectly well what Harry had

---

[17] See *Chamber of Secrets*, pp. 82-90, where a frustrated Harry tries to shake off Colin, who is determined to get a signed picture for his troubles.

[18] See *Order of the Phoenix*, pp. 565-573, where Harry trespasses on Snape's memories, and sees the teenage James putting on a show for Sirius (who had said he was bored) by taunting the 15-year-old Severus Snape.

> just refrained from saying. 'Which, given everything that has happened to you, is a great and remarkable thing. You are still too young to understand how unusual you are, Harry.'
> (*Half-blood Prince*, p. 476)

Here, the wise Dumbledore intimates that, oftentimes those who have been oppressed or abused are mostly likely to oppress others or abuse power when they get it. And perhaps this tendency is due to a predictable human urge (in those who have been wounded emotionally or otherwise), to seek compensation, or to see others undergo the pain and suffering that they themselves have had to endure.

And so, Harry has many reasons for leading a loveless life, and, like Voldemort, seeking power in order to dominate and oppress others. And it is this perception (or expectation, rather) which leads others like Cornelius Fudge and Rita Skeeter to make generalizations about him, or to expect the worst from him because of his traumatic history.

***

Unfortunately for Harry, he carries his trauma around with him in two significant ways: First, he has never learned to suppress his emotions or his painful memories. Unlike Voldemort (who has severed every human quality from himself) or Snape (who remains cold and inaccessible) Harry's emotions are always lingering near the surface. Some people might argue that this is a flaw: Indeed, as we see in *Order of the Phoenix*, this limitation has prevented him from learning Occlumency—a skill which might have enabled him to shut out Voldemort and thus avoid the trap which led to Sirius's death. Harry's inability to close his mind has even prompted Snape to slate him for being one of those

> '...fools who wear their hearts proudly on their sleeves, who cannot control their emotions, who wallow in sad memories and allow themselves to be provoked easily—weak people, in other words.'
> (*Order of the Phoenix*, p. 473)

And perhaps Harry could learn to repress his feelings if he really wanted to; however, I would argue that this emotional honesty is the underlying factor behind his persisting ability to love and empathize with others, despite all that has happened to him. Having suffered as much as he has (and lost so many people) it takes great courage for Harry to open himself up emotionally, or to face the terrible pain of his past instead of repressing it. But courage is the protagonist's defining quality; and it also proves to be his ultimate weapon.

The second way in which Harry carries around his trauma is far more out of his control: his scar. The scar symbolizes his traumatic past both in the Muggle world and in the wizarding world; and it is symbolic in many ways. First, it links him directly to Voldemort: it is the inside knowledge he gains from having direct access to the Dark Lord's mind that enables him to spy on his enemy without being detected. Second, it is a marker of rupture and loss: It is the very thing that symbolizes the fact that Harry is '*damaged.*' And it is this notion, that the protagonist carries a sort of 'permanent injury,' which has led the likes of Fudge and Skeeter to assume that he must either be deranged or delinquent.

And finally, the scar is the very embodiment of all the consequences of Voldemort's crime: for instance, the fact that Harry has no parents and was raised by the cruel Dursleys. There is also the fact that the Dementors affect him far more than anyone else, precisely because of the horrific memories linked to his infancy. And last but not least, the fact that he is famous for the scar also makes it a marker of difference: It is a permanent point of departure from his peers, who are constantly reminded—every time they look at him—that he has had a rather untypical childhood and is not like them.

It is no surprise, therefore, that people like Fudge and Skeeter have made their own erroneous assumptions about Harry. They fail to realize that Harry Potter is the total opposite of what society expects him to be. He overcomes his past by simply owning it and facing it without fear; and he does not allow the traumatic events of his life to lessen his capacity for humanity.

***

Still, one could also argue that, since Harry's parents had loved him so deeply, the hero has fewer reasons to be a child delinquent or to become a Dark wizard than his adversary, Tom Riddle, who had never known love. In addition, if we compare the social and economic circumstances of the two 11-year-old boys, we see a protagonist whose 'goodness,' some observers might argue, has been facilitated by others, and an antagonist who probably developed as a child delinquent because he had fewer positive parental figures and peers to care and provide for him. At the end of the day, the young Harry is the one with wizarding world celebrity and favorable connections. He also acquires financial empowerment very early in his life, after discovering the small fortune his parents had left him.[19] As a severe contrast, we have the boy Riddle, who was extremely poor, without notoriety or connections, and had a father whom he did not know because the latter had abandoned his mother before she died in childbirth...

And so, perhaps the reason Harry can love and Voldemort can not is simply because Harry has been raised in the assurance of his dead parents' love, while the young Riddle had been emotionally and physically abandoned by both parents even before he entered the world. As a result, he had to be raised in a Muggle orphanage by adults who probably thought his magical abilities were strange and demonic. We may deduce that the boy Riddle internalized these negative perceptions, which had been inflicted upon him since infancy. And once again, in contrast, Harry had a whole year of being adored by James and Lily Potter; and that love left a powerful impression upon him, which endured despite the Dursleys' cruelty.

And besides, as detestable as the Dursleys are, Dumbledore tries to impress upon Harry that the fact that they took him in and fed and clothed him for ten years (albeit on Dudley's leftovers) is worth a great deal. As the Headmaster informs Harry in the following, the boy's embittered aunt basically saved his life:

---

[19] See *Philosopher's Stone* (p. 58), where Hagrid accompanies Harry to his Gringotts vault and shows him the piles of gold that his parents bequeathed to him.

> '...Why could some wizarding family not have taken you in? Many would have done so more than gladly, would have been honored and delighted to raise you as a son ... [But] my priority was to keep you alive. You were in more danger than perhaps anyone but I realized. Voldemort had been vanquished hours before, but his supporters—and many of them are almost as terrible as he—were still at large, angry, desperate and violent ... And so I made my decision. You would be protected by an ancient magic of which he knows, which he despises, and which he has always, therefore, underestimated—to his cost. I am speaking, of course, of the fact that your mother died to save you. She gave you a lingering protection he never expected, a protection that flows in your veins to this day. I put my trust, therefore, in your mother's blood. I delivered you to her sister, her only remaining relative.'
>
> 'She doesn't love me,' said Harry...
>
> 'But she took you,' Dumbledore cut across him. 'She may have taken you grudgingly, furiously, unwillingly, bitterly, yet still she took you, and in doing so, she sealed the charm I placed upon you. Your mother's sacrifice made the bond of blood the strongest shield I could give you.'
>
> (*Order of the Phoenix*, pp. 736-737)

Here, we see that Dumbledore also believes that Petunia's unwilling act of kindness has left a positive mark upon Harry. The headmaster also reminds the boy that various elements of his life circumstances (such as the time of his birth, who his parents were, the fact that it was Voldemort who killed them and that his aunt gave him a home so that the protective charms could keep him safe) have facilitated both his ability and his desire to fulfill his destiny as the "Chosen One" (pp. 737-738).

Moreover, since ignorance is one of the primary causes of both prejudice and the kind of intense animosity which provokes the need for retribution, we could also argue that Harry had the 'better deal' because he was raised by people who actually knew something about the wizarding world.

Although the Dursleys tried to stifle any knowledge of his magical abilities, at least they understood *why* he was so different. Their limited knowledge of wizardkind therefore prevented them from demonizing Harry completely, the way the young Tom Riddle must have been demonized at the orphanage. We may speculate that, as a toddler or a young child just getting familiar with his own magical abilities, Tom had been suppressed and persecuted in the social setting of the orphanage—of course, as a result of fear and ignorance. And the boy obviously retaliated and defended himself.

Evidence to support these speculations appears in *Half-blood Prince*, where we see Dumbledore visiting the 11-year-old Tom at the orphanage and informing him that he is a wizard. The boy is at first extremely paranoid that his superiors intend to send him to an asylum (pp. 252-253), which suggests that the issue of his insanity had been raised prior to this event, and that the staff had tried repeatedly to contain or suppress him.

In addition, we could argue that Harry is far more privileged in terms of his wizarding world connections and friendships than Riddle ever was; and this is largely due to the fact that his parents were highly respected, well-known and loved when they were alive. And so, after arriving at Hogwarts, Harry had an admiring Dumbledore, the motherly Minerva McGonagall (who had also been the Head of Gryffindor House while Lily and James were at Hogwarts), two phenomenal best friends in Ron and Hermione (who are willing to risk their lives for him), and a loving, protective Molly Weasley, who happily assumes the role of foster parent to Harry. Molly treats him like a son, sending him Easter eggs, Christmas presents and homemade sweaters, as she does for each of her children.

In contrast, although the teenage Riddle was quite popular with his peers and most of his teachers, he did not seem to have any real, genuine friendships or parental figures to look after him in these small but wholly significant ways. Therefore, Harry certainly benefits (socially) from his parents' connections in a way that the young Tom Riddle could not profit from his own. After all, Riddle had sprung from a forbidden marriage which had been based on lies and coercion, and which ended in abandonment and his mother's ignoble and tragic death. And furthermore, the Gaunt House, to which his mother belonged, had been long bereft of wealth or respectability, despite being directly linked to the famous Salazar Slytherin.

And so, another way in which the Potters can be said to have 'facilitated' Harry's good behavior, in terms of helping him to avoid the path of severe childhood delinquency, is by providing for him financially. Many of the earlier works on juvenile delinquency cited poverty and the desire for status and money as major determinants. And Rowling herself seems to appeal to the *strain*[20] explanation of adolescent law-breaking, a theoretical approach which suggests that:

> ...some adolescents are driven to law violation in response to the frustration of experiencing or anticipating failure. The pressure to deviate from acceptable behavior norms is created by a discrepancy between culturally induced aspirations and realistic expectations. The individual internalizes the goals of society but must employ illegitimate means to obtain them when legitimate avenues to success are blocked. The causal image is the same whether the frustration or lack of opportunity involves economic success goals (Merton, 1938) or adolescent peer group status (Cohen, 1955). The frustrated, deprived, or *strained* individual violates society's rules to obtain commodities that society has convinced him or her are important to obtain.[21]

Likewise, as we delve into Voldemort's past, we discover that the teenage Tom Riddle had coveted the prestige and power of his pure-blood companions. The hierarchical setup of the wizarding world easily impressed upon Riddle that, in order to reach the very top in wizarding society, one had to either be born a dominant Pure-blood, or espouse opinions which proclaimed the innate superiority of the pure-blood master class/master race.

Take the Gringotts issue, for example. In *Chamber of Secrets* we see Hermione's parents exchanging Muggle money

---

[20] See Merton (1938), Cohen (1955) and Cloward and Ohlin (1960).

[21] Johnson, Richard E. *Juvenile Delinquency and its Origins*, CUP: 1979, pp. 1-2.

for Galleons at the bank (p. 47), which suggests that students with two Muggle parents (like Hermione) or from Muggle backgrounds (like Riddle) might not have had easy access to opening new accounts at Gringotts. Also, in *Deathly Hallows* we get a sense that the largest, most well-protected vaults belonged to the oldest and most affluent wizarding families like the Blacks, Lestranges, Malfoys, Smiths and so forth.[22] Also in the same book, Harry surmises that Voldemort wanted to be associated with peers from distinguished wizarding families, such as Bellatrix and her husband, partly because he coveted their position and wealth, as well as their access to powerful institutions like Gringotts:

> 'I think he would have envied anyone who had a key to a Gringotts vault. I think he would have seen it as a real symbol of belonging to the wizarding world.'
> (*Deathly Hallows* p. 397).

Here, even the hero acknowledges that he has always been socially and economically empowered in a way that his rival had never been as a teenager. And so, naturally, Harry is not in a position where he would be instinctively over-awed by material wealth or social status in the wizarding world; nor would he become predictably obsessed with pursuing wealth and status via the same illegitimate means used by Voldemort. And this is simply because he had parents who were successful and well-connected, and who provided for him. And on top of having had a key to a Gringotts vault since age 11, he has also had his middle-class relatives (the Dursleys) looking after him all his life—however grudgingly they might have done it.

The boy Riddle, on the other hand, never had such privileges. And it is, to a certain extent, this knowledge of his enemy's cravings and weaknesses—of basically everything Harry has always had that the boy Tom had always lacked and coveted—that ultimately gives the hero the psychological upper-hand in the final showdown.

---

[22] See *Deathly Hallows* (p. 411), where Griphook informs the trio that "The oldest wizarding families store their treasures at the deepest level, where the vaults are largest and best protected ..."

And so, I will finish off this section by stating categorically that Harry's socio-economic empowerment is one example of the many ways in which his parents, albeit deceased, continued to facilitate his life choices and, to a certain degree, his morality.

***

Nevertheless, to excuse Tom Riddle for his crimes on the basis that he never had a mother who was courageous enough to live for him would be to imply that Voldemort is not ultimately responsible for who or what he becomes. To say, for example, that he was prone to inhumanity or vengeance because his father had abandoned his mother during her pregnancy, would be an over-simplification of the facts. It would also be a damning verdict against anyone who entered the world under similar circumstances. Riddle was not '*born*' as a malignant, evil force; nor was he 'destined' to evolve into a Dark wizard. Also, any suggestion that Riddle's childhood hardships '*unavoidably*' determined his delinquency, would significantly contradict Dumbledore's (and Rowling's) apparent belief that choices matter far more than the circumstances of a person's birth.

Still, we can see that the question of how socio-economics relate to delinquency is a particularly troublesome one—even in the fictional wizarding world. In other words, would Tom Riddle have come to idolize the pure-blood class if he had had access to the same privileges that his school friends clearly benefited from? And in the same vein, are lower-class or poverty-stricken youths in our own world prone to idolizing (and envying) their middle or upper class counterparts? And how and when does this become a major factor in juvenile delinquency?

For the past seven or eight decades, sociologists have been engaged in an intellectual struggle over the very same issues. In his volume entitled *The Delinquent Solution*, Downes summarized Cloward and Ohlin's interpretation of Cohen's theory thus:

> Cohen assumes that many lower-class youth seek to affiliate with the middle-class: 'It is a plausible assumption…that the working-class boy whose status is low in middle-class terms cares about that status, that this status confronts him with a genuine problem of adjustment' (Cohen: p. 129). Indeed, Cohen suggests that delinquency results when access to this goal is limited. … Cohen's tendency to equate high levels of aspiration among lower-class youth with an orientation towards the middle class implies that lower-class youth who are dissatisfied with their position (1) internalize middle-class values and (2) *seek to leave their class of origin* and affiliate with the carriers of middle-class values.[23]

Cohen's position on socio-economics and delinquency also seemed to incriminate most youths from the lower-classes: Either they were driven to delinquency because of an obsessive ambition to attain what others had, or they were completely lacking in aspirations, desiring neither the self-sufficiency nor the status of the middle-class. We may question the universal applicability of the above theory, because it seems to automatically demonize the "lower-class" person. After all, there is a certain implication, here, that if he has any ambition at all, the lower-class youth must necessarily covet the status and wealth of his middle/upper-class counterparts. And while Cohen's theory certainly explains why some poverty-stricken youths in our own world might turn to drug dealing and prostitution in order to make a profitable living, it also overlooks others of the same class who have never been tempted to use illegitimate means to secure economic equality with the middle or upper classes.

In addition, it does not take into account the fact that others may break rules or disobey laws for reasons that have nothing to do with securing wealth or status. And, ultimately, this is what distinguishes the hero from the adversary in Rowling's work: In other words, this is why we are more inclined to pardon Harry's rule breaking and to frown upon that of Tom Riddle/Voldemort…

---

[23] Downes, 1966, p. 57.

After all, since childhood, Tom Riddle has shown signs of criminality in the Adlerian sense of causing "intentional injury to others for one's own advantage."[24] And unlike the other theorists whom I cited earlier in this chapter, Adler attributed juvenile delinquency to pampering (usually from parents):

> Criminals whom I have studied, whether in life or literature, have all been of this type. They were always children who, through pampering or self-pampering, came to an early halt in the development of their social interest.
> (Adler, 1965, pp. 258-259)

Adler's assertion that the child criminal displays a "lack of social feeling" certainly applies to Dudley, Draco and the boy Tom Riddle. But the latter is obviously the most severe case, as his un-repented delinquency...

> shows itself in the goal of superiority, which is no longer within the frame of social acceptability but merely promotes a feeling of personal satisfaction without contributing to the welfare of the general community.
> (Adler, 1965, p. 53)

Tom Riddle did not have any parents to pamper him; but, as shown in *Half-blood Prince*,[25] he certainly engaged in what Adler called "self-pampering," such as using his powers to extort things from his peers. In contrast, the child (and later, the teenager) Harry never uses his powers against others for revenge or for personal gain. And in the series finale, we see that even the distrustful goblin Griphook believes that Harry's social transgressions are not self-seeking.[26]

---

[24] Adler, 1965, p. 255.

[25] See Chapter 13 of Book 6 ("The Secret Riddle"), where Dumbledore discovers that Tom often tortured other children from the orphanage, and he stole from them. Dumbledore refers to this habit as Riddle's "magpie-like tendency." (p. 260)

[26] See *Deathly Hallows* (p. 394), where, prior to the attack on Gringotts, Griphook declares his belief in Harry's good intentions: "If there was a wizard of whom I would believe that they did not seek personal gain…it would be you, Harry Potter."

Also, earlier in the series, we see the Headmaster trying to impress upon a 12-year-old Harry that, although there are indeed many similarities between the young protagonist and the boy Riddle, the differences in their intentions and their choices are what truly matter:

> '...You happen to have many qualities Salazar Slytherin prized in his hand-picked students. His own very rare gift, Parseltongue ... resourcefulness ... determination ... a certain disregard for the rules,' he added, his moustache quivering again. 'Yet the Sorting Hat placed you in Gryffindor. You know why that was. Think.'
>
> 'It only put me in Gryffindor,' said Harry in a defeated voice, 'because I asked not to go in Slytherin ...'
>
> '*Exactly*,' said Dumbledore, beaming once more. 'Which makes you *different* from Tom Riddle. It is our choices, Harry, that show what we truly are, far more than our abilities.'
>
> (*Chamber of Secrets*, p. 245.)

Philip Nel summarizes the above by stating that Harry "wonders if some of his abilities make him a bad person."[27] For example, we have already established that his Parselmouth ability links him directly to dark wizards like Voldemort and Slytherin. But as Dumbledore explains in the above, the fact that Harry and the boy Riddle were sorted into different houses suggests that they were already on totally different life paths when each one first arrived at Hogwarts, at age 11. And furthermore, it becomes quite clear early in the series that Harry has different motivations and priorities than his adversary.

In short, Harry has somehow (miraculously) developed a strong sense of "social interest," whereas the boy Riddle is only interested in himself. For instance, when the hero sees himself surrounded by a large, loving family as he looks into the Mirror of Erised,[28] Voldemort sees himself possessing the

---

[27] Nel, 2001, p. 37.

[28] See *Philosopher's Stone*, p. 152. The inscription on the mirror reads backwards: *"I show not your face but your heart's desire."*

Philosopher's Stone, a highly coveted object which allows its owner to have unlimited riches and immortality. And moreover, the image of Tom Riddle torturing and stealing from his childhood companions is significantly different from that of Harry running away from Dudley and his gang. Both boys were harshly persecuted during their childhoods; both showed signs of having magic powers even before the letter from Hogwarts arrived; but each one responded in his own way: Whereas Riddle embraced and abused his powers, constantly seeking revenge on others, Harry (as always, unaware of his own abilities[29]) usually tried to get himself out of harm's way and keep the peace.

***

We could also argue that the boy Harry has as many reasons to crave wealth and power, or to want to inflict pain and suffering upon others. But unlike Riddle, he did not allow suffering, want or lack of material things to determine his own values. As Dumbledore reminds him later in the series, not many people in the boy's position would have seen what he saw in the Mirror of Erised:

> In spite of all the temptation you have endured, all the suffering, you remain pure of heart, just as pure as you were at the age of eleven, when you stared into a mirror that reflected your heart's desire, and it showed you only the way to thwart Lord Voldemort, and not immortality or riches. Harry, have you any idea how few wizards could have seen what you saw in that mirror?
> (*Half-blood Prince*, pp. 477-478)

Also, throughout the series, it is Harry's love and compassion for others (and *not* his wealth or fame) that ultimately propel him to success amidst seemingly insurmountable challenges. In particular, the sense of loyalty, gratitude and love which he

[29] For example, in *Half-blood Prince*, the protagonist notices that the boy Riddle was not surprised at all to find out that he was "special," or a wizard: "He believed it much quicker than I did…I didn't believe Hagrid at first, when he told me." (p. 258)

feels for Hagrid remains constant throughout all the novels. Notably, it was Hagrid who informed Harry that he was a wizard, and who introduced a baffled 11-year-old protagonist to the wizarding world.[30] In contrast, Tom Riddle was neither surprised nor moved by the news that he was "special."[31] Nor was he grateful for the help Dumbledore offered him. And, as the Headmaster informs Harry in Book 6,

> 'Riddle was already highly self-sufficient, secretive and, apparently, friendless ... He did not want help or companionship on his trip to Diagon Alley. He preferred to operate alone ... In fact, his ability to speak to serpents did not make me nearly as uneasy as his obvious instincts for cruelty, secrecy and domination.'
> (*Half-blood Prince*, p. 259)

In sharp contrast, Harry valued Hagrid's companionship; and he is also extremely appreciative of minor tokens of friendship and solidarity, such as the letters he receives from his friends. In fact, these seemingly insignificant things are worth more to him than any amount of fame or money. For instance, in *Chamber of Secrets*, we see the hero devastated when he thinks Hermione and Ron are not writing to him during the summer holidays.[32] And so, we cannot make excuses for the boy Riddle without devaluing Harry's strength and 'goodness' in choosing the path of kindness and humanity over inhumanity and vengeance.

In fact, just like Voldemort, the hero is also an orphan; and although his parents left a lingering mark of love upon the infant Harry, this could have easily been erased by anger and spite—especially considering how harshly the Dursleys treated him. We discover in Book 6 that the orphanage-raised Riddle was a very angry child, and we also see the pitiable

[30] See *Philosopher's Stone*, pp. 39-66, where Harry learns that he is a wizard and enters the wizarding world at Hagrid's side.

[31] *Half-blood Prince*, p. 258.

[32] In fact, the house-elf Dobby had been hiding Harry's letters in an attempt to protect him from harm. The elf knew that the legendary Chamber would be opened again and students might die. And Dobby thought that, by making Harry not want to return to Hogwarts or see his friends again, he could keep him safe (See *Chamber of Secrets*, pp. 19-20).

circumstances in which he entered the world. But it should not be forgotten that (between ages 1 and 11) Harry also grew up in an environment which—at least for him—was devoid of love, affection or any kind of positive emotional parental attachment. And so, he also has many reasons for being angry at the world, for desiring revenge, or for being indifferent to other people's troubles. But, of course, the hero chooses otherwise.

For example, having been teased and called "potty"[33] by even the school poltergeist, Harry refuses to join in when his peers taunt Luna Lovegood with "Loony".[34] And, having been poor all his life in the Muggle world, he does not reject Ron on the basis of his poor family background:[35] During their first trip aboard the Hogwarts Express, Harry could have easily rejected the impoverished Ron (with his second-hand robes, frayed wand and dry corned beef sandwiches) and pursued a friendship with the wealthier, cooler and far more socially affluent Draco Malfoy. Here, he could easily choose to align himself with the wizarding world's social elite. But instead, he chooses to stand up for Ron, loyally.

Also, by becoming best friends with two obvious social misfits—Ron as Pauper of the Year and Hermione as the Muggle-born Bookworm of Year—Harry empowers them (due to his own celebrity in the wizarding world); and in so doing, the hero practically redefines 'cool.'

Another miraculous facet of Harry's personality is his generosity with his newfound wealth. I think this is partly what Dumbledore was referring to when he expressed surprise at the person the hero becomes in spite of all that he has been through. Not many people in Harry's position (from such a non-privileged, abusive background) would find it so

---

[33] See *Chamber of Secrets*, p. 152, where Peeves invents a song about Harry attacking Muggle-borns because he is mad: *"Oh Potter you rotter, oh what have you done? You're killing off students, you think it's good fun."*

[34] "Potty" and "Loony" are both British colloquialisms which denote madness. In *Order of the Phoenix*, pp. 760-761, Luna tells Harry how everyone calls her "Loony." Also, Harry finds her wandering around Hogwarts, searching for her possessions, which other students have taken and hidden.

[35] See *Philosopher's Stone*, p. 75, where an embarrassed Ron thinks he has erred in revealing his family's poverty to Harry: But "Harry didn't think there was anything wrong with not being able to afford" things.

easy to spend money on others when they themselves grew up being deprived of everything except their most basic needs. In fact, the most natural, predictable instinct for one who has never had much money is to become a sort of miserly hoarder when money does become available to him. In such cases, the deprived may find it hard to give money away; they might even hesitate to spend it on their own children...

And yet, in *Goblet of Fire*, we see Harry spending thirty Galleons procuring Omnioculars (magical telescope-like instruments) for himself and his friends at the Quidditch World Cup final (p. 86). And he does so without even thinking about the amount of money he has just spent. In fact, this event proves to be a source of great annoyance for Ron (pp. 473-474), who has always been self-conscious and somewhat embarrassed about his family's poverty and his own lack of spending power.

Also, later in the same book, Harry gives all his Triwizard winnings (a thousand gold Galleons) to the Weasley twins (pp. 635-636). And on top of that, in *Half-blood Prince* we see him insisting on paying for goods in their joke shop (pp. 116-117), even though it was his own money that had funded the business in the first place.

Once again, in severe contrast, we only ever see the child or teenage Tom Riddle taking things away from others—usually through some form of coercion—and guarding them as trophies.[36] And, of course, the adult Voldemort simply trades people's lives for obedience and subservience. Therefore, although we could argue that the fortune Harry had inherited from his parents put him in a far better position than the child Tom Riddle, the hero should still be commended for being wise enough not to value wealth or power over humanity—as is symbolized by what he sees in the enchanted Mirror...

When we consider that the child Harry must have been jealous of his pampered cousin nearly all his life—as any human being in his position would have been—it is a remarkable thing that, at age 11, he values his friends and his

---

[36] After discussing Riddle's "magpie-like" tendencies, Dumbledore and Harry later discover crucial information about the Horcruxes, which are, essentially, extremely valuable and ancient trophies, with pieces of Voldemort's soul now sheltered inside them. See *Half-blood Prince*, p. 260 & pp. 463-479.

relationships over money, fame or possessions. Not only did Harry grow up without money, but he was also squashed in a tiny cupboard under the Dursleys stairs for ten years, witnessing Aunt Petunia privileging his cousin over him on a daily basis, and being verbally and physically abused by his relatives. Nevertheless, where suffering might have hardened a rancorous Snape, or turned Tom Riddle into a cold, cruel, inhuman entity, Harry retains his compassion, generosity, and free-spiritedness. And his heart remains (miraculously) pure.

***

Nevertheless, as I approach the end of the chapter, I must declare my own indecision as to whether or not Harry Potter is a child/teenage delinquent. I have devoted a lot of space to proving Harry's 'goodness'—not in terms of innateness, but rather in the choices that he makes, especially when compared with Tom Riddle's choices. But I have also questioned whether or not we should make allowances for the adversary, especially considering that the protagonist's 'good' choices have been facilitated by others (parents, friends, relatives, and so forth) who have helped and loved him throughout his life.

When we compare Harry's life circumstances with those of Tom Riddle, it seems that the boy Tom has far more compelling justifications for being a rule-breaker: Basically, the circumstances in which Riddle entered the world were highly unfavorable; and, in this regard, he is entirely disadvantaged in terms of the parents and parental care he has received since birth. And while Harry's rule-breaking may not warrant the same level of condemnation as Voldemort's murderous ways, this does not detract from the fact that Potter does indeed transgress social boundaries. Also, just like Tom Riddle, he breaks rules repeatedly and without remorse.

And so, Rowling's protagonist certainly portrays a high degree of 'delinquency' in the most rudimentary sense of the term—that is, in choosing not to abide by the rules. But if we should regard social delinquents as individuals who lightly transgress serious moral boundaries, and who are lacking in consideration for others, or who generally show contempt for human life, then Harry is certainly not a delinquent. Unlike Riddle/Voldemort, Harry has a high level of social interest: Where the young Tom's delinquent behavior was motivated by jealousy and greed, Harry's guiding force has always been compassion. And this is demonstrated, of course, in his desire to save lives and to protect the liberties of social Others.

And moreover, perhaps the whole point of Harry's adventures is to demonstrate that sometimes it is not only OK but necessary to break the rules or to contradict the social order, particularly when they infringe upon the rights and dignities of fellow human beings. After all, the author herself has encouraged her readership to "question authority,"[37] especially when it takes the form of government or media establishments seeking to justify the abuse and/or oppression of social Others.

Also, one of the main ideas put forth in the series finale is that sometimes breaking the rules is the only *humane* thing to do—"*for the greater good*."[38] As a rather striking comparison, we could use the example of 'Aryan'-looking Germans who hid and protected their Jewish friends during the Nazi regime, or who perhaps fought against the establishment in other covert ways. Indeed, they were contradicting the social order; and back then they would have been punished severely for doing so. But in retrospect, we cannot but celebrate them as heroes. And so, our own history has demonstrated the necessity of the sort of moral relativism constantly displayed in the Harry Potter novels. And this fact makes Rowling's protagonist even more of a hero, because he has been able to use his own conscience and reasoning to determine the boundaries of permissible rule-breaking.

In addition, as was highlighted in previous chapters, some people within the wizarding world believe that Harry has to become a Dark wizard (or at least learn the Dark Arts) in order to defeat Voldemort. And so, in *Chamber of Secrets*,

---

[37] Interview in October 2007 at Carnegie Hall, Manhattan, New York.

[38] After being deeply perturbed by Dumbledore's association with Grindelwald, as well as his mentor's part in coining the famous mantra, Harry finally decides that "sometimes you've *got* to think about more than your own safety…Sometimes you've *got* to think about the greater good! This is war!" (*Deathly Hallows*, p. 458).

Goblet of Fire and *Order of the Phoenix* we see that he is feared by the public and presumed either delinquent or insane by the likes of Rita Skeeter and Cornelius Fudge—all because of his history with Voldemort.

Fortunately, however, Harry does not need to become a monster in order to defeat the monstrosity of Lord Voldemort: the latter had already handed the boy the ultimate weapon by marking him, and leaving a bit of his soul inside his rival by mistake. And, of course, due to Voldemort's inability to love, the piece of his soul that remains trapped inside Harry's scar is powerless—because the hero has *also* been marked by the far greater power of his mother's love. Thus, the coincidence of Voldemort unknowingly making Harry a Horcrux has equally facilitated the boy's triumph.

But despite the fact that Harry's 'chosen-ness' has been made possible by the circumstances of his birth and Voldemort's foolish mistakes, one must admit that the boy still has the *choice* to go to the Dark Side. And the temptation is most alluring in the series finale, where we see him torn between the Horcrux hunt and the enticing pursuit of immorality through finding all three Hallows. Ironically though, it is mortality which turns the tide for the hero: After witnessing Dobby's death, he finally realizes why the Horcrux quest is more important, and prioritizes Voldemort's destruction over his own life or his own desire to conquer death. He therefore accepts the responsibilities of being the "Chosen One" for his own sake as well as for others.

And so, perhaps the most important characteristic that distinguishes Harry from Voldemort is self-acceptance: Voldemort amputates his Muggle heritage—mutilating his own soul in the process—and embraces the bigoted ideologies of the wizarding world's social/racial elite. In contrast, Harry knows that he cannot change his own past or his heritage. Nor does he want to—regardless of what Skeeter, Fudge, the Dursleys or others might say about him.

However, as I highlighted earlier in this chapter, the fact that Harry's parents had loved him and provided for him—as opposed to the abandonment, rejection and poverty that the boy Riddle had to face—has also facilitated his coming of age as the hero of the tale. Nevertheless, although Harry could be said to have fewer reasons than his adversary for being a child delinquent, he is still extraordinary for having made the choices he has made, and for accepting himself.

Similar to the boy Tom Riddle and even the young Severus Snape, Harry has also experienced tremendous suffering during his childhood. But unlike Snape (who eventually became a Death Eater) and Riddle (who transformed into a murderous and inhuman Dark Lord), Harry has never allowed his past to lead him to the Dark side. Therefore, he has overcome his abusive upbringing in a way that neither Snape nor Riddle ever could.

We could also argue that Harry's self-acceptance makes him more humane and accepting towards others—that is, when we compare the other two characters (Severus and Tom) that have had similar upbringings. Snape, for example, has been irrevocably poisoned by a lifetime of jealousy and bitterness towards James Potter and Sirius Black. And, very much like Petunia Dursley, who could never forgive her own sister for being a witch (and who subsequently took out her frustrations on Harry), Snape has never been able to judge Harry independently of his own prejudiced views about James. And so, the mere fact that Harry reconciles with Dudley and later names his own son after Snape,[39] points to the extent of the hero's capacity to look beyond even the most justified grudges and see an individual's intrinsic worth as a human being...

Harry might never become close friends with the Dursleys (or the Malfoys, for that matter), and he will probably struggle to erase the terrible memories associated with Snape; but his feelings of animosity towards these characters do not prevent him from regarding them as lives worthy of being saved. And it is this ability to empathize with people—even with those who have hurt or harmed him—which ultimately distinguishes Harry from Voldemort. Basically, Harry is able to love others because he loves and accepts himself; whereas Voldemort merely transfers his own self-loathing to everyone else, and derives immense gratification from watching others suffer.

---

[39] Named after two Hogwarts Headmasters, Harry's second son is called Albus Severus. (*Deathly Hallows*, p. 607)

Hence, we could say that Adler's concept of "social interest" is a sort of equivalent for '*empathy*,' or the ability to identify and/or sympathize with others in one's social environment. Harry's self-love and social interest, or empathy, is continuously shown in the way he regards his peers. Naturally, he looks upon his friends with a haunting wish that he, too, had a loving, supportive family of his own. But he would never want to exchange places with Ron, Hermione or anyone else—simply because he embraces his responsibility and would never wish his fate upon another person.

And this is the essence of the 'good person' that Harry has been since childhood. It is also the reason why he does not run away from the tremendous task of facing Voldemort and saving the world—knowing all the while that he may not survive the battle. And even when we see him transforming into an angry, screaming, angst-ridden teenager in *Order of the Phoenix*, Harry has still not lost that essential quality of inner 'goodness,' which is, in essence, his ability to empathize with others. For instance, we see that even while he is overwhelmed by the grief of Sirius's very recent death, he still finds it within himself to sympathize and offer assistance to the persecuted Luna Lovegood (pp. 759-761). And in *Half-blood Prince*, we see him showing resolute loyalty to social outcasts such as Neville Longbottom, when most of his peers expect him to have much "cooler friends" (p. 133). Therefore, by accepting his own oddity and 'outsider' status as "The ('Damaged') Boy Who Lived," the hero is able to show acceptance and compassion to others who fall into the same '*non*-normal' category. Most importantly, Harry values the people in his life who have stood by him, regardless of blood status (or race), popularity, or how socially or economically empowered they are.

A true testament to his capacity for empathy is the way he reacts to discovering the contents of the Prophecy, and finding out that Voldemort had a choice between the Potters and the Longbottoms. In the following, we witness the hero's sense of inner torture, as he wonders what his life might have been like if Voldemort had gone after Neville's family instead of his own:

> Had Voldemort chosen Neville, it would be Neville sitting opposite Harry bearing the lightening-shaped scar and the weight of the prophecy ... or would it? Would Neville's mother have died to save him, as Lily had died for Harry? Surely she would ... but what if she had been unable to stand between her son and Voldemort? Would there, then, have been no 'Chosen One' at all? An empty seat where Neville now sat and a scarless Harry who would have been kissed goodbye by his own mother, not Ron's?
> (*Half-blood Prince*, pp. 133-134)

Evidently, Harry is as tortured by the idea of Neville's death as his own. As I suggested before, he recognizes that no one—including himself—deserves the pain that he has suffered. And it is quite remarkable that, despite the horrific tragedy of losing his parents and growing up in a loveless environment, Harry is still able to feel tremendous compassion for another human being who perhaps only narrowly missed his own fate.

***

Finally, since I also briefly raised the issue of Harry's scar earlier in this chapter, as part of my concluding argument that self-acceptance ultimately distinguishes the hero from Riddle/Voldemort I would like to emphasize the fact that, from as early as *Philosopher's Stone*, we learn that Harry liked his scar.[40] This is a good sign, because it suggests that, even at this early stage, the hero has accepted himself, his past and his fate as Voldemort's ultimate adversary. And although throughout the series we sometimes see Harry wishing his life were less complicated, he accepts the truth about himself, regardless of how harshly other people (like the Dursleys) have judged him.[41] Furthermore, after discovering that his wand shares a twin core with Voldemort's wand, it does not

---

[40] "The only thing Harry liked about his own appearance was a very thin scar on his forehead which was shaped like a bolt of lightning." (*Philosopher's Stone*, p. 20).

[41] See *Philosopher's Stone*, p. 23, where Aunt Petunia gives Harry a bad haircut but leaves a fringe "to hide that horrible scar," and *Goblet of Fire*, pp. 611-615, where Fudge disparages Harry's sanity because of his "curse scar" (p. 613).

affect Harry's self-perception or his will to choose Good over Evil. And although he feels "contaminated"[42] when he learns that his scar is the mark of a Horcrux, Harry continues to think of himself as Voldemort's opposite, ultimately deciding to lay down his life rather than choose an unnatural, ill-gotten immortality.

And so, to sum up, Harry acknowledges that he has been robbed of his childhood and victimized by Voldemort; and he knows that the tragic events of his past continue to have a profound effect on him emotionally (as demonstrated by his scar as well as the Dementors' attraction to him). But he does not allow himself to be defined by victimhood; he fights it constantly and ultimately overcomes it. One example of this is the fact that it is Harry who insists that Lupin teach him the Patronus Charm so that he can fight the Dementors.[43] This suggests that the hero is not just pro-active about self-defense but also about self-improvement: He recognizes that the fear of the Dementors paralyzes him (and also that, due to his own harrowing history, these creatures will always be attracted to him). But instead of resorting to the safety of Hogwarts or depending on Dumbledore and others to protect him, he learns to protect himself, and in doing so, he triumphs over his Dementor-related 'disability,' if we might call it that.

And moreover, his ability to produce a corporeal Patronus later enables him to save Dudley's life, and it also qualifies him to lead and teach his peers to fight the Dark Arts. Thus, by empowering himself, Harry also facilitates the empowerment of others—again, in sharp contrast with Voldemort, who has always sought power so that he could dominate, silence and oppress everyone else.

And so, whatever his relatives or the rest of society might expect from Harry as a "should-be-delinquent," his choices and his good heart are what ultimately determine his fate.

---

[42] Actually, the word "contaminated" is used in *Order of the Phoenix* (p. 435), after Harry overhears others speculating on whether or not he has been possessed by Voldemort. But he actually discovers that he is a Horcrux in the penultimate chapter of *Deathly Hallows*, pp. 550-551.

[43] See *Prisoner of Azkaban* (p. 141), where Harry implores Professor Lupin to show him how to protect himself against Dementors because "I need to be able to fight them—"

Harry Potter is therefore a symbol of hope for anyone who has ever been 'damaged' (physically or emotionally), abandoned, tortured, abused, or otherwise persecuted and oppressed. And perhaps it is this fact, more than anything else, which explains the appeal of Rowling's work, not only to the mainstream audience, but also to those individuals who may have found themselves trapped in the margins of society.

Conclusion

As I approach the end of this volume I am even more aware of its limitations: It is even clearer now how unfeasible it is to do justice to all the topical issues related to prejudice in one short book, whilst critiquing seven novels at the same time. For example, I would have liked to spend more time on the sexism issue, which I briefly raised in Chapter 6. Heilman and Gregory have expressed objections about how gender roles and family life are depicted in the series, with a sort of inferior positioning of women in maternal, domestic roles or as deputizing officials to more powerful men. My own personal view on this issue is that the *Harry Potter* novels, in many ways, reflect the societal conventions of our own world. However, I would not go as far as saying that they "promote and perpetuate dominant culture," as Heilman and Gregory suggest,[1] but rather that their formulaic structure and conventional content serve the purpose of helping the author to construct an effective societal metaphor.

Moreover, for this volume, I set out to examine the prejudice ***themes*** in Rowling's work: Rather than analyzing her portrayal of current societal conventions, I wished to take a closer look at the metaphors of prejudice in our own world, which she has created and developed throughout the series.

***

I would also have liked to address the religion topic in far greater detail, particularly in the modern context of Islamic terrorism. Allport's take on religion was that "it makes and unmakes prejudice."[2] And, as Batson and Stocks explain:

> ...All major religions teach universal tolerance and compassion. In practice, however, these same religions often promote intolerance and hatred."[3]

---

[1] The quote has been paraphrased. See essay entitled "Images of the Privileged Insider and Outcast Outsider" (Heilman, 2002, p. 257)

[2] Allport, 1954/1979, p. 444.

[3] From the essay entitled "Religion and Prejudice" in *On the Nature of Prejudice*. (Edited by Dovidio et al., 2005, p. 413)

And so, it might have been useful to explore the religious (doctrinal) model of prejudice, as it relates to patterns of "making and unmaking prejudice" in the *Harry Potter* novels.

Nevertheless, I think I have sufficiently addressed this model in terms of developing the themes that were most relevant to the concept of "acting out" prejudice in society—whether in the real world or in the fictional wizarding world. For example, factors concerning race are sometimes (though not always) applicable to cases where a person is the subject of religion-based prejudice. In other words, the prejudice is based on similar principles, which are basically notions of perpetual outsiderhood: The social Other is considered to be irreconcilably different because of what he or she believes.

***

Another topic that I would have liked to address in greater detail is the role that the State plays in sustaining prejudice—whether by fuelling the propaganda machine (through media censorship and manipulation) or by passing discriminatory laws. I have very briefly addressed the 'false doctrine' issue as it relates to anti-werewolf stigma and legislation. However, there were also some other crucial subverted references to statehood (in an almost Orwellian sense) that I have not addressed. These include Dolores Umbridge's repressive regime in *Order of the Phoenix*, plus the Muggle-born trials in which she plays a crucial role in *Deathly Hallows*. Also, Dolores's "Inquisitorial Squad" (in *Order of the Phoenix*) references numerous historical events, including the Spanish Inquisition and the more modern instances of torturing and questioning political detainees.

Also, I did not spend a lot of time discussing the repressive politics of Rufus Scrimgeour, who so unwittingly perpetuates the same mistakes as his predecessor (former Minister for Magic Cornelius Fudge). The new Minister goes to extraordinary lengths to conceal the truth from the wizarding public, while the Death Eaters quietly infiltrate the Ministry right under his nose. Unfortunately, Scrimgeour is yet another example of a politician with good intentions but questionable methods.

***

And finally, I would have liked to discuss the 'scapegoat' issue in greater detail. This is a subject matter to which Allport devoted a lot of space in his book. Due to the recentness of the Holocaust at the time he was writing about prejudice, the scapegoating of Jews throughout history was quite a topical and relevant issue. And in the introduction to his commentary on Allport's chapter on scapegoating, Glick also cites the more recent example of the Tutsi genocide in Rwanda, where the neighboring Hutu tribe blamed the Tutsis for the country's economic and social problems.[4]

But while there is certainly a dynamic of scapegoating in the *Harry Potter* series (particularly in terms of Pure-bloods blaming Muggle-borns for diminishing the wizard race), it was difficult to develop this topic due to a lack of textual evidence. For instance, we know that there were envy-related socio-economic reasons behind the Nazis' persecution of Jews. But there is very little evidence in the *Harry Potter* books to support the claim that Muggles or Muggle-borns were generally wealthier than wizards: They vastly outnumber wizards; but they are not necessarily portrayed as richer or more affluent. In fact, there are poverty-related, middle-class and upper-class dynamics on both sides. And so, any text-to-world analysis in this regard would be limited by the mere complexity of the scapegoating issue, as well as the lack of textual evidence from Rowling.

And besides, we cannot forget that the primary aim of any piece of fantasy literature is to entertain, rather than to instruct or to create perfect metaphors of society.

***

As I stated in the *Foreword*, one of my aims for this work was simply to highlight the 'general perceptions' of social Others that lead to prejudice and discrimination in the *Harry Potter* novels. Also, I wished to comment on how Rowling's

[4] From the essay entitled "Choice of Scapegoats" in *On the Nature of Prejudice*. (Edited by Dovidio et al., 2005, p. 244)

construction of wizarding world hierarchies reflects an understanding of some of the societal issues currently plaguing our world. Admittedly, there are many ways of interpreting literature; and so, other *Harry Potter* enthusiasts might have understood the same subplots highlighted in this book in entirely different ways. Nevertheless, we cannot deny the shrewdness of Rowling's gaze upon society. Whether or not she had meant to do so, she has managed to create an effective metaphor for some rather complex real-world social issues through her so-called "magical community" or "wizarding world." And, in doing so, she has demonstrated an acute understanding of human nature, as well as the politics of difference...

In several interviews in which the author answered questions related to the series, she has repeatedly declared an intention to send a message of tolerance to her readership; and the message is not exactly subtle. And still, no one could accuse her of being 'preachy': If she were an obvious brow-beater campaigning for social change, then perhaps far less people would have bought or read her books. And perhaps we would not enjoy them as much as we do?

But it is one thing to create entertaining metaphors in popular fantasy literature of real-world societal issues, and an entirely different matter altogether to offer real solutions to the problems that currently plague all modern societies. In the end, we are all reminded that this is just a story: The mere fact that it has a happy, complete, conclusive ending makes it a sort of '*too-good-to-be-true*' fairytale, despite the many personal tragedies experienced by some of its characters. After all, as I stated in previous chapters, the author has gone as far as revealing to her readership (following the release of the series finale) that the Ministry of Magic is purged of its discrimination after the last war against Voldemort.

And so, basically, we are to accept that Harry accomplishes the impossible by keeping his soul in tact whilst fighting the monstrosity of Lord Voldemort, surviving the battle and then waltzing off into the sunset with two unscathed sidekicks and the girl of his dreams. In fact, apart from "Albus Severus," Harry's second son, we are only left to speculate on the middle-names of his other children and the names of his grandchildren. But no clues are given as to how exactly the trio go about creating "a better world"—in which they clearly live by the time we get to the end of the Epilogue ("19 Years Later").

It is certainly the perfect ending for a fairy-tale; but it is by no means typical of the real world, where stories such as Harry's rarely have neat, positive, conclusive endings. It is safe to say that the fate of revolutionaries in the real world is far more complex and far less optimistic than Harry Potter's situation, especially in terms of the kind of resistance they encounter from corrupt governmental systems that have sustained social injustice for decades, if not centuries. After all, the fall of Hitler did not bring about the total eradication of anti-Semitism in Europe. Likewise, the rise of Nelson Mandela and the end of Apartheid in South Africa did not signal the end of racist abuse against Blacks in that country—or across the world for that matter. Neither does new legislation legalizing gay marriage diminish the level of persecution which homosexuals continue to face in conservative social settings.

Therefore, although Rowling has created a valuable metaphor of some of the world's most troublesome social issues, she is limited by her role as a storyteller to offer clear solutions that can be instituted in order to bring about tangible or immediate social changes in the real world.

The writer appears to be operating on the assumption that she can change the world by changing the way people think. And although it is not a perfect strategy, especially considering how easy it is for the mainstream to rationalize guilt, or to turn a blind eye to the sort of glaring social injustices inflicted upon some minority groups in our own world, it is, nonetheless, a good start. It certainly takes a brave kind of honesty and, in the words of the character Mad-Eye Moody, *constant vigilance* to spot the kinds of injustice and inequality that are so easily overlooked by society.

This is particularly the case when—as we see with the house-elves in the *Harry Potter* series—overwhelming disparities between social groups (in terms of basic privileges or inalienable rights) have become the social 'norm.' George Orwell echoed similar sentiments in the censored Preface to *Animal Farm*, in which he warned that "tolerance and decency are deeply rooted in England, but they are not indestructible, and they have to be kept alive partly by conscious effort."[5] This is, essentially, the message that Rowling is trying to send, decades later. But more often than not, people are likely to miss the point, or change the subject altogether.

For example, over the years, the absence of ethnic minority lead characters in the *Harry Potter* books and films has been the subject of various commentaries in the media, as some critics have slated Rowling for having three Caucasian lead characters and restricting tokenized ethnic minorities to minor roles. But, clearly, the same commentators would have hardly found the occasion (or had the inclination) to make this criticism if the books and films had never become the global franchising success that they are. And where the marketing and franchising successes of the so-called "Harry Potter phenomenon" are concerned, the author herself is highly irrelevant.

And moreover, we ought to ask ourselves if it is a good idea to extend the political constraints (and the hypocrisy) of "affirmative action" to literature. Can we, in all honesty, scapegoat a writer with the fact that ethnicity is still restricted to the margins in popular literature and in the visual media (television, cinema and so forth)? Surely, as literary critics we must see that burdening any writer with the responsibility of 'racially diversifying' literature compromises the integrity of the story-telling process. And furthermore, it does not correct the obvious imbalances within the bookselling industry, where ethnic minority fiction writers are still vastly underrepresented on bookshop shelves targeting the so-called "mainstream" audience. Clearly, it is not the absence of ethnic characters in Rowling's work that is the problem, but rather the mainstream's disposition towards ethnicity. And neither J.K. Rowling nor any other popular writer should be made to account for the perceived public tastes, which are largely determined by cultural bias, and reverently catered to by an exceedingly conventional, White-dominated book publishing industry.

---

[5] The banned Preface can be found in the latest editions of *Animal Farm*, and also on several internet sites.

In fact, we can see Rowling ridiculing the publishing industry and media's habits of privileging celebrity and physical appearance over quality and substance in *Chamber of Secrets*. Here, we meet the talent-less Gilderoy Lockhart: a shallow, self-obsessed charlatan and plagiarist who is prolifically published and exceedingly adored by the wizarding public—simply because of his good looks and perfect smile.

Of course, this is *not* to say that either the physical appearance or the ethnic backgrounds of authors is a crucial (or the only) criterion when publishers decide which stories to publish or heavily promote as popular fiction ... Such a statement would be a gross generalization about the operations of the publishing world in gauging mainstream tastes, or identifying works that appeal to the mainstream audience. But it goes without saying that, whether it is the author's or the protagonist's physical appearance, "looks" do sometimes play a part in the decision-making process. For example, in a talk given at the 2004 Cheltenham Book Festival, Malorie Blackman[6] admitted that, when she first started out as a writer, she was often asked by publishing editors (some of whom would later reject her work) to write Caucasian lead characters, so that her stories would be more appealing to the mass market...

There is also the rather complex issue of the subject matters that ethnic minority writers are most inclined to write about, and how these may or may not appeal to the so-called "mass market." But unfortunately, I cannot address this issue here without over-generalizing; and so, I will refrain from discussing it at all...

***

Of course, other fantasy writers such as G. P. Taylor have jumped on the disapproving bandwagon, citing *Harry Potter* as the prime example of ethnic deficiencies in popular children's literature in Britain. In two separate 2003 interviews with the BBC and NPR radio, Taylor declared:

---

[6] Author of the acclaimed novel, *Noughts and Crosses*.

> "There [was] no good, positive black characters in children's literature over here. We have Harry Potter who is white, Anglo-Saxon, protestant, with his dark hair. We've got Hermione and Ron. But there is no place in English literature where people of color have been used as positive role models. And I did consciously want to do that."[7]

Here, Taylor is referring to his first novel *Shadowmancer*, for which he created the character Raphah, a multilingual African who joins forces with two Yorkshire teenagers in the fight against the evil vicar Demurral at some point during the sixteenth century. But unfortunately, like so many others of his race and social standing had done before him, Taylor sought a simple solution for a rather complex social issue.

In addition, there is an unmistakable tone of self-congratulation in the above quote, as Taylor asserts a sort of '*condescension*' to '*include*' an ethnic minority lead in a work with a mainstream target audience—presumably in contrast to other English writers who have so far neglected to do so. But his declaration shows extraordinary naivety and an almost endearing (though thoroughly frustrating) lack of understanding of the racial divide, or even the publicity or marketing strategies employed by the publishing industry.

For example, although Raphah is supposed to be one of Taylor's '*leads*,' the character is almost completely overlooked in most of the initial reviews for *Shadowmancer*. For example, the BBC North Yorkshire Book Club review identified only the two English teenagers (Kate and Thomas) as "two attractive heroes who will, no doubt, feature in future adventures."[8] And Raphah—the third and crucial member of Taylor's trio—is not mentioned until the end of the article, where there is no mention at all of him being black or African. In fact, he is simply described as "the mysterious friend who offers a tantalizing glimpse of another country and culture."[9] Here, we see that Taylor's valiant attempt to empower the ethnic

---

[7] BBC and NPR Radio broadcast. Real Audio Keyword: "Shadowmancer."

[8] Book Review entitled "*Shadowmancer* Touted as 'Hotter than Potter'" (2004).

[9] Ibid.

minority character is thwarted by the mainstream reviewer's instinctive urge to not only mystify and exoticize him, but also to conceal from the potential reader the very thing that Taylor considered to be the most integral part of the character's identity: his race.

Similarly, in the first *Harry Potter* movie,[10] we can see the film industry not only marginalizing race, but also appealing to overriding racial stereotypes. For example, while Harry's black classmate, Dean Thomas, is given only one or two lines in the entire film, the Centaur character called Firenze is portrayed as a black man, despite the fact that Rowling specifically describes him in the books as a blond man with a Palomino body and blue eyes.[11]

And so, I think G.P. Taylor might have deluded himself in thinking he can control how race is portrayed in the media. And furthermore, he has failed to create a veritable Black protagonist in Raphah, whose character is underdeveloped and shrouded in deep mysticism. The mere fact that the most positive reviews for the story use words such as "mysterious" and "tantalizing" to describe the character confirms and legitimizes Taylor's very own (mainstream) perceptions of the so-called '*exotic*.' Without realizing it, he has obviously been socialized to view himself—a white author of popular fiction—as the social norm, and to regard ethnicity as '*otherness*' and 'non-mainstream.' And, rather unfortunately, such notions of entitlement do come across in his work, despite his (commendable) efforts to be racially inclusive.

Therefore, mainstream Caucasian writers taking up the task of 'diversifying' popular literature with minority characters (ethnic, religious or otherwise) will not correct the obvious imbalances in the popular fiction market. Rather than promoting or encouraging diversity in literature, such an approach to writing creates an awkward, contrived sense of characterization, with rather obvious designs for futile political correctness.

---

[10] The Warner Brothers Film was released in the US as *Harry Potter and the Sorcerer's Stone* and in Great Britain as *Harry Potter and the Philosopher's Stone*. (2001)

[11] See *Philosopher's Stone*, p. 187.

And so, it seems to me that, instead of wondering why a writer as popular as J.K. Rowling did not create ethnic minority leads, we should rather be asking ourselves why more ethnic minority writers, or perhaps even works with ethnic lead characters like Raphah, rarely achieve the status of being in the phenomenally popular league—alongside works by Tolkien, Lewis, Blyton, Pratchett, Pullman, Rowling, and so forth. (And, once again, being able to cite the few canonized (or other) examples will not eliminate the overall disparity). If we are brave enough, we might even ask ourselves why fictional ethnic minority characters rarely get converted into Hollywood blockbuster phenomena (alongside Frodo, Lyra and Harry[12])...

It is either because there is a general perception that the vast majority of ethnic minority writers do not possess the skills necessary to write for a popular audience, or, that publishers (and Hollywood)—believing themselves to acquainted with mainstream tastes—are convinced that the mass audience is really not that interested in ethnicity ... And therefore, they might limit their investment in works with ethnic minority leads or by ethnic minority writers.

Clearly, these are uncomfortable truths which still need to be spoken. After all, silence is the most effective form of oppression. And furthermore, as Patricia Williams writes,

> If race is something about which we dare not speak in polite social company the same cannot be said of the viewing of race.
> (Williams, 1997, p. 17)

And so, the racial biases latent in the publishing industry are perceived and casually accepted, but never openly acknowledged: This is really where the real problem lies; and it certainly will not be rectified by putting popular Caucasian authors under pressure to write ethnic minority leads.

Furthermore, one might enquire: Who is it that determines what causes deserve more attention, or which marginalized groups should be given greater visibility in the

---

[12] The three protagonists from Tolkien's *The Lord of the Rings*, Pullman's *His Dark Materials* trilogy and J.K. Rowling's *Harry Potter* series, respectively.

printed or visual media? In other words, if we are going to criticize J.K. Rowling for not having any ethnic minority leads, should we not also berate her for not putting Ron or Hermione in a wheelchair,[13] or for neglecting to portray Dumbledore's character as a flaming homosexual,[14] or for not making any of her other characters Muslim, and so forth?

Of course, such contrivances would defeat the purpose of creating metaphors of prejudice, which is what the "wizarding world" or "magical community" is all about. They would also undermine the clear message that Rowling is trying to send to society through a fictional world that has its own parameters of racial hierarchy and social difference: Simply, that physical appearance (including race, disability, and so forth) should not determine a person's worth or hinder their progress in society—Nor should sexuality, age, socio-economics, or any of the other factors which cause human beings to marginalize each other.

The whole point of the *Harry Potter* series is to send the message that no one should ever be required to 'perform' a pre-determined, designated role (based on what they look like or where they come from) in order to receive social acceptance, respect or humane treatment. And this message is constantly restated throughout the novels. Whether through the Muggle-born subplot or those pertaining to giants, werewolves or house-elves, Rowling implicitly implores her audience not to place too much stock in outward appearance, social stereotypes or pecking orders based on blood or race.

***

The rigid, static structure of Rowling's wizarding world points to the sustained disadvantaged position of certain groups in the hierarchical set-up of the real world. In most modern societies, social hierarchies are sometimes—but not always—linked to race, blood or other biological elements.

---

[13] See Christina Papamichael's BBC article "Harry Potter and the Curse of Disability." (See the *Bibliography* of this volume for a URL reference).

[14] Some fans were disturbed after Rowling's recent revelation that Dumbledore is gay. One news article called for Rowling to "Put Dumbledore back in the Closet." (Cloud, *Times Online*, 2007)

And, indeed, institutional racism exists; but nowadays it is not nearly as pronounced—or as unsubtle—as it seems to be in Rowling's fictional world. And yet, there are unmistakable trends that justify certain generalizations about race and social status, in the same way that generalizations about elves and Muggle-borns have, to a certain degree, reflected and/or determined their social status within the magical community.

Take the healthcare issue in our own world as an example: In *Whitewashing Race* (2003), the co-authors explain that there is a marked difference in the level of access to basic healthcare for the majority of America's Latino and Black population, in comparison with Whites.

Another example pertains to education. Statistics show that, in the United States, children who come from broken homes or who grow up in underprivileged neighborhoods are most likely to come from ethnic minority groups, and that they are also less likely to apply to university. As Rattansi iterates, it is not surprising—given the disparities in educational achievement—that "while nearly half of all white men are in 'white-collar' jobs, the portion for Blacks is less than one-third."[15]

Here, we see education operating as a social ladder in both the literal and figurative sense. Likewise, if we observe certain social trends in Rowling's fictional world, we see that despite their wizard blood, Squibs and werewolves are unable to climb the wizarding world's social ladder, partly due to their lack of access to magical education. Hence, we could say that these groups are '*kept in their place*' by their social status and/or personal misfortunes. In much the same way, many of the underprivileged are socially immobile in our own world due to their lack of access to education. And, unfortunately, in the United States in particular, this social trend tends to correlate with the racial background of the people in question.

Although many Whites in the United States experience severe socio-economic problems as well, the figures (percentage-based ratios) suggest that poverty and lack of opportunities for social advancement affect ethnic minority persons far more than the Caucasian group. For example, as Rattansi explains:

---

[15] Rattansi, 2007, p. 142.

> Striking disparities between American Whites and Blacks are to be found in crime and the criminal justice system. While Blacks make up around 12% of the total population, they constitute 50% of the prison population, a figure that has risen from 29% in 1950.
> (Rattansi, 2007, p. 142)

And so, even though notions of 'privilege' in our world are sometimes non-racial, they are still fraught with socio-economic consequences for the racial and/or cultural Other.

Non-visible minority groups such as the gay community or the mentally ill also struggle for social equality because of prevailing negative perceptions, or stereotypes. But physical appearance is usually the first and most obvious marker of difference.[16] Furthermore, physical features such as obesity, disability, permanent disfigurement, unconventional or religious clothing, and so forth, sometimes operate as resistant social barriers, even though they are sometimes unrelated to racial background...

A social privilege might simply be the fact that, by virtue of one's appearance or obvious religious or cultural allegiance, family, racial or socio-economic background, a person is perceived in a positive light, is expected to do and accomplish great things, or simply be '*a good person*.' In the meantime, other individuals with the same qualifications and motives but different appearance, background or connections are almost irrevocably cast in a negative light. Thus, traditional perceptions are maintained and prejudgments are made to the detriment of the individual who finds him or her self in an undesirable social category.

J.K. Rowling's call for tolerance pertains to all of the aforementioned groups. But we need more than mere tolerance if we are to work towards improving the world. At the least, we need the right definition of tolerance because, as Allport explained, mere tolerance cannot be an appropriate anti-dote to *intolerance*:

---

[16] For example, in the last chapter, I outlined the reasons why Harry Potter's scar is of such great symbolic importance.

> Tolerance may seem to be a flabby word. When we say that we tolerate a headache, or our shabby apartment, or a neighbor, we certainly do not mean that we like them. To tolerate newcomers in a community is merely a negative act of decency
> (Allport, 1954/1979, p. 425).

Rowling's magical community provides some good example of the wrong kind of tolerance, plus the dangers it poses to social harmony. For example, prior to Voldemort's first rise to power, and even after his fall in the early 1980s, the wizarding world was 'tolerant' towards Muggle-borns, in that the group was no longer violently persecuted, and it had become 'politically *in*correct' to use the "Mudblood" epithet. Nevertheless, as demonstrated through characters like Cornelius Fudge and Horace Slughorn, many Half-bloods and Pure-bloods continued to perpetuate negative stereotypes about the innately inferior ability of witches and wizards born to two Muggle parents. In much the same way, modern social researchers such as Herrnstein and Murray continue to perpetuate ideas regarding the inferior intellectual ability of Blacks[17] ...

Perhaps the likes of Fudge and Slughorn even secretly resented the rise of a few Muggle-borns to higher social circles—the so-called *exceptions that proved the rule*. Although they would never go as far as calling a Muggle-born a "Mudblood", they were still deeply racist: They 'tolerated' the presence of Muggle-borns in the wizarding world, but they neither respected nor accepted them as social equals.

Meanwhile, other out-groups within the magical community, particularly those unfortunate enough to be categorized as "sub-human" or "part-human," were facing bigotry that went beyond mere perception. Werewolves were being deprived of the most basic rights; elves were being shamefully abused and exploited; goblins carried serial numbers like mere objects; and the giants, most notably, were nearly persecuted into extinction.

---

[17] In *The Bell Curve*, Herrnstein and Murray argue that Blacks have genetically derived inferior IQs compared to Whites and Asians (Rattansi, 2007, p. 142).

For most of these so-called "sub-human" and "part-human" magical beings, their presence in the magical community was only acceptable according to terms laid down by wizards. The very essence of their beings—as in not being "*fully human*"—was dictated by wizards. And so, the wizard race used the rhetoric of diminished humanity to justify exploiting and persecuting their fellow magical beings. ... This sounds so dreadfully familiar when we consider some of the justifications for the Trans-Atlantic Slave Trade.

Therefore, if wizards were to say that they 'tolerated' other magical beings, even when the wizarding world was in a relatively peaceful state, what they would really be saying is that they '*put up with*' them despite their personal feelings of *insecurity* about these social Others in their midst. Despite their *ignorance* of their customs, and despite their *indifference* to matters that truly concerned them, they 'tolerated' their presence. ... We can certainly see some very important parallels when we look at social pecking orders and the separation of ethnic and religious communities in our own world, or the way society often mislabels individuals who lead alternative lifestyles, or underestimates people from disadvantaged family backgrounds or those of low socio-economic standing...

And so, as Rowling aptly demonstrates throughout the *Harry Potter* series, mere tolerance cannot be the antidote for *intolerance*. We must adopt what Allport called the "more rugged" meaning of being tolerant, which takes into account not our indifference but our most purposeful judgments, making "no distinction of race, color, or creed,"[18]and we may easily add to that: "physicality, gender, sexuality, or socio-economic background." In order to eradicate prejudice and intolerance in the real world, we must develop and embrace a more inclusive and far more "comfortable" sense of *acceptance*.

[18] Allport, 1954/1979, p. 425.

Afterword

'You take *Harry Potter* way too seriously,' said an American colleague once, as I discussed the "Squib" and "Mudblood" subplots with her. At that time, she had still not read any of the *Harry Potter* novels, and I myself had not got very far in the series. But even then, I felt that there were some deep, heavy politics lurking beneath the surface in Rowling's fictional wizarding world. It has always amazed me whenever critics commented on how "subtle" J.K. Rowling's messages were. In my view, not only are the messages emphatically and clearly expressed, but a seething anger at all forms of social injustice also percolates through the series. And besides, the author has made countless public declarations that the *Harry Potter* books are "a prolonged argument for tolerance."[1] And so, in a sense, her efforts to send a message to society will have proved futile if readers fail to take the books seriously.

Of course, there is a saying that, *when one's only tool is a hammer, everything looks like a nail.* And I suppose that, since my life's work has largely centered around postcolonial issues (which in a sense scrutinize many of the prejudice and discrimination trends in most modern societies), and since my main aim when I set out to write this book was to highlight and comment on the social issues in the *Harry Potter* novels, naturally, I would have been looking for signs of prejudice in each sentence and in every figure of speech ... Quite the opposite, the average *Harry Potter* reader simply picks up the novels for entertainment or a bit of light reading.

Indeed, I sometimes wondered if I was taking the books "too seriously," or simply seeing things that were not there or that the author never meant to say or imply. One such instance (when I thought, "Maybe I am reading too much into it") was when I read *Chamber of Secrets* for the first time: It struck me as really odd that, after being coerced by Malfoy into suspending Dumbledore, the Hogwarts body of school

[1] See the interview report in a news article by Hillel Italie (*Times* Online). The URL reference can be found in the *Bibliography* section of this volume.

governors obviously regretted their decision, especially when the attacks on Muggle-borns continued. But they were only able to find the courage to stand up to Malfoy and reinstate Dumbledore when a Pure-blood (Ginny Weasley) finally disappeared.

I instantly read this subplot as a typical example of one social group (Pure-bloods, in this case) inspiring far greater sympathy—both in the hearts of the mainstream as well as in the political agenda of the authorities—than out-groups such as Ethnic Minorities. In other words, I thought that although the governors were not exactly indifferent to the fact that Muggle-borns were being attacked—after all, Lucius Malfoy had used the fact that they *cared* about student welfare to manipulate them into getting rid of Dumbledore—they were obviously not as alarmed about the Muggle-borns being targeted as they were when Ginny Weasley became a victim. And so, it became clear to me that at some point in wizarding history, Muggle-borns must have been severely persecuted on the basis that they were innately inferior.

Still, citing this one example as a demonstration of wizarding world racism made me feel a bit like the boy who cried "wolf." So I then attempted to rationalize my way out of assuming that the governors' hesitancy was related to traditional wizarding prejudice against Muggle-borns—that is, if we should interpret relatively reduced sympathy as prejudice (which it certainly is). And I told myself that the previous attacks were merely "petrifications"; the monster had never before "taken" a student into the chamber, as it had done with Ginny. And so, naturally, Ginny's situation should be perceived as far more serious ... But the sheer immediacy of Dumbledore's return (following Ginny's disappearance) convinced me that my initial conclusion was right: The truth of the matter is that it was not until a Pure-blood became singled-out for persecution that the governors and the wider wizarding public realized that no one was safe.

And furthermore, the development of the "Muggle-born persecution" subplot in subsequent *Harry Potter* novels has demonstrated the group's traditionally disadvantaged position within the wizarding world.

Alongside the Muggle-born issue, Rowling satirizes all kinds of prejudiced attitudes towards out-groups in the real world. And she does so through the subplots involving other persecuted magical species or targeted magical "beings": "Squibs," "werewolves," "giants," "elves," "goblins," and so forth. And with the release of the final book in the series (*Harry Potter and the Deathly Hallows*), the readership finally witnesses the extent and the severity of 'old-time' wizarding prejudice against out-groups (especially towards Muggle-borns). And so, there is no doubt left in my mind that the *Harry Potter* books are just as political as they are entertaining.

In this volume, I have avoided discussing the literary merits of Rowling's work because they are, in fact, irrelevant to my discussion of the prejudice and discrimination themes in the series. And besides, various critics have already committed themselves to the task of evaluating the books' literary qualities; but so far, no one has scrutinized their politics in depth. And I suspect that part of the reason for this trend is that the *Harry Potter* books are so 'mainstream' in their appeal and so committed to the realm of magical fantasy—and some would argue that they are so "subtly" written—that it is easy to overlook or to simply ignore their considerable social relevance to the modern world.

Most importantly, it is not always easy to talk about prejudice and discrimination in the modern context of enforced political correctness: For some reason, we feel the need to 'tip-toe' around these so-called 'negative' issues. And we live in an age when activism carries a certain degree of stigma. After all, celebrity gossip is far more discussable than the fact that human beings are still being side-lined in our world due to age, race, disability, sexuality and so forth; and never mind the fact that children are dying from malnutrition and very curable diseases in the developing world...

We may even find that, many people who are being victimized by overt prejudice and discrimination in the developed world struggle to find a voice. After all, citing cases of "sexism," "racism," and so forth, has become almost as "taboo" as witches and wizards saying "Voldemort" in the context of Rowling's wizarding world. And so, I took it upon myself to scrutinize these prickly subject matters for the section of the *Harry Potter* audience that has been as intrigued and impassioned by them as much as I have—and even for those who just read the books for fun but never thought too much about their political significance or their social relevance...

If you took the trouble of opening this book at all, then it is my sincere hope that you have found the discussion to be lively and engaging, even if you should hesitate to agree with the arguments put forth in it—or even if you refuse to take any of it too seriously.

Bibliography

Ackerman, N.W. and Marie Jahoda. *Anti-Semitism and Emotional Disorder*. New York: Harper, 1950.

Adam, Heribert & Kogila Moodley. *The Opening of the Apartheid Mind: Options for the New South Africa*. Berkeley, London & Los Angeles: University of California Press, 1993.

Adler, Alfred. *Superiority and Social Interest: A Collection of Later Writings*. (Edited by Heinz and Rowena Ansbacher with biographical essay by Carl Furtmüller). London: Routledge and Kegan Paul, 1965, c1964.

Aitken, Paul. "The Appropriation of "Gay." April 23, 2007. URL: http://www.altpenis.com/penis_news/gay.shtml.

Alford, Richard D. *Naming and Identity: A Cross-cultural Study of Personal Naming Practices*. New Haven, Connecticut: HRAF Press, 1988.

Allison, Kevin W. "Stress and Oppressed Social Category Membership" in *Prejudice: The Target's Perspective*. (Edited by Janet Swim and Charles Stangor). San Diego, London et al: Academic Press, 1998, pp. 145-170.

Allport, Gordon W. *The Nature of Prejudice*. New York: Perseus Publishing, 1954, 1958 & 1979.

Appiah, Anthony. "Identity, Authenticity, Survival" in *Multiculturalism: Examining the Politics of Recognition*. (Edited by Amy Gutmann). Princeton, NJ: Princeton University Press, 1994, pp. 149-163.

Barsamian, David. "Liberating the Mind from Orthodoxies: An Interview with Noam Chomsky." May, 2001. URL: http://zmag.org/Zmag/articles/may01barsamian.htm.

Batson, Daniel C & E. L. Stocks. "Religion and Prejudice" in *On the Nature of Prejudice*. (Edited by Dovidio et al.). Malden, MA: Blackwell Publishing, 2005, pp. 413-427.

Beechey, V. "On Patriarchy." *Feminist Review, No. 3*. (1979), pp. 66-82.

—"What's so special about women's employment? A review of some recent studies of women's paid work." *Feminist Review, No. 15*. (1986), pp. 130-159.

Beker, Avi. *The Plunder of Jewish Wealth During the Holocaust: Confronting European History*. Basingstoke: Palgrave, 2001.

Black, P. and R.D. Atkins. "Conformity versus prejudice as exemplified in White-Negro relations in the South: some methodological considerations. *Journal of Psychology* (1950), *Vol. 30*, pp. 109-121.

Blackman, Malorie. *Noughts and Crosses*. London: Random House, 2002.

Boeckmann, Robert J. & Carolyn Turpin-Petrosino. "Understanding the Harm of Hate Crime." *Journal of Social Issues, Vol. 58, No 2*, pp. 207-225. Oxford: Blackwell Publishing, 2002.

Boeckmann, Robert J. & Jeffrey Liew. "Hate Speech: Asian American Students' Justice Judgements and Psychological Responses." *Journal of Social Issues, Vol. 58, No 2*, pp. 363-381. Oxford: Blackwell Publishing, 2002.

Brown, M., M. Carnoy, E. Currie, T. Duster, D. Oppenheimer, M. Shultz & D. Wellman. *Whitewashing Race: The Myth of a Color-Blind Society*. Berkeley & London: University of California Press, 2003.

Brown, Rupert. *Prejudice: Its Social Psychology*. Oxford: Blackwell, 1995.

Browne, Anthony. "The Last Days of a White World." Guardian Online Archives. Guardian Newspapers Limited, 2004. URL: http://www.guardian.co.uk/racism/Story/0,,363783,00.html

Butler, Judith. *Gender Trouble: Feminism and the Subversion of Identity*. London and New York, Routledge, 1990.

Butler, Judith. *Bodies that Matter: On the Discursive Limits of Sex*. London and New York, Routledge, 1993.

Chomsky, Noam. "Dominance and Dilemmas" [News article]. *Le Monde diplomatique*. August, 2003. Also October 10, 2003. URL:

http://zmag.org/content/showarticle.cfm?SectionID=1 1&ItemID=4332.

—"Selective Memory and False Doctrine." [News article December 21, 2003]. URL: http://zmag.org/content/showarticle.cfm?SectionI D=15&ItemID=4736

—"What Makes Mainstream Media Mainstream." [From a talk at Z Media Institute]. June, 1997. URL: http://zmag.org/chomsky/articles/z9710-mainstream-media. html

Cloud, John. "Put Dumbledore Back in the Closet" [News Article] *Times Online*. October 22, 2007. URL: http://www.time.com/time/arts/article/0,8599,167455 0,00.html

Cohen, Albert K. *Delinquent Boys*. Glencoe, III: Free Press, 1955.

Cloward, Richard A. and Lloyd E. Ohlin. *Delinquency and Opportunity*. New York: Free Press, 1960.

Conger, John Janeway and Wilbur C. Miller. *Personality, Social Class and Delinquency*. Mew York, London & Sidney: John Wiley & Sons, Inc., 1966.

Cowan, Gloria, Miriam Resendez, Elizabeth Marshall and Ryan Quist. "Hate Speech and Constitutional Protection: Priming Values of Equality and Freedom." *Journal of Social Issues, Vol. 58, No. 2,* pp. 247-263. Oxford: Blackwell Publishing, 2002.

Crompton, Rosemary and Michael Mann (Editors). *Gender Stratification*. Cambridge: Polity Press, 1986

Dalton, Annie. *Naming the Dark*. London: Methuen Children's Books, 1993.

De Tocqueville, A. *Democracy in America*. New York: George Dearborn, 1838.

Devine, Patricia G. "Stereotypes and Prejudice: Their Automatic and Controlled Components." *Journal of Personality and Social Psychology, Vol. 56* (1989), pp. 5-18.

— "Breaking the Prejudice Habit: Allport's 'Inner Conflict' Revisited" in *On the Nature of Prejudice*

(Edited by Dovidio et al). Malden, MA: Blackwell Publishing, 2005, pp. 327-342.

Dovidio, John F, Peter Glick and Laurie A. Rudman. *On the Nature of Prejudice: Fifty Years Later*. Malden, MA: Blackwell Publishing, 2005.

Downes, David M. *The Delinquent Solution*. London: Routledge and Kegan Paul, 1966.

Dugan, Emily. "Modelling Agencies Blamed for Racist Culture." [News Article: *The Independent* (United Kingdom).] October 10, 2007. URL: http://www.independent.co.uk/news/uk/politics/modelling-agencies-blamed-for-racist-culture-396454.html

Esses, Victoria M., Lynne M. Jackson, John F. Dovidio & Gordon Hodson. "Instrumental Relations Among Groups: Group Competition, Conflict and Prejudice" in *On the Nature of Prejudice*. (Edited by Dovidio et al). Malden, MA: Blackwell Publishing, 2005, pp. 227-243.

Fiske, Susan T. "Social Condition and the Normality of Prejudgment" in *On the Nature of Prejudice* (Edited by Dovidio et al). Malden, MA: Blackwell Publishing, 2005, pp. 36-53.

Flaubert, Gustave. *Madame Bovary*. Translated by Mildred Marmur. New York: Penguin Putnam, 1964.

Foucault, Michel. "The subject and power", Afterword to H. L. Dreyfus and P. Rabinow, *Michel Foucault: Beyong Structuralism and Hermeneutics* (Chicago: University of Chicago Press, 1982).

Freud, Sigmund. [James Strachey (Translator)]. *Totem and Taboo*. London and New York: Routledge Classics, 2001.

Freud, Sigmund. *Totem und Taboo*. Vienna: Hugo Heller, 1913.

Glick, Peter. "Choice of Scapegoats." *On the Nature of Prejudice*. (Edited by Dovidio et al.). Malden, MA: Blackwell Publishing, 2005, pp. 244-261.

Gluek, Sheldon & Eleanor. *Delinquents in the Making*. New York: Harper & Brothers, 1952.

Gupta, Suman. *Re-reading Harry Potter*. Basingstoke and London: Palgrave Macmillan, 2003.

Gutmann, Amy (Ed.). *Multiculturalism: Examining the Politics of Recognition*. New Jersey: University of Princeton Press, 1994.

Haley, Alex. *Roots*. New York: Doubleday, 1976.

Hall, Alex. "Shadowmancer Touted as 'Hotter Than Potter'" (Book Review and Audio file) [Real Audio & Windows Media Keyword: "Shadowmancer"]. URL: http://www.bbc.co.uk/northyorkshire/culture/bookclub/reviews/2003/07/shadow2.shtml.

Haller, Beth A. "Confusing Disability with Tragedy," [News article]. *The Sun*. Baltimore, Maryland. April 29, 2001. URL: http://www.bic-un.bahai.org/88-0806.htm

Harvey, Robert. *The Fall of Apartheid*. New York: Palgrave, 2001.

Heilman, Elizabeth E. & Anne E. Gregory. "Images of the Privileged Insider and Outcast Outsider." *Harry Potter's World* (Edited by Heilman). London & New York: RoutledgeFalmer, 2002, pp. 241-258.

Heilman, Elizabeth E. (Editor). *Harry Potter's World: Multidisciplinary Critical Perspectives*. London & New York: RoutledgeFalmer, 2002.

Herrnstein, Richard J. & Charles Murray. *The Bell Curve*. New York & London: The Free Press, 1994.

Hirschi, Travis. *Causes of Delinquency*. [New edition with Introduction by Author: First published in 1969]. New Brunswick & New Jersey: Transaction Publishers, 2002.

Hutton, John, MP, Rt. Hon. "Ethnic Minority Employment in Britain–Recognizing Women's Potential." Women's Enterprise Project - Bethnal Green (Wednesday, 28th February 2007). URL: http://www.dwp.gov.uk/aboutus/2007/28-02-07.asp.

Italie, Hillel. "Rowling: Potter's Dumbledore Gay." [News article: *Times Online* Article. October 20, 2007. URL: http://www.time.com/time/arts/article/0,8599,1674069,00.html .

Johnson, Richard E. *Juvenile Delinquency and its Origins.* Cambridge, London, New York, Melbourne: Cambridge University Press, 1979.

Jones, James M. "Mechanisms for Coping with Victimization: Self- Protection Plus Self-Enhancement." *On the Nature of Prejudice,* (Edited by Dovidio et al.) Malden, MA: Blackwell Publishing, 2005, pp. 155-171.

Jost, J.T. & Banaji, M.R. "The Role of Stereotyping in System Justification and the Production of False Consciousness." *British Journal of Social Psychology, Vol. 33*, pp. 1-27. (1994)

Katz, P. A. "The Acquisition of Racial Attitudes in Children." *Towards the Elimination of Racism,* (Edited by P. A. Katz). New York: Pergamon, 1976, pp. 125-153.

—"Racists or Tolerant Multiculturalists. How Do They Begin?" *American Psychologist, Vol. 58* (2003), pp. 897-909.

La Piere, R. T. "Attitudes versus Actions." *Journal of Social Forces, Vol. 13,* (1934) pp. 230-237.

—"Type-rationalizations of group antipathy." *Journal of Social Forces, Vol. 15,* (1936) pp. 232-237.

Leets, Laura. "Experiencing Hate Speech: Perceptions and Responses to Anti-Semitism and Antigay Speech." *Journal of Social Issues, Vol. 58, No 2,* pp. 341-361. Oxford: Blackwell Publishing, 2002.

Le Guin, Ursula. *A Wizard of Earthsea.* London: Puffin Books, 1974.

Lenski, G. *Power and Privilege.* New York: Harper and Row, 1966.

Levin, Brian. "From Slavery to Hate-Crime Laws: The Emergence of Race and Status-Based Protection in American Criminal Law." *Journal of Social Issues, Vol. 58, No 2,* pp. 227-245. Oxford: Blackwell Publishing, 2002.

Litwack, Leon F. *North of Slavery: The Negro in the Free States, 1790-1860.* Chicago and London: Chicago University Press, 1961.

Lynch, William. "The Willie Lynch Letter: The Making of a Slave. "Transcript URL:

http://www.itsabouttimebpp.com/BPP_Books/pdf/The_Willie_Lynch_Letter_The_Making_of_a_Slave!.pdf

Maccoby, E. and Jacklin, C. *The Psychology of Sex Difference.* Stanford: Stanford University Press, 1974.

Merton, Robert K., "Social Structure and Anomie." *American Sociological Review* No. 26 (October 1938), pp. 672-682.

Mitford, Jessica. *Hons and Rebels*. London: Golancz, 1989, c1961.

Murgatroyd, L. "Gender and occupational stratification." *Sociological Review, Vol. 30, No. 4.* 1982.

—"Women and the social grading of occupations." *British Journal of Sociology, Vol. 35, No. 4.* 1984.

—"Gender and occupational stratification" in *Localities, Class and Gender*. London: Pion, 1984.

Nazer, Mende and Damien Lewis. *Slave.* London: Virago Press, 2004.

Nel, Philip. *J.K. Rowling's Harry Potter Novels: A Reader's Guide*. New York & London: Continuum, 2001.

Orwell, George. *1984*. London: Secker and Warburg, 1949.

—*Animal Farm: A Fairy Story*. London: Secker and Warburg, 1971.

—"Banned Preface to *Animal Farm*" (1945). URL: http://home.imprimus.com.au/korob/Orwell.html.

Ouseley, Herman (Foreword Contributor) and Ali Harris (Introduction Contributor). *Profiles of Prejudice: An in-depth analysis of the nature of prejudice in England.* [MORI survey report]. Published in London by Greenhouse and Citizenship 21, a 21st Century Project of Stonewall, 2001. URL: http://www.stonewall.org.uk/docs/finalpop.pdf

Papamichael, Christina. "Harry Potter and the Curse of Disability." [News Article—*BBC-Ouch!-Close Up*]. URL: http://www.bbc.co.uk/ouch/closeup/harrypotter.shtml

Rattansi, Ali. *Racism: A Very Short Introduction*. New York: Oxford University Press, 2007.

Rothbart, M. & John, O.P. "Social Categorization and Behavioral Episodes: A Cognitive Analysis of Effects of Intergroup Contact." *Journal of Social Issues, Vol. 41*, pp. 81-104. Blackwells, 1985.

Roy, Arundhati. *The God of Small Things*. London: Flamingo (HarperCollins), 1997.

Rowling, J.K. *Harry Potter and the Philosopher's Stone*. London: Bloomsbury, 1997.

– *Harry Potter and the Chamber of Secrets*. London: Bloomsbury, 1998.

– *Harry Potter and the Prisoner of Azkaban*. London: Bloomsbury, 1999.

– *Harry Potter and the Goblet of Fire*. London: Bloomsbury, 2000.

– *Harry Potter and the Order of the Phoenix*. London: Bloomsbury, 2003.

– *Harry Potter and the Half-blood Prince*. London: Bloomsbury, 2005.

– *Harry Potter and the Deathly Hallows*. London: Bloomsbury, 2007.

– [Interview] Live Chat, Bloomsbury.com. July 30, 2007 (2.00-3.00pm BST). Transcript URL: http://www.accio-quote.org/articles /2007/0730-bloomsbury-chat.html

– [Interview] Carnegie Hall, Manhattan, New York. October, 2007. Transcript URL: http://www.the-leaky-cauldron.org/2007/10/20/ j-k-rowling-at-carnegie-hall-reveals-dumbledore-is-gay-neville-marries-hannah-abbott-and-scores-more.html

Rudman, Laurie A. "Rejection of Women? Beyond Prejudice as Antipathy." *On the Nature of Prejudice*. Malden, MA: Blackwell Publishing, 2005, pp. 106-120.

Saïd, Edward. *Out of Place: A Memoir*. London: Granta Books, 1999. Sancho, Jane. "Disabling Prejudice: Attitudes towards disability and its portrayal on television." A report of research undertaken by the British

Broadcasting Corporation (BBC), the Broadcasting Standards Commission and the Independent Television Commission. London: Office of Communications (OfCom), 2003. URL: http://www.ofcom.org.uk/static/archive/bsc/pdfs/research/disability.pdf

Siltanen, Janet. "Domestic Responsibilities and the Structuring of Employment." *Gender Stratification* (Edited by Rosemary Crompton and Michael Mann). Cambridge: Polity Press, 1986, pp. 97-118.

Singer, Jefferson A., Laura A. King, Melanie C. Green, Sarah C. Barr. "Personal Identity and Civic Responsibility: 'Rising to the Occasion' Narratives and Generativity in Community Action Student Interns." *Journal of Social Issues, Vol. 58, No 3,* pp. 535- 556. Oxford: Blackwell Publishing, 2002.

Spencer, Margaret Beale & Frances Degen Horowitz. "Effects of Systematic Social and Token Reinforcement on the Modification of Racial and Color Concept Attitudes in Black and in White Preschool Children." *Journal of Developmental Psychology, Vol. 9, No. 2,* University of Kansas Press, 1973, pp. 246-254.

Sinclair, Stacey, Elizabeth Dunn and Brian S. Lowery. "The Relationship Between Parental Racial Attitudes and Children's Implicit Prejudice." *Journal of Experimental Social Psychology, Vol. 41* (2005), pp. 283-289.

Swim, Janet K. and Charles Stangor (Ed.) *Prejudice: The Target's Perspective*. San Diego, London et al: Academic Press, 1998

Taylor, Charles. *The Ethics of Authenticity*. Cambridge, MA: Harvard University Press, 1991.

—"The Politics of Recognition." *Multiculturalism: Examining the Politics of Recognition* (Edited by Amy Gutmann). Princeton, NJ: Princeton University Press, 1994, pp. 25-73.

Taylor, G.P. *Shadowmancer*. London: Faber and Faber, 2003.

– *Wormwood*. London: Faber and Faber, 2004.

– *Shadowmancer: The Curse of Salamander Street*. London: Faber and Faber, 2006.

Tolkien, J.R.R. *The Lord of the Rings* [Collector's Edition Complete Trilogy]. London: Harper Collins, 1991.

Williams, Patricia J. *Seeing a Color-blind Future: The Paradox of Race*. New York: The Noonday Press, 1997.

Yusuf, Huma. «Culte de la blancheur au Pakistan et en Inde: Vive les visages pales!» *Courier International*, 2-8 September, 2004, pp. 42-43.

Zuckerman, D.M. Singer, D.G. and Singer, J.L. "Children's Television Viewing, Racial and Sex-role Attitudes." *Journal of Applied Psychology, Vol. 10,* Issue 4 (August, 1980), pp. 281-294.

Index

**=only work/co-author mentioned*

Prejudice in *Harry Potter*'s World

Written by

Karen A. Brown
Oxford University

Crisp, insightful, engaging, and thoroughly researched, *Prejudice in* Harry Potter'*s World* turns the tables on literary critique. Brown shows uncommon, in-depth knowledge of the *Harry Potter* canon. And she delves straight into her analysis of social themes in J.K. Rowling's work without pulling any punches. First, the book provides a detailed outline of the social hierarchy in the so-called "wizarding world." Then, the author offers perceptive and highly relevant commentaries. Each chapter focuses on how a select group contributes to wizarding society and helps to maintain the social order ... whether by embracing their own oppression or by oppressing others.

***

What are some of the consequences of institutional discrimination in *Harry Potter*'s world, and how do they compare with social trends in the real world? This book provides all the answers.

LaVergne, TN USA
03 January 2011
210744LV00001B/63/P